WORLD
REVOLUTIONARY
LEADERS

WORLD
REVOLUTIONARY
LEADERS

Mostafa Rejai

Kay Phillips

RUTGERS UNIVERSITY PRESS

New Brunswick, New Jersey

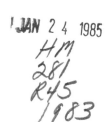
Copyright © 1983 by Rutgers, The State University

All rights reserved

Manufactured in the United States of America

Library of Congress Cataloging in Publication Data

Rejai, M. (Mostafa)
 World revolutionary leaders.
 Bibliography: p.
 Includes index.
  1. Revolutions. 2. Revolutionists.
3. Revolutionists — Psychology. 4. Leadership.
I. Phillips, Kay. II. Title.
HM281.R45 1983   303.694   82-13231
ISBN 0-8135-0975-0

Contents

List of Tables

Acknowledgments

A study of this magnitude could not have been completed without the assistance and support of a variety of individuals and institutions. In developing the code sheets* I drew much inspiration from the work of Harold D. Lasswell and his associates (see bibliography of theoretical literature). A relatively large number of research assistants diligently participated in the tedious process of data collection: David Arredondo, Keith Atlas, Elaine Bruestle, Susan Carroll, William Carroll, Pio Celestino, Candace Conrad, Patrick Costigan, Stuart Gilman, Jeffrey Kranz, Karen Leander, Mack Leftwich, Mary Maloney, Kirby McMillan, Robert Miller, Susan Moyer, Mekki Mtewa, Brian Murphy, Rebecca Nash, Julius Nyang'oro, Otieno Okelo, Antony Ruprecht, Bruce Spector, Jerry Sukys, Wayne Torrey, John Vitullo, Steven Wainscott, Janet West, David Wyatt, John Young, Philip Zampini.

In addition, Candace Conrad rendered important assistance with translation of Spanish and Portuguese materials, as did Josette Thévenin with translation of French texts, and Frank Van Mierlo with translation of Dutch sources. The Vietnam Working Group of the U.S. Department of State provided usable data on the Vietminh and Vietcong revolutionaries.

Much of the research for this work was conducted at the Center for International Affairs, Harvard University, and the Hoover Institution, Stanford University. I am indebted to the officers and staffs of these organizations for superbly fruitful opportunities.

Sarah Barr, Jennifer Cargill, Martin Miller, Mary Persyn, and Patricia Ormiston of Miami University Libraries have, consistently for over a decade, demonstrated admirable resourcefulness in locating a variety of source materials from a host of collections throughout the United States and abroad. Suzanne Adlon of Miami University's Scripps Foundation for Population Research and Christine Noble of the Academic Computer Services rendered assistance with programming and computer runs, in addition to providing important help with problems of methodology.

---

*Since both the general code sheet and the code sheet for factor analyses have already appeared in M. Rejai and K. Phillips, *Leaders of Revolution* (Beverly Hills: Sage, 1979), it seems redundant (and costly) to reprint them here as well.

ACKNOWLEDGMENTS

The American Philosophical Society provided a grant from its Penrose Fund. Miami University and its Faculty Research Council have been more than generous in supporting my work in every conceivable way throughout the years.

My political science colleagues Warren Mason and Herbert Waltzer have been extremely helpful with comments and suggestions concerning this project, as have been my psychology colleagues Donald Parker and Richard Sherman. Dorothy S. Pierson typed successive drafts of the manuscript with characteristic patience, dispatch, and good humor.

Marlie Wasserman of Rutgers University Press proved to be an editor's editor. A thorough professional and a demanding taskmaster, she contributed a great deal to whatever merit this book might have. Janet Mais's copyediting was simply the most meticulous and the most impressive I have known. Leslie Mitchner skillfully steered the manuscript through production.

Having joined the project in 1977, Kay Phillips, a sociologist, became a full partner on this volume. The Introduction has been written in the first person singular since, among other things, it describes the twelve-year history of the project (1970–1982) as experienced by Rejai.

Although we have been exceedingly fortunate to have had the assistance of so many individuals and institutions, we alone remain responsible for what appears in this book.

Mostafa Rejai
Oxford, Ohio

INTRODUCTION

Introduction

This volume continues work begun in *Leaders of Revolution.*[1] The earlier book* reported on 64 leaders of twelve revolutionary movements, beginning with the English Revolution of the 1640s and ending with the French upheaval of 1968. The present volume reports on an additional 71 leaders of nineteen revolutionary movements which took place in the 1960s and the 1970s (whether successful or abortive) or which were active as of December 1978 (our closing date for data collection). The initial objective of this study was to present (1) a comparative analysis of the 71 revolutionaries of the 1960s and 1970s with their 64 earlier counterparts and (2) and overall analysis of the 135 leaders. For reasons discussed in Chapter 3, however, the first task proved unproductive.

This work continues the search for answers to two interrelated sets of questions about revolutionary elites,** one dealing with their social characteristics and traits, the other with their motivation and emergence upon the scene:

(1) Who are men who lead revolutions? How old—or how young—are they? Are they urban dwellers or do they come from rural areas? What level of education do they have? What socioeconomic and occupational backgrounds do they come from? What socialization experiences do they share? What sorts of family life do they have? Where and how do they acquire social awareness and political experience? What ideological postures do they adopt? What attitudes do they hold about man and society?

(2) Under what conditions do men turn revolutionary? What makes men risk their lives to challenge the established order? What

*Throughout the present study, all references to "earlier book," "earlier work," "earlier volume," "its predecessor," and the like are to *Leaders of Revolution.*

**Throughout this volume, I use "elite" to refer to a single revolutionary group (for example, the Angolans) and "elites" to refer to more than one (for example, the Angolans and the Peruvians). On occasion, as the context makes clear, I use the two words in a generic sense as well.

forces or circumstances provide impetus to the emergence of revolutionary leaders? What are the dynamics—situational, social, psychological—that propel men toward revolutionary action?

The several steps taken in the execution of the study require elaboration. To begin with, I define *political revolution* in such a restrictive fashion that relatively few historical upheavals qualify for inclusion. Briefly, I see political revolution as *illegal mass violence aimed at the overthrow of a political regime as a step toward overall societal change.*[2] This definition, it is clear, accommodates successful as well as unsuccessful revolutionary movements—that is to say, one need not look at the outcome in order to identify the event (note the idea of *intent*). Moreover, though restrictive, this definition is useful in identifying political revolutions as a class of events sharply to be distinguished from such other phenomena as riots, rebellions, coups d'etat, and the like.

Employing this definition, a comparatively small number of events qualify for consideration. Specifically, the present volume reports on thirty-one revolutionary upheavals spanning four centuries and covering all major regions of the world (see below).

My list of revolutions, I hasten to add, is neither exhaustive nor representative of the entire universe of revolutions, as other scholars may wish to include a variety of other violent events. My list is admittedly tilted toward the more dramatic and the best documented revolutions. Even so, problems of data availability have beset me at every turn.

The next step in the preparation of the study was the identification of the principal leaders of each revolutionary movement. By "principal leaders" I refer to persons who risk their lives by playing a *prominent, active,* and *continuing role* throughout the revolutionary process. By "throughout the revolutionary process" I mean *during* and perhaps immediately *before* the revolution, but not necessarily *after* the success or failure of the movement. My intention here is to distinguish the "real" revolutionary from the dilettante, the propagandist, the pamphleteer.

The identification of principal leaders in any thorough and definitive sense turned out to be an impossible task. The procedure adopted in the earlier volume, it may be recalled, was the relatively

4

convenient one of drawing up a tentative list of leaders for each revolution and then subjecting the list to the judgment of a panel of experts. Difficult as those judgments eventually proved to be, they simply were infeasible for the present volume. Reasons include: (1) dearth of data about leaders of the more recent revolutions; (2) major fluctuations in leadership positions over time: having been around since 1916, for example, the Irish Republican Army has seen the passage of many leadership groups; similarly, "Palestine"* and Quebec have experienced major discontinuities in leadership; (3) the presence of intense fragmentation and rivalry both between and within revolutionary groups: Angola, Mozambique, "Palestine," Peru, South Africa, and Zimbabwe are cases in point.

These and related difficulties left us with the alternatives of either abandoning the project altogether or being satisfied with a less rigorous procedure for identification of the newer leadership groups. Having naturally selected the latter course, we include on our list—without regard to faction, organization, or ideology—any revolutionary who meets our conception of "principal leader" or who is so identified by unquestionably authoritative sources (for example, Basil Davidson and John Marcum on Angola, Colin Legum on South Africa, Paul Langer and Joseph Zasloff on Laos, William Quandt on "Palestine," Douglas Pike on South Vietnam, and the like). Organized by region as well as country, our list of thirty-one revolutionary movements and 135 revolutionary leaders is as follows:

AFRICA

Angola 1975	*South Africa 1978*
Mário de Andrade	Stephen Bantu Biko
Viriato da Cruz	Manus Buthelezi
António Agostinho Neto	Nelson Mandela
Holden Roberto (José Gilmore)	Robert Sobukwe
Jonas Malheiro Savimbi	Oliver Reginald Tambo

*Although as of this writing there is no such country as "Palestine" with recognized international boundaries, I use this designation (with quotation marks) for stylistic convenience.

Algeria 1962†

    Hussein Ait Ahmed
    Ahmed Ben Bella
    Mustafa Ben Boulaid
    Mohammed Labri Ben M'Hidi
    Rabah Bitat
    Mohammed Boudiaf
    Mourad Didouche
    Mohammed Khider
    Belkassem Krim

Guinea-Bissau 1974

    Raphael Barbosa (Zain Lopez)
    Amilcar Cabral

Mozambique 1975

    Marcelino Dos Santos
    Samora Moises Machel
    Eduardo Mondlane

Namibia (South West Africa) 1978

    Sam Nujoma
    Herman Toivo ja Toivo

Zimbabwe (Rhodesia) 1978

    James Robert Chickerema
    Herbert Chitepo
    Robert Mugabe
    Joshua Nkomo
    Ndabaningi Sithole

ASIA AND THE MIDDLE EAST

China 1949†

    Ch'en Yi
    Chou En-lai
    Chu Teh
    Lin Piao
    Liu Shao-ch'i
    Mao Tse-tung

Kampuchea (Cambodia) 1975

    Ieng Sary
    Khieu Samphan
    Saloth Sar (Pol Pot)

North Vietnam 1954†

    Ho Chi Minh (Nguyên Sinh Cung)
    Lê Duân
    Pham Van Dong
    Truong Chinh (Dang Xuan Khu)
    Vo Nguyên Giap

Laos 1975

    Kaysone Phomvihan
    Nouhak Phongsavan
    Phoumi Vongvichit
    Singkapo Chounramany
    Sithon Kommadam
    Souk Vongsak
    Souphanouvong

South Vietnam 1975

    Ho Thu
    Huynh Tan Phat
    Nguyên Huu Tho
    Nguyên Van Hieu
    Phung Van Cung
    Tran Buu Kiem
    Tran Van Tra (Tran Nam
      Trung)
    Vo Chi Cong

† Indicates revolutions (and revolutionaries) covered in *Leaders of Revolution.*

"Palestine" 1978

> Yasir Arafat (Abu Amar) (né Rahman el-Qudwa el-Husayni)
> George Habash
> Nayif el-Hwatmah
> Saleh Khalef (Abu Iyad)
> Ahmad Asaad Shukairy
> Khalil el-Wazir

Philippines 1978

> Bernabé Buscayno (Commander Dante)
> José Mariá Sison (Amado Guerroro)

LATIN AMERICA

Brazil 1969

> Carlos Marighella

Colombia 1966

> Camilo Torres Restrepo

Cuba 1959†

> Fidel Castro Ruz
> Raul Castro Ruz
> Camilo Cienfuegos
> Ernesto (Che) Guevara
>   de la Serna

Uruguay 1972

> Raúl Sendic Antonaccio
>   (Rufo)

Bolivia 1952†

> Juan Lechín Oquendo
> Víctor Paz Estenssoro
> Hernán Siles Zuazo

Guatemala 1978

> César Maciás Mayora
>   (César Montes)
> Luís Augusto Turcios Lima
> Marco Antonio Yon Sosa

Peru 1965

> Héctor Béjar Rivera
> Hugo Blanco Gladós
> Guillermo Lobatón Millé
> Luis de la Puente Uceda

EUROPE AND NORTH AMERICA

America 1776†

> John Adams
> Samuel Adams
> Patrick Henry
> Thomas Jefferson
> James Otis
> George Washington

England 1640s†

> Oliver Cromwell
> Robert Devereux,
>   third earl of Essex
> John Hampden
> John Pym
> Henry (Harry) Vane

France 1789†

    Georges Jacques Danton
    Jean Paul Marat
    Honoré Gabriel Riqueti, comte de Mirabeau
    Maximilien François Marie Isidore de Robespierre
    Emmanuel Joseph Siéyès

France 1968†

    Daniel Cohn-Bendit
    Alain Geismar
    Alain Krivine
    Jacques Sauvageot

Hungary 1956†

    Ernö Gerö
    Janós Kadar (Janós Csermanck)
    Pál Maletér
    Imre Nagy
    Matyas Rakosi

Mexico 1910†

    Venustiano Carranza
    Francisco Indalecio Madero
    Alvaro Obregón
    Francisco (Pancho) Villa (Doroteo Arango)
    Emiliano Zapata

Northern Ireland 1978

    Joseph Cahill
    Cathal Goulding
    Sean MacStiofáin (né John Stephenson)
    Joseph McCann
    Ruairi O'Bradaïgh (né Rory Brady)
    Daithi (né David) O'Connell

Puerto Rico 1978

    Juan Mari Bras

Quebec/Canada 1970

    Charles Gagnon
    Gabriel Hudon (Roger Dupuis)
    François (né Frenec) Schirm
    Georges Schoeters
    Pierre Vallières
    Raymond Villeneuve

Russia 1917†

    Vladimir Alexandrovich Antonov-Ovseyenko
    Lev Davidovich Bronstein (Leon Trotsky)
    Joseph Vissarionovich Dzhugashvili (Joseph Stalin)
    Lev Borisovich Kamenev
    Jakov Mikhailovich Sverdlov
    Vladimir Ilyich Ulyanov (Nikolai Lenin)
    Grigori Evseyevich Zinoviev

Several aspects of the list require comment and clarification. First, since South West Africa is commonly known as Namibia (indeed, it has been so called at the United Nations since 1968), we too use the shorter name. Second, Zimbabwe is unusual among our revolutionary movements in that, following years of struggle, the British, consistent with their historic policy of "devolution," effected a relatively peaceful power transfer. Whether—and for how long—the situation remains calm is anybody's guess. Moreover, independence came in 1980, following our closing date for data collection.

Third, although Quebec is not a country, it warrants consideration in its own right. To begin with, Quebec's population of over six million is about the same as the populations of such countries as Angola, Bolivia, Guatemala, and Zimbabwe and substantially larger than the populations of such other countries as Guinea-Bissau, Laos, Uruguay.[3] Moreover, needless to say, Quebec is quite distinctive among the ten Canadian provinces in terms of language and culture. Finally, any potential objections to inclusion could be overcome simply by changing "Quebec" to "Canada."

Fourth, although from a strictly geographic standpoint Puerto Rico should be listed among Latin American countries, geopolitical considerations dictate otherwise. In fact, virtually every writer lists Puerto Rico as a "United States Territory" or a "commonwealth within the United States" and hence a part of North America.[4]

Fifth, a number of prominent recent revolutionary movements had to be excluded for the sheer absence of usable data. Particularly notable in this regard are Iran and Nicaragua, as well as El Salvador, Thailand, Burma, and others. Sixth, even for the revolutionary movements that *are* included, the same data problems forced the exclusion of some prominent leaders. Specifically, data were collected for over twenty additional revolutionaries from throughout Africa, Asia, Latin America, Europe, and North America. In the end, the data proved so sparse as to be unusable. By contrast, despite the wealth of available information, we exclude Albert Luthuli of South Africa because he does not qualify as a revolutionary leader in our sense. Indeed, as one authority has written, Luthuli was "a passionate believer in nonviolent passive resistance."[5] On the other hand, although at times Prince Souphanouvong of Laos played a figurehead role, his inclusion was unavoidable.

Seventh, the names in parentheses are real names, nicknames, aliases, or noms de guerre, as the context makes clear. A few revolutionaries legally changed their names, and these too are duly noted (by designation né) for the record.

Eighth, the determination of the date of revolution appearing after each country name is governed by the realization that the thirty-one revolutionary movements fall into three groups: (1) Those that as of December 1978 (closing of data collection) had succeeded. In all these instances, the date used is that of actual power seizure. (2) Those that as of December 1978 were still "currently active" or "in process." In all these instances, the date used is 1978. (3) Those that by December 1978 had failed. In all these circumstances, the date used is the year of effective decline or disintegration of the movement. (In two cases—Brazil and Colombia—the dates used are those of Marighella's and Torres's deaths, respectively.)* In the light of the foregoing distinctions, we may summarize the status of our thirty-one revolutionary movements, *as of December 1978*, as follows:

Successful (16)	*In process (9)*	*Abortive (6)*
Algeria	Colombia	Brazil
America	Guatemala	France 1968
Angola	Northern Ireland	Hungary
Bolivia	Namibia	Peru
China	"Palestine"	Quebec
Cuba	Philippines	Uruguay
England	Puerto Rico	
France 1789	South Africa	
Guinea-Bissau	Zimbabwe	
Kampuchea		
Laos		
Mexico		
Mozambique		
North Vietnam		
Russia		
South Vietnam		

---

*In addition to Marighella and Torres, we should note, six other revolution-

Finally, since some of the names (for example, the Palestinians) are spelled in a variety of ways, I have adopted the policy of using the simplest spelling. Moreover, the Introduction is the only place in the study where all names appear in full; in the balance of the text, short or popular names are used.

The next step in the execution of the study was the gathering of data for each leader of each revolution on a uniform code sheet running over fifty data items (see the Acknowledgments). The code sheet was kept as consistent as possible with that used in *Leaders of Revolution* so as to afford maximum replication and comparability.

Parenthetically, we should note that in reexamining the data for the earlier volume, we discovered two errors which, happily however, do not appreciably affect our findings. Specifically: (1) Robert Devereux's socioeconomic status should have been punched as upper (not middle) class; (2) Ho Chi Minh's socioeconomic status should have been marked as middle (not lower) class. These errors have now been corrected.

As for the actual collection of relevant data, the process proved far more arduous and time consuming than it had been for the earlier volume, due in large measure to the relative newness of the nineteen upheavals of the 1960s and 1970s. Beginning in June 1971—with the help of the team of research assistants named in the Acknowledgments—I undertook a thorough scrutiny of the available literature in a variety of languages and locales (see Acknowledgments and Bibliography).

Simultaneously, I initiated correspondence with a variety of governmental and quasi-governmental organizations, foreign ministries in Washington, private and quasi-private research institutes, some prominent newspapers (concerning their "morgue files"), and some individual scholars specializing in particular countries.

---

aries were assassinated, ambushed, or killed in action: Biko 1978, Cabral 1973, Mc-Cann 1972, Mondlane 1969, de la Puente 1964, Yon Sosa 1970. A ninth leader, Turcios Lima, died in an automobile accident in 1966.

In only a single instance, the U.S. Department of State pleasantly surprised me by providing usable data on the Vietnamese leaders; all other correspondence proved in vain, as not a solitary datum was forthcoming.*

Nearly eight years later—in December 1978—I called a halt to data collection, having resigned myself to the proposition that further search would not yield appreciable results. As of this writing, I have had no reason to question that decision. Some years hence, however, the situation may change, in which case an update will be forthcoming, as appropriate.

The gathering of social background data on revolutionary elites went hand in hand with—but quite distinct from—the examination of historical, social, and psychological conditions under which the leaders emerge. The latter endeavor involved close scrutiny of primary and secondary sources with heavy reliance on autobiographical and biographical materials. Although such sources could not be located for all the 135 leaders, usable—but not uniformly even—information has been collected for 50 revolutionaries. Constituting 37 percent of the larger group, and representing twenty-two countries and all regions, they are:

AFRICA

Algeria

    Ben Bella

Angola

    Roberto

Mozambique

    Machel

    Mondlane

Guinea-Bissau

    Cabral

South Africa

    Biko

Zimbabwe

    Nkomo

    Sithole

---

*Some of the fruits of my pleas for assistance are worth noting: (1) no response at all. (2) The polite "No." (3) The blunt "No." (4) The run around: "If you were to write the foreign ministry at. . . ." (5) The denial: "We have no problems here. . . ." (6) The evasion: providing inappropriate (usually propaganda) materials.

ASIA AND THE MIDDLE EAST

China

    Chou
    Chu
    Lin
    Liu
    Mao

Laos

    Souphanouvong

North Vietnam

    Ho
    Giap

"Palestine"

    Arafat
    Habash

LATIN AMERICA

Bolivia

    Paz Estenssoro

Colombia

    Torres

Cuba

    F. Castro
    Guevara

Brazil

    Marighella

Peru

    Blanco
    De la Puente

Uruguay

    Sendic

EUROPE AND NORTH AMERICA

America

    J. Adams
    S. Adams
    Henry
    Jefferson
    Otis
    Washington

Mexico

    Madero
    Villa
    Zapata

Quebec/Canada

    Schirm
    Schoeters
    Vallières

England

    Cromwell
    Devereux
    Hampden
    Pym
    Vane

France 1789

    Danton
    Marat
    Mirabeau
    Robespierre

Russia

    Lenin
    Stalin
    Trotsky

The questions of validity and reliability of the data collected for this work have been given careful consideration. As for validity, as noted in the Acknowledgments, the data items used in this volume are adapted from the general literature of elite analysis; in fact, these items are by now part of the "conventional wisdom" of the literature, representing considerable scholarly consensus. Moreover, the variables for which data are collected interrelate to a large extent. Thus, demographic, ideological, attitudinal, psychological, and situational variables not only cohere as distinct groups; they intersect and interface at many points as well.

As far as reliability is concerned, every effort has been made to minimize possible errors. While there is probably no such thing as an error-free study, a series of precautions was taken in data collection and coding. First, as the Bibliography indicates, a wide range of data sources was employed. Second, while the initial data gatherings were in hands of the research assistants listed in the Acknowledgments, each assistant was provided with a detailed code sheet and with detailed instructions. Third, I personally reviewed every data item on every code sheet against the many sources indicated, thus arriving at a final determination. These precautions apparently stood us in good stead, since as noted above, a thorough reexamination of over four thousand data items for the first volume unraveled only two errors.

In all instances, problems of conflicting data were resolved by relying on two yardsticks: (1) the frequency with which a datum appeared in independent sources and (2) the authenticity of the source or person giving the datum. Needless to say, the second yardstick was given preference throughout.

Although by nature a study of this kind lends itself to convoluted treatment, every effort has been made to keep organization and presentation as straightforward as possible. Part I sets forth the theoretical foundations of the enterprise. Chapter 1 examimes and evaluates the psychoanalytic, psychohistorical, and sociological (using the concept of charisma) approaches to the study of revolutionary elites. Each approach having been found wanting in some respect, Chapter 2 proposes a "situational" theory, stressing the interplay between demographic, sociological, and psychological factors in the emergence of revolutionary leaders.

Part II undertakes a quantitative analysis of a range of data for the 135 revolutionaries, in the light of the propositions and hypotheses developed in Chapter 2. It examines over fifty variables concerning age, birthplace, socioeconomic status, family life, ethnicity, religion, education, occupation, foreign travel, revolutionary organization and agitation, arrest and imprisonment, ideologies and attitudes, and the like. It postulates a series of independent variables in order to determine variations among revolutionary elites. It employs factor analysis in an effort to arrive at a typology of revolutionary leaders.

Part III presents a qualitative analysis of the situational, sociological, and psychological dynamics underlying the emergence of the fifty revolutionaries for whom adequate autobiographical and biographical data are available. Looking at patterns of radicalization, it examines formative years, school socialization, new experiences and cultures, and purely situational dynamics. In considering psychological dynamics, it pays particular attention to vanity and egotism, asceticism and puritanism, relative deprivation and status inconsistency, marginality and inferiority complex, oedipal conflict writ large, and estheticism and romanticism.

Part IV synthesizes the study and presents its principal findings and conclusions. In a systematic and step-by-step fashion, it funnels the quantitative and qualitative analyses and findings of Parts II and III into the theoretical posture adopted in Chapter 2. In so doing, it confirms our situational theory of revolutionary leadership.

To achieve maximum comparability and to present as comprehensive a study as possible, this volume replicates the theoretical and methodological operations of *Leaders of Revolution*. The theoretical apparatus is synthesized, condensed, and revised in Chapters 1 and 2. Although I have made every effort to keep the methodological operations identical, some modifications and unanticipated findings (for instance, the temporal patterns introduced in

15

Chapter 3 and carried throughout the entire work) are dictated by the nature of the available data. These modifications and findings are noted in the appropriate chapters of the study.

The Bibliography is in four parts: theoretical literature, general data sources, regional studies, country studies. The third and fourth parts, it should be stressed, are by no means exhaustive of any of the revolutions examined. Specifically, they incorporate two types of sources: (1) those containing data relevant to the presentations in Parts II and III and (2) those important for understanding the context of a particular revolution as that context shapes the outlook of the revolutionaries.

This book, together with its predecessor, rounds out, at least for the time being, our examination of revolutionary elites throughout the world and across the centuries. To explore that which is quintessentially "revolutionary" about revolutionary elites, however, it is necessary to compare them with their establishment political counterparts. Such a control group would provide, at least in principle, a strong element of prediction, hence possibly advancing our understanding of leadership in general. At the moment, theoretical and methodological problems associated with such an endeavor appear overwhelming. Nonetheless, I propose to remedy this lacuna in a future work, by undertaking a comparative analysis of revolutionary and establishment elites—to the extent comparable data permit.

Reading *World Revolutionary Leaders* will naturally prompt the question as to how this study relates to, or differs from, our earlier work, *Leaders of Revolution*. Although this isssue is explicitly addressed at several junctures in the manuscript, for the reader's convenience, the main points are summarized here:

1. *World* is the concluding volume of our wide-ranging study (if we may say so) of revolutionaries. As such, it supersedes *Leaders* in every respect. Since the present study replicates the earlier volume (a well-established scholarly tradition), however, the theoretical foundations are altogether indispensable to the integrity of the en-

terprise—and they are condensed, synthesized, and revised in Chapters 1 and 2.

2. *Leaders* dealt with only 64 revolutionaries from twelve "old" countries; *World* covers 135 leaders from thirty-one revolutionary movements from the 1640s through the 1970s, covering all major regions of the world.

3. *World* offers new data, findings, interpretations, and conclusions about our revolutionaries. Specifically, first appearing in Chapter 3, a theoretically significant distinction between prewar and postwar leaders permeates the entire volume. New materials on regional variations, ideological orientations, life experiences, and psychodynamics of revolutionary elites throw light on the processes of radicalization.

4. *World* confirms our "situational" theory of revolutionary leadership as revised.

PART I

THEORY

1
The Psychological and Sociological Approaches*

Three theoretical approaches to the study of revolutionary elites may be identified: the psychoanalytic, the psychohistorical, the sociological. The psychoanalytic approach focuses on the inner dynamics of human personality, and it seeks to locate the impulse to revolution in the early psychological experiences of individuals. The psychohistorical approach seeks to move beyond the purely psychoanalytic theories by placing personality dynamics in the context of society and history; it attempts to combine psychological motivation with actual life experiences of an individual through time. The sociological approach—which is most prominently associated with the concept of charisma—stresses certain exceptional or supernatural qualities of individual leaders that sharply distinguish them from the masses while at the same time eliciting the latter's commitment and devotion.

THE PSYCHOANALYTIC APPROACH

The Leader as Ego Ideal

Pioneered by Sigmund Freud, the psychoanalytic approach constitutes the foundation of some influential contemporary studies of leadership. Though not concerned with revolutionary leaders as such, Freud's *Group Psychology and the Analysis of the Ego* presents a theory of leadership in general. More explicit applications of the Freudian theory to political and revolutionary person-

*More elaborate treatments of these approaches will be found in M. Rejai and K. Phillips, *Leaders of Revolution* (Beverly Hills: Sage Publications, 1979), Chaps. 1–3.

alities have been undertaken by Harold D. Lasswell and E. Victor Wolfenstein, among others.

Since group behavior is characterized by irrationality and emotionality, according to Freud, leadership is the key to understanding collective phenomena. He writes: "A group is . . . as intolerant as it is obedient to authority. It respects force and can only be slightly influenced by kindness, which it regards merely as a form of weakness. What it demands of its heroes is strength, or even violence. It wants to be ruled and oppressed and to fear its masters."[1]

The mutual ties binding together the members of a group are based upon their common libidinal/emotional (but desexualized) ties to the leader. This, Freud believes, is "the essence of the group mind," determining its cohesiveness and unity. The followers' common identification with the leader shapes their mode of identification toward each other as well.

The followers' emotional ties to the leader stem from persistent tension within their personalities. Specifically, within their psychic apparatus, the ego (rationality principle) is too weak to resolve the eternal conflict between the id (instinctual forces) and the superego (social or moral imperatives). Since the followers are unable to measure up to their own "ego ideal"—as represented by the superego—they come to substitute the leader for the ego ideal.

The psychology of the leader, on the other hand, stands in sharp contrast to that of the members of the group. Most significantly, the leader has no emotional ties to any one: "he may be of a masterful nature, absolutely narcissistic, self-confident and independent."[2]

The Displacement Hypothesis

Acknowledging the "spectacular and influential nature of Freud's work,"[3] Lasswell focuses directly upon the psychological dynamics of the political man. Specifically, he views the political personality as the power-centered personality: the political man compensates for his feelings of inadequacy and low self-esteem by a relentless pursuit of power. He values power above all else, for only through the pursuit and exercise of power can he maintain his personal "integrity." Moreover, this private need or motive is displaced upon public objects and rationalized in terms of the public interest.[4]

Lasswell's groundbreaking work on a wide range of clinical case studies led him to postulate several political personality types, most notably the agitator, the administrator, and the theorist. (Although Lasswell uses the term *theorist* in his early work, the context makes clear that what he has in mind is the "ideologue.")

The agitator is committed to principle, highly narcissistic (cf. Freud), and dependent upon the emotional acclamation of the people. The administrator displaces his private motives upon impersonal and concrete objects; his primary value lies in "the coordination of effort in continuing activity." The ideologue is riddled by doubt, preoccupied by trivialities, and dogmatic: "Deep doubts about the self are displaced onto doubts about the world outside, and these doubts are sought to be allayed by ostentatious preoccupation with truth."[5]

Lasswell sees persons involved in social movements—revolutions included—in the same light: they displace private motives upon public objects. Anticipating the work of Wolfenstein, he writes: "The affects which are organized in the family are redistributed upon various social objects, such as the state. Political crises are complicated by the concurrent reactivation of specific primitive impulses."[6]

Oedipal Conflict Writ Large

Wolfenstein's study of the "revolutionary personality" is in essence a specific application and amplification of Lasswell's displacement hypothesis, focusing upon the Oedipus complex.[7] Whereas in Freud rebellious sons channel their aggression directly against the fathers, in Wolfenstein they externalize their hostilities onto larger arenas.

Wolfenstein employs Erik H. Erikson's model of the eight stages of personality development—oral, anal, genital, latency, adolescence, young manhood, adulthood, maturity—in an effort to locate the motivational dynamics that impel men toward revolutionary action. He searches for similarities and differences in the early life experiences of Lenin, Trotsky, and Gandhi in an attempt to account for their emergence as revolutionary personalities in later years.

According to Erikson, each stage of personality development is marked by a distinctive crisis the successful resolution of which is a prerequisite for a "mature" transition to the succeeding stage. Focusing upon the genital stage, Wolfenstein identifies the inability to manage its unique crisis—the Oedipus complex—as the root motivation of the revolutionary. This uniformity, he finds, contrasts sharply with the dissimilarities in the life experiences of Lenin, Trotsky, and Gandhi in the other stages of personality development.

Wolfenstein concludes that the revolutionary personality represents the externalization of the parental rebellion associated with the oedipal conflict and its projection at the societal level. Thus:

> The basic attribute of this personality is that it is based on opposition to governmental authority; this is the result of the individual's continuing need to express his aggressive impulses vis-à-vis his father and the repressive action of governmental officials. The latter permits the individual to externalize his feelings of hatred. . . . Now the situation is much less ambivalent; governmental authority is clearly malevolent . . . and hence can be fought with a clear conscience.[8]

Governmental authority, then, is the functional equivalent of a surrogate father. Each of the three revolutionaries, Wolfenstein notes, fashioned an ideological framework which, among other things, juxtaposed the functional equivalent of a benevolent father (communist society, national independence) to that of a malevolent one (tsarism, British imperialism). The resolution of guilt and ambivalence permits all hate to be directed toward the government, all love toward the "people."

Critique

Intriguing though they are, psychoanalytic theories of political and revolutionary personalities are beset by a series of insurmountable difficulties. First, these studies are highly speculative, intuitive, and not always amenable to scientific criteria (for example, replication and verification). This is as true of Freud's super-ego and ego ideal as it is of Lasswell's power seeking and displacement hypothesis and of Wolfenstein's propositions concerning the Oedipus complex and the surrogate father. Second, these studies provide at best parochial explanations of revolutionary leadership, since they are limited to very few individuals and since they leave out considerations of historical and socioeconomic variables. Finally, the sheer wealth and variety of psychological data necessary for conducting these studies are staggering and more than likely unavailable in most instances.

THE PSYCHOHISTORICAL APPROACH

While the psychoanalytic perspective deals predominantly with the inner dynamics of human personality, the psychohistorical approach attempts to move beyond psychoanalysis by placing personality dynamics in the context of society and history. As pioneered by Erikson and practiced by many others, the psychohistorical approach represents, by definition, a fusion of psychology and history. In particular, in Erikson's interpretation, it seeks to juxtapose and interrelate the personality conflicts of a "great man" with the historical problems of a particular era.

Personal Crisis and Historical Drama

According to Erikson, as we have noted, the human life cycle consists of eight distinct and successive stages of development, each of which evolves in a sociohistorical setting and each of which contributes toward the progressive differentiation—and whole-ness—of the human personality as it unfolds through time. Each stage is marked by a distinct "crisis" or "turning point," the successful addressing of which contributes toward the development of a fully psychosocial personality.

Whereas Wolfenstein's approach to Lenin, Trotsky, and Gandhi centers on the genital stage and the oedipal conflict, Erikson's

25

groundbreaking studies of Martin Luther and Mahatma Gandhi focus on the turning points of adolescence (Luther) and adulthood (Gandhi).[9] In Luther's case, the central concern is "identity crisis," the successful resolution of which results in personal wholeness, integrity, and continuity. In Gandhi's case, the focus is "generativity crisis," that is, whether or not one develops the capacity to establish and guide the next generation—either in terms of actual fatherhood or symbolically in terms of accomplishments or "works." In each case, Erikson uses a pivotal "Event" around which to organize his study.

Erikson's work on Luther opens with the account of the Event: a fit Luther is supposed to have had in the choir of his monastery, most likely in his early twenties. Falling to the ground, according to two or three eyewitnesses, Luther raved: "It isn't me!" (German version) or "I am *not!*" (Latin version). Erikson treats this incident as the exemplar of Luther's identity crisis; and he searches for its dynamics in Luther's home life and childhood.

Luther's parents were strict disciplinarians, as were the teachers under whom he studied. Young Martin himself was brooding and aloof, lacked feelings, was rebellious and given to violent moods, and demonstrated a bad temper and an intense capacity to hate. At the University of Erfurt he studied under radical theologians who questioned the strict teachings of the Catholic Church. Having obtained a master's degree, he underwent an abrupt "conversion": in an act of outright defiance of his father, Luther terminated his academic studies and determined to become a monk. Having joined a harsh and austere monastery, he was ordained a priest in 1507, at the age of twenty-three.

Luther's training for priesthood—itself a form of ideological indoctrination—provided him with an opportunity to formulate his distinctive theology as a legitimate weapon with which to attack the Catholic Church. In 1517 Luther nailed his ninety-five theses on the church door in Wittenberg.

Luther's reformulation of Christianity, his emphasis upon the priesthood of all believers, his attack upon church hierarchy—in all this, according to Erikson, he spoke for countless thousands who had shared the same sentiments but had not dared challenge the established order. As such, Luther was one of those great men who was "called upon . . . to lift his individual patienthood to the level of a universal one and to try to solve for all what he could not solve for himself alone."[10]

The Event around which Erikson constructs his study of Gandhi is the Ahmedabad textile strike of 1918. Although other authorities—Gandhi himself included—have not assigned such signal importance to the strike, Erikson sees it not only as the cornerstone of labor unionism in India but also as critical in Gandhi's life and in the fate of nonviolence as a transformative technique.[11] The strike, he notes, occasioned the first time Gandhi—then forty-eight years old—fasted for a political issue. A year later, he led the mass movement of national civil disobedience, thereby establishing a spiritual belief in nonviolence as a ritual.

In expounding and practicing nonviolence, according to Erikson, Gandhi was responding to a crisis of generativity characteristic of his adulthood. In fashioning a following, a vast retinue, an extended family, and a nonviolent technique, Gandhi was involved in a process of nation building as well as of self-creation. In transforming the negative Indian identity of inferiority vis-à-vis the British, he at the same time transformed a negative self-image based upon persistent feelings of depression, personal despair and humiliation, and an intense feeling of guilt toward the father (note the famous episode of Gandhi having sexual intercourse as his father lay on his deathbed in another room in the same house). In any event, we witness once again the coalescence of historical imperative and personal drama. And we see once again a great man stepping out of conventional boundaries to adapt the historical setting to his personal needs.

Asceticism and Displaced Libido

A specific psychohistorical study of revolutionary leaders has been undertaken by Bruce Mazlish. Mazlish's starting point is that "there is a cluster of traits" which epitomizes the "revolutionary ascetic" as an ideal type. In delineating this concept, he relies upon the work of Freud and Max Weber.

Asceticism, Mazlish argues, has two components: (1) narcissism and (2) self-denial, self-control, self-sacrifice. Mazlish's discussion of the first component draws directly on Freud's *Group Psychology and the Analysis of the Ego* (see above). Thus, as Freud has indicated, the leader has few libidinal ties to others; he is incapable of feelings and emotions; he is "masterful" and "absolutely narcissistic." For Freud's idea of "few libidinal ties," however, Mazlish substitutes the notion of "displaced libido," meaning that the individual has displaced his libidinal ties onto an abstraction. Thus, "it is the Revolution, the People, Humanity, or Virtue which the leader glorifies and extols."[12]

In treating the second component of asceticism, Mazlish draws upon Weber. In his *Protestant Ethic and the Spirit of Capitalism,* Weber shows how asceticism as an initially religious concept was transformed into a worldly one and placed at the service of capitalism. These traits, Mazlish maintains, were "later put under the banner of revolutionary activity."[13]

When combined, according to Mazlish, asceticism and displaced libido are highly functional to the vocation of the revolutionary: "We are postulating, in fact, that there is an enormously explosive power in 'revolutionary asceticism,' that the traits of displaced libido and asceticism are highly functional in the real world of revolution."[14]

Having applied the concept of the revolutionary ascetic to Cromwell, Robespierre, Lenin, and Mao, Mazlish concludes that the four are very much alike in the pattern of behavior they exhibited, differing only in the sociohistorical context in which they found themselves.

Critique

By introducing sociohistorical variables into the discussion of great leaders, the psychohistorical approach overcomes some of the problems of the purely psychoanalytic theory. At the same time, it creates fresh problems of its own. To begin with, much of the intuitive and nonscientific aspects of the psychoanalytic theory remains, as there remain enormous problems of operationalizing many of the psychological categories and of locating the requisite psychohistorical data. Similarly, the problem of the range of explanation remains unresolved, as these works, too, are limited to very few individuals.

As far as Erikson's work is concerned, his studies of Luther and Gandhi are characterized by such "neatness" as to raise questions about their scientific rigor. In each case, as we have seen, he uses an Event that is, at best, suspect as the turning point that he presents it to be but that nonetheless provides a seemingly compelling logic around which a tight interpretation is constructed. Thus, in each case, we end up with the fortuitous coalescence of personal trauma and historical crisis. In this context, one appreciates Paul Roazen's reference to the "novelistic" quality of Erikson's work.[15]

Mazlish's study of the revolutionary ascetic, though informed by a more elaborate theoretical apparatus, is hardly as sophisticated as he claims. Put simply, to state that the life of a revolutionary leader is characterized by self-discipline, self-denial, and self-control is to say very little, for these qualities are *definitional components* of such a personality. A stoic, austere, puritanical life style is widely adopted by revolutionary leaders and widely commented upon by any number of writers (see Chapter 8).

THE SOCIOLOGICAL APPROACH

The most prominent sociological theory of revolutionary leadership revolves around the concept of charisma. Although *charisma* has become a widely abused term in the English language, finding expression in a variety of forms, our treatment is limited to the professional literature.

Weber's Formulation

The word *charisma* was originally coined by the church historian Rudolf Sohm, who associated it with divinely inspired leaders and used it in an exclusively religious context. According to Sohm, "The charisma is from God . . . and the service to which the charisma calls is a service imposed by God, and an office in the service of the church, and not of any local community."[16]

Weber—with whom the concept of charisma is most prominently associated—accepted the original religious meaning while adding a secular dimension. Acknowledging that charisma is "often . . . most clearly developed in the field of religion," he proceeded to suggest that "in principle, however, the same state of affairs recurs universally."[17] Specifically, according to Weber, charisma refers "to certain quality of an individual personality by virtue of which he is set apart from ordinary men and treated as endowed with supernatural, superhuman, or at least specifically exceptional powers or qualities. These are . . . regarded as of divine origin or as exemplary, and on the basis of them the individual concerned is treated as a leader."[18]

Charisma, it follows, is a leader–follower relationship: without the voluntary recognition of disciples and followers, there would be no charisma. "Psychologically," writes Weber, "this 'recognition' is a matter of complete personal devotion to the possessor of the [charismatic] quality, arising out of enthusiasm, or of despair and hope."[19]

Lying outside the established structures of social, political, and economic rationality, charisma involves fundamental innovation and change. Writes Weber: "Within the sphere of its claims, charismatic authority repudiates the past, and is in this sense a specifically revolutionary force." Not bound by the existing order, the charismatic leader "transvalues everything." As such, charismatic authority is most likely to emerge "in times of psychic, physical, economic, ethical, religious, political distress."[20]

Charisma and Political Revolution

Weber's conception of charisma has set off a controversy of major proportions in social science literature. Scholars have variously accepted Weber's formulation, rejected it, revised it, and applied it in various contexts. Some have discussed charisma in the context of political development, which may involve revolutionary upheavals. Of interest in this regard is the work of Ann R. Willner.

Accepting Weber's delineation of charisma, Willner stresses

the conditions of crisis under which charismatic leaders emerge in colonial or developing societies. Thus, "situations of economic deprivation, social stress, political crisis, and psychic stress can crystallize into a collective call by the people for a leader to come to their rescue."[21] These leaders, she finds, come from diverse social backgrounds. They possess high levels of energy and vitality, high intelligence and motivation, a capacity for originality and innovation, composure under stress, an ability to evoke cultural myths, symbols, and values. Crisis, in short, leads to the emergence of charisma; charisma, in turn, produces stability and order.

A relatively extensive analysis of revolutionary charisma has been undertaken by Robert C. Tucker. The concept of charisma, he maintains, "is virtually indispensable, particularly for students of revolutionary movements of various kinds." Specifically, Tucker sets out "to develop the theory of charisma into a more workable tool of understanding and research."[22] His principal contribution in this regard is to equate charismatic leadership with charismatic movement:

> Charismatic leadership . . . typically appears in the setting of a social *movement* of some kind or creates such a movement. The charismatic leader is not simply any leader who is idolized and freely followed for his extraordinary leadership qualities, but one who demonstrates such qualities in the process of summoning people to join in a movement for change and in leading such a movement. . . . To speak of charismatic leaders, then, is to speak of charismatic movements; the two phenomena are inseparable.[23]

Allowing that a charismatic leader may appear at the outset of a movement or sometime thereafter, Tucker claims that his focus on "movement" has important implications by placing the emphasis on the leader's early career: "For the student of charisma . . . the pre-power stage of a leader's career is of critical significance."[24] Stressing that charismatic leaders appear in periods of stress, Tucker writes: "The charismatic leader is one in whom, by virtue of unusual personal qualities, the promise or hope of salvation—deliverance from distress—appears to be embodied. . . . He is in essence a savior, or one who is so perceived by his followers. *Charismatic leadership is specifically salvationist or messianic in nature.*"[25]

A systematic attempt to revise Weber's concept of charisma has been undertaken by James V. Downton, who approaches charisma as "psychological exchange" in which both the leader and the follower come to fulfill certain personality needs.[26] Relying on Freud and Erikson (see above), he identifies the sources of the follower's commitment as tensions within his personality. These tensions result from the inability of the ego effectively to mediate the conflict between the id and the superego. On the part of the follower, in other words, ego weakness is the basic stimulus for psychological exchange.

The primary personality need of the leader is deference: "the leader comes to see himself as charismatic and lives from day to day on the deferential treatment he sees as rightfully his." In return for deference, the charismatic leader performs three roles: (1) he is a "comforter" by offering security; (2) he provides an "ideal" by offering a role model; (3) he is a "spokesman" for a transcendent authority.[27]

As such, Downton maintains, there are two types of charismatic leadership: revolutionary and institutionalized. Charisma is not only an agent of change; it is also a conservative force. Thus, "Weber was wrong in assuming that charismatic authority was synonymous with personal rulership."[28]

Critique

The concept of charisma has come under a barrage of criticisms from all directions. Many scholars have pointed to the ambiguous and elusive nature of Weber's formulations, particularly as they regard the qualities of charisma. Some have called into question the social-scientific utility of the term altogether. For example, K. J. Ratnam argues that the looseness with which "charisma" is used has encouraged "wrong explanations." It has provided some scholars with "the easy way out" by enabling them simply to attribute success to "charisma" without considering that their "explanations follow no recognized criteria."[29]

The application of the concept of charisma to the analysis of revolutionary leadership is even more problematical. While the concept is of some intuitive value, its empirical utility is seriously limited. Thus, in his massive *Handbook of Leadership,* Ralph M. Stogdill omits the coverage of charisma altogether. His rationale reads: "This important variant of the leadership role has not been a willing or frequent subject of research that involves measurement and experimentation. Numerous biographical studies of charismatic leaders are available, but they provide comparatively little information that adds to an understanding of leadership."[30]

Finally, while charismatic figures have appeared in most—perhaps all—revolutions, it is quite clear that not all revolutionary leaders are charismatic, nor are all charismatic leaders revolutionary. Considering the revolutionary movements of the twentieth century, for example, we can identify a handful of leaders who may have possessed charismatic qualities—for example, Lenin, Mao, Ho, Castro, Guevara—but by far the majority cannot be called charismatic by any stretch of the imagination.

2
The Situational Approach

We have discussed the psychoanalytic, psychohistorical, and sociological approaches to the study of revolutionary elites, and we have indicated their weaknesses for purposes of theoretical understanding. In this chapter we propose a situational theory of revolutionary leadership.[1] This theory is synthetic in two respects: (1) it draws upon the strong points of the approaches we have criticized, and (2) it combines sociological and psychological considerations in the analysis of revolutionary leaders.

Although we have not changed our theory in any fundamental way, we have appropriately modified it in order to take into account our findings in the earlier volume. Our operating premise in this regard is that, ideally, theory is a guide to research, while research in turn helps refine and sharpen theory. Whether our modified theory is a more powerful guide to the research reported in this volume is a question to which we return in the concluding chapter.

Our theoretical position is stated in terms of two interrelated sets of propositions and hypotheses about revolutionary elites, one relating to their emergence upon the scene, the other to their social background. These propositions and hypotheses are derived— both inductively and deductively—from selected studies of leaders, revolutions, and revolutionaries considered as a *composite* literature. (Clearly we cannot rely on any *single* source for any proposition or hypothesis because we know of no other study with a data base comparable to ours.) Important contributors to this literature include Paul Berman, James H. Billington, Crane Brinton, James M. Burns, James C. Davies, Jerome Davis, James V. Downton, Jr., Lewis J. Edinger, Erik H. Erikson, Sigmund Freud, Ted Robert Gurr, Margaret G. Hermann, Samuel P. Huntington, Daniel Katz, John H. Kautsky, Harold D. Lasswell, Harold D. Lasswell and

Daniel Lerner, Harold D. Lasswell et al., Ming T. Lee, James K. Martin, Bruce Mazlish, Barrington Moore, Jr., Glenn D. Paige, Robert D. Putnam, William B. Quandt, Robert A. Scalapino, David C. Schwartz, Philip Selznick, Edward Shils, Ralph M. Stogdill, Charles Tilly, Robert C. Tucker, Max Weber, Ann R. Willner, and E. Victor Wolfenstein (for details, see bibliography of theoretical literature).

EMERGENCE OF REVOLUTIONARY ELITES

Our initial postulate is commonsensical: revolutionary leaders grow out of a particular social-historical context. Their social background and socialization experiences imbue them with a set of norms and values and prepare them for the political roles they will be called upon to play in the future. By the same token, they are in a position convincingly to capture, internalize, and articulate the fears, frustrations, hopes, and aspirations of their peoples. In this context, as one scholar has written, "leadership is clearly a relationship between followers with needs and wishes and leaders who conceptualize, symbolize, satisfy or promise satisfaction of these needs."[2]

Revolutionary leadership, we propose, is primarily situational. A situation of crisis—whether political, military, social, economic, or psychological—catapults the leaders into prominence and provides them with ready and willing followerships. Political crises may consist of interelite rivalries or coups d'etat, riots or rebellions, nationalist movements set in motion by imperialist penetration and control, widespread governmental corruption and ineptitude. Military crises are represented by defeat in war or army mutiny. Social crises include the disintegration of the prevailing ideology, normative order, and social institutions. Economic crises are represented by severe inflation or depression. Psychological crises consist of widespread frustration, alienation, and relative deprivation. It is difficult if not impossible to propose a general rule concerning the precise crisis that generates a revolutionary situation in our sense. It seems clear, however, that the greater the intensity and coalescence of various crises, the greater the likelihood and the more rapid the emergence of revolutionary leaders.

Situations of uncertainty, unpredictability, anxiety, and stress, in turn, rally the people and mobilize them in a common search for safety and security. In this context, Erik H. Erikson has proposed three forms of distress which may set the stage for the emergence of revolutionary elites: (1) "fear"—for example, of impending doom; (2) "anxiety"—for example, associated with persons in an "identity vacuum"; (3) "existential dread"—for example, experienced by persons whose routines of life have collapsed. Correspondingly, revolutionary leaders emerge to offer people salvation in the form of safety or identity or ritual.[3]

A second type of situation may account for the emergence of other revolutionaries. Specifically, the persistent turbulence and large-scale violence characteristic of the history of such countries as China, Colombia, Cuba, Guatemala, Northern Ireland, and Vietnam set the stage for—and facilitate the emergence of—revolutionary elites.

A third form of situational variable relates to personal traits or characteristics that are "external" to the leader himself and over which he has little or no control. Among these are: (1) birthplace, (2) urban culture, (3) socioeconomic status, (4) legitimacy status, (5) number of siblings, (6) age ranking among siblings, (7) quality of family life, (8) ethnicity, (9) religious background. Some of these variables—particularly urban exposure, socioeconomic status, and age ranking among siblings—are significantly associated with the emergence of revolutionary elites.

Though critical, situation alone does not account for the emergence of revolutionary elites; it is a necessary but not a sufficient condition. For a revolutionary leader to emerge, it is imperative that the situation coincide with the presence of a certain kind of person or personality. This person or personality has two essential characteristics: (1) a mental set or a psychology that propels him toward revolutionary action and (2) a set of skills—particularly verbal and organizational—that enables him to perform his tasks.

The mental set or psychology to which we refer takes a variety of forms. The sense of vanity, egotism, and narcissism of revolutionary leaders has been noted by any number of observers and scholars. This self-aggrandizement, in turn, may be ignited by feelings of persecution—real or imagined—and a desire for revenge.

Revolutionary elites are motivated by varieties of nationalism and patriotism. They may seek to maintain the independence and integrity of their nations. They may set out to free their countries from the oppression and exploitation of other nations.

Revolutionary leaders are driven by a sense of justice–injustice and a corresponding mission to "set things right." This syndrome is most pronounced in colonial contexts, where it coincides with the feelings of nationalism and the hatred of the outsider.

To be convincing in their drive for justice, revolutionary elites must adopt a posture of virtue and purity. Thus, it is not surprising that many revolutionary leaders adopt a simple, spartan life style. They shun luxuries, even comfort, stressing sacrifice and hard work instead. The reign of virtue and purity, in turn, may be impossible without the massive exercise of violence and terror.

In their attempt to right the wrongs they perceive, some revolutionaries begin as reformers: they try to bring about change by working within the system. Since the system is typically unresponsive, frustration and disillusionment set in. Rejecting the system, the reformers turn to revolutionary politics.

Relative deprivation and status inconsistency may serve as other sources of revolutionary motivation. Where there is a felt discrepancy between aspiration and achievement (relative deprivation), one may set out to redress the situation accordingly—whether by reformist or by revolutionary means. Similarly, where there is discrepancy between one's socioeconomic status and one's political power (status inconsistency), reformist or revolutionary politics may offer relief.

Some revolutionary leaders are driven by a compulsion to excel, to prove themselves, to overcompensate. This compulsion is likely due to feelings of low self-esteem or inferiority complex. How this condition comes about is a question that requires examination on a case-by-case basis.

The Oedipus complex and its attendant consequences may

play roles in the emergence of some revolutionary elites. The displacement of an internal psychological drama onto the political realm provides a compelling motivation for some revolutionaries, for it reduces feelings of ambivalence and guilt and makes life more manageable. But this too must be analyzed on an individual basis.

In short, any number of dynamics may play roles in shaping the mental set of revolutionary elites. We hazard the proposition, however, that no single motivation or dynamic is sufficient to explain the formation of all revolutionary personalities. Nor do we anticipate an invariant "mix" of dynamics universally explanatory of the psychology of revolutionary leaders. A "mix" there will be, to be sure, but we expect it to vary from revolutionary to revolutionary.

Revolutionary elites require a set of skills with which to approach their calling. In particular, they have the capacity to devise and propagate an appropriate ideology and to create the necessary organizational apparatus.

Revolutionary leaders denounce the established order by appealing to "higher" norms and principles. They evoke, conjure, and assimilate onto themselves myths and values of a transcendent nature, and they communicate these values through rhetoric, symbolism, and imagery—all appropriately simplified for popular consumption.

Revolutionary elites articulate an alternative vision of society embodying a superior order. This alternative vision frequently includes a utopian image or a grand myth—the Fatherland, the Classless Society, the Golden Age. The grand myth elicits emotional response and becomes a rallying cry for the masses.

Revolutionary leaders propose plans and programs designed to realize the alternative order. In other words, the mere delineation of a utopian vision is not enough; the new vision must be concretized in a plan of action promising success in the foreseeable future.

In doing all this, revolutionary elites highlight grievances and injustices, undermine the legitimacy and morale of the ruling regime, mobilize the masses to the cause, and lend dignity to revolutionary action. They evoke reverence and devotion among a large following. They generate commitment and elicit sacrifice from a small group of dedicated cadres. They promote unity, solidarity, and cohesion in the revolutionary ranks.[4]

To be most effective, the verbal skills of revolutionary leaders must be complemented by an ability to fashion an appropriate revolutionary organization. In effect, revolutionary leaders translate ideology into action through the medium of organization. Ideology helps mobilize the masses; organization functions to tap their energies and channel them toward the realization of revolutionary objectives. Philip Selznick writes: "Although ideology, to be translated into power, requires organization, effective organization also requires ideology."[5] Samuel P. Huntington has laid down the general principle that "organization is the road to power. . . . In the modernizing world [as elsewhere?] he controls the future who organizes its politics."[6]

Employing organizations of various kinds—political, military, paramilitary—revolutionary elites perform a number of critical functions. They keep in touch with the masses; recruit, socialize, and train cadres; motivate members and supporters by dispensing appropriate rewards and inducements; maintain internal discipline and control; carry out communication and propaganda functions; and conduct intelligence activities by collecting and utilizing information about the enemy. In a word, they lay the groundwork for the eventual seizure of power.[7]

To summarize to this point, we have stressed the close interplay among three variables in the emergence of revolutionary leaders: a revolutionary situation, a mental set of psychology, a range of skills. Taken together, the three variables demonstrate why it is that (1) not all revolutionary situations give rise to revolutionary leaders and (2) not all persons with the appropriate psychology and skills emerge as leaders of revolution.

Stated differently, revolutionary leadership is a function of coalescence of time, place, social conditions, psychological dispositions, and verbal and organizational skills. The revolutionary leader emerges in a particular context, by virtue of a psychology that drives him toward action and a set of skills that enables him to address the needs of the situation. It is clear that the theoretical posture advanced here combines trait theories of leadership with situational theories.

CHARACTERISTICS OF REVOLUTIONARY ELITES

The mere possession of verbal and organizational skills suggests a certain social background which revolutionary leaders share. It also points to an appropriate social setting—and an appropriate set of life experiences—in which these skills are acquired. It further implies a period of time over which these skills are sharpened and refined. It finally requires a degree of freedom from daily labor. To clarify these and related matters, we turn to a series of propositions and hypotheses concerning revolutionary elites.* Our general postulate is that the behavior of revolutionary leaders is a function of their social background plus their experiences as they go through life.

Revolutionary elites are neither very young nor very old, most of them being in their thirties and forties. Though they may become exposed to revolutionary ideologies (and participate in revolutionary activity) at much earlier ages, the development of the requisite skills—and the assumption of leadership positions—require periods of gestation and refinement. The twentieth century has marked a tendency toward younger revolutionary leaders, a phenomenon which may be a function of the increasing education and enlightenment available in recent times—including awareness of experiences of earlier and contemporary revolutionaries.

Revolutionary leaders either come from the urban centers, or if born and raised in rural environments, they quickly acquire extensive urban exposure and orientation. Early involvement in national

*In a prepublication review of the manuscript, a colleague suggested that the propositions and hypotheses advanced in this section "taste more like a preview of the empirical findings." In fact, however, these propositions and hypotheses were formulated well in advance of data analysis, most of them having appeared in much earlier works. See M. Rejai, "Leaders of Revolution," paper presented at the annual meeting of the American Political Science Association, Washington, D.C., September 1972; idem, *The Strategy of Political Revolution*, chap. 3.

politics in the urban areas is essential to the development of revolutionary elites.

Revolutionary leaders typically belong to the main ethnic groups in their societies; they are full-fledged members of the peoples they seek to lead. Their religious background, too, is of the mainstream variety, though their evolving religious orientation is highly fluid and unstable.

Revolutionary elites are broadly middle class in origin, with substantial representation from the lower class. The latter phenomenon is primarily associated with twentieth-century revolutions in underdeveloped and semideveloped countries.

Leaders of revolution constitute a well-educated group, many of them having obtained university or other advanced training. Accordingly, they are concentrated in the professions, particularly law, medicine, education, journalism and related fields. An impressive number of individuals are professional revolutionaries pure and simple, or they combine another occupation with that of the professional revolutionary. Although they may not have received professional training in the military, most leaders acquire military experience as a necessary tool of revolution and a necessary component of their skills. Generally "intellectuals," revolutionary elites write extensively, typically on revolutionary theory and practice.

Leaders of revolution have extensive histories of involvement in clandestine or open radical activity. They actively participate in revolutionary organizations of various kinds. They are in frequent difficulty with the established authorities, and they have records of arrest, imprisonment, and exile.

Whether voluntarily or involuntarily, revolutionary elites acquire substantial exposure to foreign cultures, languages, and ideologies. These experiences provide a variety of base lines against which to judge the realities of their own societies. Beyond this, revolutionary leaders are typically indigenous to the countries in which they operate.

The ideologies of revolutionary elites are typically eclectic, combining indigenous and foreign elements. The most prominent revolutionary ideologies have been democracy of various types, nationalism of various forms, Marxism of various shades, or some combination of the three.

Leaders of revolution have a generally positive or optimistic attitude toward human beings ("the nature of man") and toward their own countries. By contrast, their image of the international society is dualistic: they see it as divided into unmistakable friends and unmistakable foes.

PART II

CHARACTERISTICS OF REVOLUTIONARY LEADERS

3
General and Temporal Patterns

To test the hypotheses and propositions concerning the demographic, experiential, ideological, and attitudinal attributes of revolutionary elites advanced in Chapter 2, we gathered data on the aforementioned variables for 135 leaders from thirty-one revolutionary movements. The data came from a variety of sources, as discussed in the Introduction and detailed in the Bibliography.

In reporting our findings in this volume, we initially postulated a dual task: (1) a comparative analysis of the 71 revolutionaries of the 1960s and 1970s with the 64 leaders of the earlier times and (2) an overall analysis of our 135 revolutionary elites. Upon closer examination, however, the temporal distinction underlying the first task proved artificial and unproductive. For one thing, the distinction involves some overlap, since two of our "earlier" revolutions (Algeria and France) also occurred in the 1960s. More important, extensive data analyses unraveled a marked paucity of meaningful or theoretically significant distinctions between the two groups.

The temporal distinction that *is* of crucial significance concerns the revolutionaries who are active before the Second World War and those who appear upon the scene after that watershed event. In the earlier volume, it will be remembered, we find important variations between twentieth-century revolutionary elites and all their earlier counterparts. The *prewar–postwar distinction* is an even sharper variation on the same theme, and it recurs throughout this volume.

In particular, as we shall see, a series of significant differences separate the 107 leaders of revolutionary movements that unfolded or culminated after World War II from the 28 revolutionaries that preceded them. (Of the 28 leaders, it will be recalled, 5 each are from England, France, and Mexico; 6 from America; and 7 from Russia.) The Second World War and its consequences left an indelible imprint on the theory and practice of revolution. The disintegration of the great empires shattered the myth of white invincibility: it demonstrated conclusively that in principle the white man was vulnerable. Initial Japanese successes further showed (as had Japanese victory in the Russo-Japanese War of 1904–1905) that the nonwhite could even *prevail* over the white.

Anti-Western national revolutionary movements mushroomed throughout Africa, Asia, and Latin America, and they were led, ironically enough, by men who had been educated in Western countries. Indeed, the genesis of many postwar revolutions can be traced to student and émigré groups from various colonies who met, planned, and organized in London, Paris, and other European cities and then transported the revolution, as it were, to their native countries. Revolutionary leaders of widely divergent cultures and backgrounds shared knowledge and experience as they enriched and reinforced one another.

Advances in technology (particularly transportation and communication), coupled with the "knowledge explosion," made Western learning accessible to people in every part of the earth, the colonials included. Having returned to their native lands, revolutionary leaders were in a position to intensify awareness among their peoples, many difficulties (e.g., illiteracy) notwithstanding.

To be sure, some revolutions were defeated, and others remain in various states of dormancy. On the other hand, a great many colonial revolutionary movements succeeded. As new countries emerged, membership in the United Nations more than tripled, from 51 at its founding in 1946 to nearly 160 at this writing. In a word, the Second World War gave rise to new revolutions and new breeds of revolutionaries. In this context, the Chinese Revolution may have served as a pivotal example.

In the pages that follow, we present our findings concerning the general characteristics of our 135 revolutionary elites, organized to correspond as much as possible with our treatment in *Leaders of Revolution*. Simultaneously, we report our findings relative to a series of variations between prewar and postwar revolutionary elites. This temporal dimension is one of the key independent variables we employ to highlight heterogeneity among revolutionaries (see Chapter 4). We incorporate the two sets of findings in this chapter in an effort to streamline presentation and avoid repetition. Where no significant variations occur between prewar and postwar leaders, the frequency distribution alone is reported.

We note for the record that throughout the course of this study, we have come across findings that, although "statistically significant," carry little or no theoretical substance or meaning. In all such instances, we have refrained from reporting our "findings."

FINDINGS

Tables 3.1 through 3.6 incorporate all the relevant data concerning our 135 revolutionaries. One finding is so evident as to require only a bare mention: there is not a single woman among our leaders. Although women have begun to play increasingly significant roles in recent times, none appears among the top leaders of the thirty-one revolutionary movements we studied.

Age and Birthplace

Revolutionary elites tend to be older than we had anticipated, as shown in Table 3.1, section A; in fact, a surprising 40 percent are over the age of forty-five. Nor is there a trend toward younger leaders in more recent times, as no significant variations emerge in this respect for prewar and postwar elites.

As far as exposure to revolutionary ideologies is concerned, as Table 3.1.B indicates, our elites run the entire spectrum, with a distinct concentration (76 percent) in the three youngest age groups (twenty-four years or younger). In fact, such diverse figures as Arafat, Ben Bella, Buscayno, Cahill, F. Castro, Chou En-lai, Cohn-Bendit, Guevara, and de la Puente are exposed to revolutionary ideology *before* age fifteen. On the other hand, nearly 22 percent of postwar leaders develop radical orientations after the age of twenty-five, as compared to over 32 percent of prewar elites.

47

Table 3.1. Frequency Distribution of Hypothesized Characteristics of Prewar and Postwar Leaders: Age and Birthplace

(A) LEADER'S AGE AT TIME OF REVOLUTION

	16–19		20–24		25–34		35–44		45–64		65+		Total	
	N	%	N	%	N	%	N	%	N	%	N	%	N	%
	1	0.7	1	0.7	40	29.6	34	25.2	54	40.0	5	3.7	135	100.0

(B) AGE FIRST EXPOSED TO REVOLUTIONARY IDEOLOGY

LEADERS	0–15		16–19		20–24		25–34		35–44		45–64		Total	
	N	%	N	%	N	%	N	%	N	%	N	%	N	%
Prewar	3	10.7	13	46.4	3	10.7	5	17.9	1	3.6	3	10.7	28	20.7
Postwar	21	19.6	36	33.6	27	25.2	20	18.7	3	2.8	0	0.0	107	79.3
Total	24	17.8	49	36.3	30	22.2	25	18.5	4	3.0	3	2.2	135	100.0

Gamma = −.13 Chi square = 15.61 $p < .008$

(C) AGE FIRST TOOK PART IN REVOLUTIONARY ACTIVITY

LEADERS	0–15		16–19		20–24		25–34		35–44		45–64		Total	
	N	%	N	%	N	%	N	%	N	%	N	%	N	%
Prewar	0	0.0	7	25.0	0	0.0	11	39.3	7	25.0	3	10.7	28	20.7
Postwar	6	5.6	30	28.0	34	31.8	28	26.2	8	7.5	1	0.9	107	79.3
Total	6	4.4	37	27.4	34	25.2	39	28.9	15	11.1	4	3.0	135	100.0

Gamma = −.50 Chi square = 25.16 $p < .0001$

(D) BIRTHPLACE

	Urban		Rural		Total	
	N	%	N	%	N	%
	58	46.0	68	54.0	126	100.0

(E) EXPOSURE TO URBAN LIFE IF NONURBAN BORN

	1–3 years		4 or more years		Total	
	N	%	N	%	N	%
	5	7.5	62	92.5	67	100.0

(F) AGE EXPOSED TO URBAN LIFE

	0–14		15–19		20–24		25–29		Total	
	N	%	N	%	N	%	N	%	N	%
	22	32.4	27	39.7	17	25.0	2	2.9	68	100.0

Note. Totals do not correspond due to missing data.

As Table 3.1.C demonstrates, our leaders first participate in revolutionary activity across all age categories. The difference between prewar and postwar elites is dramatic, however. Whereas only 25 percent of the former engage in radical activity by the age of 24, over 65 percent of the latter are so engaged by the same age.

Revolutionary elites are either urban born (46 percent) or, if born in rural contexts, acquire early and sustained exposure to urban life (Table 3.1.D, E, F). "Revolutionariness," in other words, is an urban phenomenon, which may then be "exported" to nonurban areas. These findings appear to hold across time, as no significant variations occur for prewar and postwar revolutionaries.

Socioeconomic Status and Family Life

The socioeconomic status of revolutionary elites, Table 3.2.A illustrates, is well within the anticipated range: about 19 percent are from the upper class, 52 percent from the middle class, and 26 percent from the lower class. Postwar revolutionaries, however, come from significantly different social backgrounds than prewar ones. Specifically, while the proportion from the middle class remains relatively constant, upper-class representation is sharply down for postwar elites (14 percent as compared to 36 percent for prewar leaders), whereas lower-class representation is dramatically up (30 percent as compared to 11 percent). These variations are no doubt due to the undeveloped or semideveloped nature of the societies or regions with which many of our revolutionaries are associated.

Revolutionary elites are typically of legitimate birth, and they come from relatively large families, with over 65 percent having three to nineteen siblings (Table 3.2.B and C). The temporal variation is significant, however, in that prewar elites come from much larger families. Specifically, nearly 55 percent of prewar elites come from families of seven or more siblings, the corresponding figure being only 18 percent for postwar leaders. Moreover, as can be seen, fully 34 percent of postwar revolutionaries have only one sibling or none at all, the corresponding figure being a mere 5 percent for their earlier counterparts.

As for age ranking among siblings, as Table 3.2.D documents, our revolutionaries tend to be either the oldest child (27 percent) or the youngest child (21 percent) or the only child (11 percent) or the oldest son (10 percent). Only 26 percent are middle children. This disproportionate representation—particularly in the light of the large families from which many of the leaders come—is an intriguing subject to which we shall have occasion to return.

Revolutionary elites tend to enjoy "tranquil" family lives, as seen in Table 3.2.E. Specifically, whereas nearly 60 percent fit this category, 22 percent have turbulent childhoods and 19 percent come from broken homes. This characteristic, as well as the one preceding it (age ranking among siblings), remains constant across time, there being no significant variations among prewar and postwar leaders on either score.

Ethnicity and Religion

Leaders of revolution tend to be of mainstream variety with respect to ethnicity and religion. As for ethnicity, as Table 3.3.A demonstrates, 57 percent of our elites belong to the major groupings in their societies, while 31 percent belong to a large minority, and only 12 percent to a small one. Similarly, 71 percent of our leaders belong to the main religions in their countries, and only 29 percent to a minority religion (Table 3.3.B). Moreover, ethnicity and religion are among characteristics that do not appreciably change over time, there being no significant variations for prewar and postwar revolutionaries.

As a whole, Table 3.3.C shows, the religious background of revolutionary elites is characterized by considerable variety: Catholic (37 percent), Protestant (23 percent), Buddhist (16 percent), Muslim (13 percent), Jewish (7 percent). There are important differences among the two groups, however. Specifically, prewar leaders are predominantly Protestant (46 percent) or Catholic (31 percent) or Jewish (over 15 percent). Postwar elites are a much more diverse group. Catholics, primarily from Latin American countries, represent a somewhat higher proportion (over 38 percent), and Protestants and Jews much smaller ones (17 and 4 per-

Table 3.2. Frequency Distribution of Hypothesized Characteristics of Prewar and Postwar Leaders: Socioeconomic Status and Family Life

(A) SOCIOECONOMIC STATUS

LEADERS	Upper class		Middle class		Lower class		Other		Total	
	N	%	N	%	N	%	N	%	N	%
Prewar	10	35.7	15	53.6	3	10.7	0	0.0	28	20.9
Postwar	15	14.2	55	51.9	32	30.2	4	3.8	106	79.1
Total	25	18.7	70	52.2	35	26.1	4	3.0	134	100.0

Cramer's $V = .27$ Chi square $= 9.80$ $p < .03$

(B) LEGITIMACY STATUS

Legitimate		Illegitimate		Illegitimate, parents married		Total	
N	%	N	%	N	%	N	%
107	97.3	2	1.8	1	0.9	110	100.0

(C) NUMBER OF SIBLINGS

LEADERS	None		One		Two		Three		Four		Five		Six		Seven or more		Total	
	N	%	N	%	N	%	N	%	N	%	N	%	N	%	N	%	N	%
Prewar	1	4.5	0	0.0	1	4.5	3	13.6	3	13.6	2	9.1	0	0.0	12	54.5	22	33.3
Postwar	6	13.6	9	20.5	6	13.6	2	4.5	4	9.1	3	6.8	6	13.6	8	18.2	44	66.7
Total	7	10.6	9	13.6	7	10.6	5	7.6	7	10.6	5	7.6	6	9.1	20	30.3	66	100.0

Gamma = −.51   Chi square = 18.17 $p < .02$

(D) AGE RANKING AMONG SIBLINGS

	Only child		Youngest		Middle		Oldest		Oldest son		Other		Total	
	N	%	N	%	N	%	N	%	N	%	N	%	N	%
	7	11.3	13	21.0	16	25.8	17	27.4	6	9.7	3	4.8	62	100.0

(E) FAMILY LIFE: CHARACTER

	Broken Home		Tranquil		Stormy		Very stormy		Total	
	N	%	N	%	N	%	N	%	N	%
	13	19.1	40	58.8	9	13.2	6	8.8	68	100.0

Note. Totals do not correspond due to missing data.

Table 3.3. Frequency Distribution of Hypothesized Characteristics of Prewar and Postwar Leaders: Ethnicity and Religion

(A) ETHNICITY

	Majority		Large minority		Small minority		Total	
	N	%	N	%	N	%	N	%
	75	57.3	41	31.3	15	11.5	131	100.0

(B) RELIGIOUS AFFILIATION

	Main group		Minority group		Total	
	N	%	N	%	N	%
	80	70.8	33	29.2	113	100.0

(C) RELIGIOUS BACKGROUND

LEADERS	Protestant		Catholic		Christian, other		Jewish		Muslim		Buddhist		Other		Total	
	N	%	N	%	N	%	N	%	N	%	N	%	N	%	N	%
Prewar	12	46.2	8	30.8	2	7.7	4	15.4	0	0.0	0	0.0	0	0.0	26	22.2
Postwar	15	16.5	35	38.5	1	1.1	4	4.4	15	16.5	19	20.9	2	2.2	91	77.8
Total	27	23.1	43	36.8	3	2.6	8	6.8	15	12.8	19	16.2	2	1.7	117	100.0

Cramer's V = .47   Chi square = 25.33 $p < .0003$

(D) RELIGIOUS ORIENTATION

LEADERS	Atheist		Protestant		Catholic		Christian, other		Muslim		Other		Total	
	N	%	N	%	N	%	N	%	N	%	N	%	N	%
Prewar	7	25.0	9	32.1	4	14.3	1	3.6	0	0.0	7	25.0	28	24.8
Postwar	53	62.4	13	15.3	8	9.4	0	0.0	11	12.9	0	0.0	85	75.2
Total	60	53.1	22	19.5	12	10.6	1	0.9	11	9.7	7	6.2	113	100.0

Cramer's V = .57   Chi square = 36.99 $p < .00001$

Note. Totals do not correspond due to missing data.

Table 3.4. Frequency Distribution of Hypothesized Characteristics of Prewar and Postwar Leaders: Education and Occupation

(A) EDUCATION: HIGHEST LEVEL ATTAINED

LEADERS	None, to through high school		Some college, to B.A.		Professional		Trade, religious, military		Total	
	N	%	N	%	N	%	N	%	N	%
Prewar	5	17.9	6	21.4	9	32.1	8	28.6	28	21.5
Postwar	22	21.6	25	24.5	50	49.0	5	4.9	102	78.5
Total	27	20.8	31	23.8	59	45.4	13	10.0	130	100.0

Cramer's V = .33 Chi square = 13.92 $p < .003$

(B) PRIMARY OCCUPATION

LEADERS	Professional		Professional revolutionary		Politician, businessman, landlord		Working class		Combination		Total	
	N	%	N	%	N	%	N	%	N	%	N	%
Prewar	8	29.6	6	22.2	4	14.8	0	0.0	9	33.3	27	20.6
Postwar	25	24.0	55	52.9	5	4.8	2	1.9	17	16.3	104	79.4
Total	33	25.2	61	46.6	9	6.9	2	1.5	26	19.8	131	100.0

Cramer's V = .29 Chi square = 11.35 $p < .03$

(C) FATHER'S PRIMARY OCCUPATION

LEADERS	Professional		Politician, businessman, landlord		Working class		Combination		Tribal chief		Total	
	N	%	N	%	N	%	N	%	N	%	N	%
Prewar	6	23.1	8	30.8	4	15.4	8	30.8	0	0.0	26	25.5
Postwar	13	17.1	25	32.9	30	39.5	4	5.3	4	5.3	76	74.5
Total	19	18.6	33	32.4	34	33.3	12	11.8	4	3.9	102	100.0

Cramer's $V = .39$ Chi square $= 15.85$ $p < .004$

Note. Totals do not correspond due to missing data.

cent, respectively). Moreover, Buddhists (21 percent) and Muslims (nearly 17 percent) are new to the postwar group. These variations are due no doubt to the great variety of regions and locales with which postwar revolutionaries are associated, a topic to which we return in Chapter 4.

The religious *orientation* of our revolutionaries is more homogeneous than their religious background, with 53 percent becoming atheists (Table 3.3.D). Again, there are important differences among our two groups. To begin with, only 25 percent of prewar leaders abandon their religious beliefs, as compared to over 62 percent for postwar elites. Moreover, some religious affiliations are more stable than others. Thus, for example, all Buddhists become atheists, as do all Jewish leaders (both prewar and postwar) and a large proportion of Catholics. By contrast, only four Muslim revolutionaries discard their religious heritage.

These shifts, in turn, are likely related to the type of ideology to which our elites subscribe. In general, revolutionaries with Marxist ideologies are more likely to abandon their religious beliefs than are other leaders. Indeed, some religions—particularly Islam—tend to reinforce ideological beliefs: the Muslim revolutionaries see their adversaries not only as aliens but as infidels as well.

Education and Occupation

As anticipated, revolutionary leaders are well educated. As Table 3.4.A indicates, nearly 70 percent have college or professional education, and another 10 percent are trained in trade, religious, or military institutions. Once again, there are some variations among the two groups. Postwar elites are more likely to have had postgraduate education in the professions (law, medicine, journalism, education) than prewar leaders (49 percent and 32 percent, respectively). Similarly, postwar elites are less likely to have had parochial training in trade, religious, or military institutions than their earlier counterparts (5 percent and 29 percent, respectively). In general, then, postwar elites are more broadly and professionally educated.

The primary occupations of our elites are inconsistent with

their education. As Table 3.4.B demonstrates, only 25 percent remain in their chosen vocation, whereas nearly 47 percent become professional revolutionaries, their previous education and training notwithstanding. As for postwar and prewar elites, the only meaningful variations include a dramatic rise in the number of professional revolutionaries (53 percent and 22 percent, respectively) and a moderate drop in the "politician, businessman, landlord" category (5 percent as compared to 15 percent).

The primary occupations of the *fathers* of our revolutionaries are rather heterogeneous. As seen in Table 3.4.C, over 33 percent have working-class occupations; 32 percent are politicians, businessmen, or landlords; and 19 percent are in the professions. As for our two groups, the only significant distinction is a sharp rise in the number of working-class occupations for fathers of postwar elites (nearly 40 percent as compared to only 15 percent for prewar leaders). Correspondingly, we note a small decline (6 percentage points) in the professional occupations of fathers of postwar elites. The four postwar leaders whose fathers are tribal chiefs are Buthelezi and Mandela of South Africa, Mondlane of Mozambique, and Sithon Kommadam of Laos.

Activities before and during Revolution

Revolutionary elites have impressive publication records, chiefly on matters of revolutionary theory and practice. As Table 3.5.A indicates, fully 64 percent may be considered prolific writers; another 28 percent have "few" or "some" pieces; and only 7 percent have no publication to their credit.

Revolutionary leaders divide virtually evenly as far as participation in legal activities and organization are concerned (Table 3.5.B). As may be anticipated, however, an overwhelming 97 percent have engaged in illegal organization and agitation (Table 3.5.C). Moreover, the foregoing three characteristics (publication record, legal activity, revolutionary activity) hold constant across the centuries, there being no significant variation for prewar and postwar groups.

Given their heavy and sustained involvement in radical activi-

Table 3.5. Frequency Distribution of Hypothesized Characteristics of Prewar and Postwar Leaders: Activities before and during Revolution

(A) PUBLICATION RECORD

	None	Few (1–3)	Some (4–6)	Many (7+)	Total
N	7	16	11	61	95
%	7.4	16.8	11.6	64.2	100.0

(B) MEMBERSHIP IN LEGAL POLITICAL ORGANIZATIONS

	None	Yes, moderate	Yes, intense	Total
N	57	28	30	115
%	49.6	24.4	26.1	100.0

(C) MEMBERSHIP IN REVOLUTIONARY ORGANIZATIONS

	None	Yes, moderate	Yes, intense	Total
N	1	3	131	135
%	0.7	2.2	97.0	100.0

(D) ARREST RECORD

LEADERS	None		Some (1–3 times)		Moderate (4–6 times)		Frequent (7 or more)		Total	
	N	%	N	%	N	%	N	%	N	%
Prewar	18	64.3	5	17.9	4	14.3	1	3.6	28	23.0
Postwar	9	9.6	63	67.0	19	20.2	3	3.2	94	77.0
Total	27	22.1	68	55.7	23	18.9	4	3.3	122	100.0

Gamma = .59   Chi square = 38.95 $p < .00001$

(E) DURATION OF IMPRISONMENT

LEADERS	None		1 year or less		2–9 years		10 or more years		Total	
	N	%	N	%	N	%	N	%	N	%
Prewar	18	64.3	3	10.7	3	10.7	4	14.3	28	23.0
Postwar	9	9.6	20	21.3	56	59.6	9	9.6	94	77.0
Total	27	22.1	23	18.9	59	48.4	13	10.7	122	100.0

Gamma = .59   Chi square = 41.56   p < .00001

(F) FOREIGN LANGUAGES

LEADERS	None		One		Two		Three		Four		Five		Six+		Bilingual		Total	
	N	%	N	%	N	%	N	%	N	%	N	%	N	%	N	%	N	%
Prewar	4	16.7	6	25.0	6	25.0	6	25.0	1	4.2	1	4.2	0	0.0	0	0.0	24	21.1
Postwar	1	1.1	25	27.8	20	22.2	6	6.7	4	4.4	0	0.0	2	2.2	32	35.6	90	78.9
Total	5	4.4	31	27.2	26	22.8	12	10.5	5	4.4	1	0.9	2	1.8	32	28.1	114	100.0

Cramer's V = .51   Chi square = 29.44   p < .0001

(G) FOREIGN TRAVEL BEFORE REVOLUTION: EXTENT

LEADERS	None		Little (1 country)		Moderate (2–3 countries)		Extensive (4 or more countries)		Total	
	N	%	N	%	N	%	N	%	N	%
Prewar	13	46.4	4	14.3	2	7.1	9	32.1	28	21.7
Postwar	5	5.0	13	12.9	30	29.7	53	52.5	101	78.3
Total	18	14.0	17	13.2	32	24.8	62	48.1	129	100.0

Gamma = .55   Chi square = 33.45   p < .00001

Table 3.5, *continued*

(H) FOREIGN TRAVEL BEFORE REVOLUTION: PLACE

LEADERS	None		Europe		U.S.A.		Asia		Africa		Latin America		Combination		Total	
	N	%	N	%	N	%	N	%	N	%	N	%	N	%	N	%
Prewar	13	46.4	10	35.7	1	3.6	0	0.0	0	0.0	1	3.6	3	10.7	28	21.7
Postwar	5	5.0	9	8.9	1	1.1	7	6.9	6	5.9	7	6.9	66	65.3	101	78.3
Total	18	14.0	19	14.7	2	1.6	7	5.4	6	4.7	8	6.2	69	53.5	129	100.0

Cramer's V = .65   Chi square = 54.90 $p < .00001$

(I) FOREIGN TRAVEL BEFORE REVOLUTION: DURATION

LEADERS	None		Less than 1 year		1–3 years		4 + years		Total	
	N	%	N	%	N	%	N	%	N	%
Prewar	13	46.4	5	17.9	1	3.6	9	32.1	28	21.9
Postwar	5	5.0	18	18.0	24	24.0	53	53.0	100	78.1
Total	18	14.1	23	18.0	25	19.5	62	48.4	128	100.0

Gamma = .56   Chi square = 33.34 $p < .00001$

(J) CONTINUING FOREIGN CONTACTS

LEADERS	None		Few (1–3)		Some (4–6)		Many (7 or more)		Total	
	N	%	N	%	N	%	N	%	N	%
Prewar	14	70.0	1	5.0	0	0.0	5	25.0	20	21.7
Postwar	4	5.6	6	8.3	12	16.7	50	69.5	72	78.3
Total	18	19.6	7	7.6	12	13.0	55	59.8	92	100.0

Gamma = .72   Chi square = 42.15 $p < .00001$

ty from an early age, we would expect our revolutionaries to have accumulated substantial arrest records. This expectation is substantiated in Table 3.5.D and E. Fully 78 percent of all our leaders are arrested one or more times, and they spend up to twenty years (as in the case of Lenin) in prison or exile. A sharp variation occurs for our two groups: only about 10 percent of postwar elites have no arrest or imprisonment record, as compared to 64 percent for prewar leaders.

Revolutionary elites are cosmopolitan in many senses. They travel widely, spend long periods of time in other countries, develop foreign contacts, and speak foreign languages, as shown in Table 3.5.F–J. Specifically: (1) an overwhelming 96 percent speak one or more foreign languages; (2) 86 percent have records of foreign travel of considerable variety and duration, with 48 percent visiting four or more countries over a period of four or more years; (3) over 53 percent visit a combination of countries in Africa, Asia, Europe, and the Americas; and (4) over 80 percent maintain a variety of contacts outside their own countries.

A series of impressive variations emerges when we compare our two groups: (1) only 1 percent of postwar revolutionaries do not speak a foreign language, as compared to nearly 17 percent of prewar elites; (2) only 5 percent of postwar revolutionaries have no record of foreign travel, as compared to over 46 percent of prewar leaders; (3) fully 82 percent of postwar revolutionaries travel to two or more countries, 77 percent of them for at least one year, as compared to only 39 percent of prewar elites, of whom 36 percent stay abroad at least one year; and (4) only about 6 percent of postwar revolutionaries have no foreign contacts, as compared to 70 percent of prewar leaders.

In all respects, in short, postwar revolutionaries are more cosmopolitan than their earlier counterparts.

Ideologies and Attitudes

Given their cosmopolitanism, it is not surprising that the ideologies of our revolutionaries tend to have a foreign source. As Table 3.6.A demonstrates, 73 percent of the leaders adapt a foreign ideol-

63

Table 3.6. Frequency Distribution of Hypothesized Characteristics of Prewar and Postwar Leaders: Ideologies and Attitudes

(A) SOURCE OF IDEOLOGY

LEADERS	Indigenous		Foreign		Foreign/indigenous		Total	
	N	%	N	%	N	%	N	%
Prewar	13	48.1	0	0.0	14	51.9	27	20.1
Postwar	19	17.8	4	3.7	84	78.5	107	79.9
Total	32	23.9	4	3.0	98	73.1	134	100.0

Cramer's V = .29   Chi square = 11.44   p < .004

(B) TYPE OF IDEOLOGY

LEADERS	None		Demo-cratic		Marxist-Leninist		Nation-alist/Marxist-Leninist		Nation-alist/Marxist-socialist		Nation-/alist/other		Leftist/other		Right-ist/other		Other		Total	
	N	%	N	%	N	%	N	%	N	%	N	%	N	%	N	%	N	%	N	%
Prewar	1	3.6	11	39.3	5	17.9	0	0.0	0	0.0	2	7.1	5	17.9	2	7.1	2	7.1	28	20.7
Postwar	0	0.0	0	0.0	5	4.7	66	61.7	9	8.4	21	19.6	6	5.6	0	0.0	0	0.0	107	79.3
Total	1	0.7	11	8.1	10	7.4	66	48.9	9	6.7	23	17.0	11	8.1	2	1.5	2	1.5	135	100.0

Cramer's V = .83   Chi square = 92.09   p < .00001

(C) PERSONALITIES ADMIRED

Yes		Unknown		Total	
N	%	N	%	N	%
61	45.2	74	54.8	135	100.0

(D) ATTITUDE TOWARD MAN

LEADERS	Strongly negative		Mildly negative		Fluctuating		Mildly positive		Strongly positive		Total	
	N	%	N	%	N	%	N	%	N	%	N	%
	6	7.5	6	7.5	7	8.8	20	25.0	41	51.3	80	100.0

(E) ATTITUDE TOWARD OWN COUNTRY

LEADERS	Strongly negative		Mildly negative		Fluctuating		Mildly positive		Strongly positive		Total	
	N	%	N	%	N	%	N	%	N	%	N	%
Prewar	2	8.0	0	0.0	9	36.0	1	4.0	13	52.0	25	20.3
Postwar	1	1.0	3	3.1	2	2.0	6	6.1	86	87.8	98	87.8
Total	3	2.4	3	2.4	11	8.9	7	5.7	99	80.5	123	100.0

Gamma = .70   Chi square = 33.75 $p < .00001$

(F) ATTITUDE TOWARD INTERNATIONAL COMMUNITY

LEADERS	Strongly negative		Mildly negative		Fluctuating		Mildly positive		Strongly positive		Dualistic		Total	
	N	%	N	%	N	%	N	%	N	%	N	%	N	%
Prewar	2	9.1	5	22.7	4	18.2	2	9.1	5	22.7	4	18.2	22	17.6
Postwar	0	0.0	0	0.0	0	0.0	1	1.0	0	0.0	102	99.0	103	82.4
Total	2	1.6	5	4.0	4	3.2	3	2.4	5	4.0	106	84.8	125	100.0

Cramer's V = .87   Chi square = 93.86 $p < .00001$

Note. Totals do not correspond due to missing data.

ogy to local needs; only 24 percent work with an indigenous ideology. Comparing our two groups, we readily see that almost half of prewar leaders subscribe to an indigenous ideology, the other half to a foreign/indigenous one. By contrast, nearly four-fifths of the postwar revolutionaries adapt a foreign ideology to local conditions; only 18 percent develop an exclusively indigenous ideology.

Table 3.6.B depicts the types of ideologies our revolutionary elites hold. Of the 135 revolutionaries, only one leader (Devereux of England) appears to have held no particular ideology, the others subscribing to a variety of democratic, nationalist, socialist, Marxist, and nationalist/Marxist ideologies (nearly half subscribe to the last-mentioned ideology). (For this particular classification of ideologies, see chapter 4.) Turning to our two groups, we see that *all* leaders with a democratic ideology fall in the prewar category, *all* elites with a nationalist/Marxist ideology in the postwar one. In general, shades of Marxist ideology run through 75 percent of our postwar revolutionaries; strands of nationalism are present in a commanding 91 percent; and a combination of Marxism and nationalism in an impressive 94 percent. The postwar period, in short, marks the triumph of Marxism and nationalism as revolutionary ideologies.

Reflecting upon the ideologies of our revolutionaries is their identification with or admiration for certain historic personalities. As Table 3.6.C shows, 45 percent of the revolutionaries for whom we have data do admire other personalities (the other 55 percent fall in the "unknown" category). Generally speaking, the historic figures admired are theorists and practitioners of revolution. The largest group, which we label "national liberators," include such diverse figures as José Marti, George Washington, Abraham Lincoln, Mao Tse-tung, Ho Chi Minh, and Fidel Castro. To this topic, we return in Chapter 5.

The attitudes of our revolutionaries toward man, society, and the international community are also likely shaped by the ideologies they hold, as exhibited in Table 3.6.D,E,F. Revolutionary leaders tend to have an optimistic view of human nature (76 percent), with only a handful (15 percent) expressing a negative view. Similarly, our leaders have a decidedly positive view of their own countries (80 percent). Postwar leaders are even more positive than pre-war elites: 88 percent to 52 percent. Only 2 percent of postwar leaders vacillate between the positive and the negative, as compared to 36 percent of prewar elites.

As may be expected, the attitudes of our revolutionaries toward the international community are dualistic, 85 percent seeing it as made up of friends to be cultivated and enemies to be fought. This dualism becomes even more pronounced when we focus on our two groups: 99 percent of postwar elites see the world in this light, as compared to a mere 18 percent of prewar leaders. Only one postwar revolutionary holds a mildly positive attitude toward the international order; prewar revolutionaries run the gamut from strongly negative to strongly positive.

SUMMARY

The hypotheses and propositions advanced in Chapter 2 relative to the general characteristics of revolutionary elites are supported by the data, with modifications and qualifications. A series of distinctions between prewar and postwar leaders adds dimensions to our findings not anticipated in our initial thinking about revolutionaries.

As a whole, revolutionary elites turn out to be somewhat older at the time of their revolutions than we had anticipated; nor is it the case that the twentieth century has witnessed the emergence of younger revolutionaries.

Contrary to expectations, revolutionary leaders tend to have normal family lives. Though typically from large families, they tend, however, to be either oldest or youngest children.

Although well-educated (as anticipated), occupations of revolutionary elites are inconsistent with their education. Many simply abandon their professions (whether medicine, law, teaching, or the ministry) to become professional revolutionaries.

4
Regional Patterns

METHODOLOGICAL NOTE

The findings presented in Chapter 3 make clear that revolutionary elites do not constitute a homogeneous group. A series of demographic, situational, ideological, and attitudinal associations is related to significant differences among our leaders. As a starting point, we postulated a set of four independent variables that may account for further heterogeneity among revolutionaries. These are: (1) the time period in which the revolution occurs, (2) the region in which the revolution unfolds, (3) the type of country in which the revolution takes place, (4) the type of ideology to which the leaders subscribe. Having examined the temporal variable in the previous chapter, we now turn to a discussion of the other three.

The regions of the world in which revolutions occur turn out to have a bearing on differences among revolutionary elites. Our thirty-one sets of leaders conveniently group into four major regions: Africa (seven cases), Asia and the Middle East (seven cases), Latin America (seven cases), Europe and North America (ten cases)* (for details, see Introduction).

The countries in which our revolutions occurred are grouped into three types: developed, semideveloped, undeveloped. The standard criterion used in determining the level of development of a country is the relative proportion of labor force engaged in agriculture. Countries with more than 67 percent of their labor force in agriculture are classified as undeveloped; those with 34 to 66 per-

---

*We dispense with the region conventionally labeled "Middle East and North Africa" because it would incorporate only two of our thirty-one cases: Algeria and "Palestine."

cent as semideveloped; and those with less than 34 percent as developed.[1] Applying the criterion of labor force in agriculture uniformly to all our thirty-one countries,* *as of the time of their revolutions,* we end up with the following breakdown:[2]

Developed	Semideveloped	Undeveloped
France 1968	Bolivia	Algeria
Northern Ireland	Brazil	America
Puerto Rico	Colombia	Angola
Quebec	Cuba	China
South Africa	Hungary	England
Uruguay	Namibia	France 1789
	"Palestine"	Guatemala
	Peru	Guinea-Bissau
	Philippines	Kampuchea
	Zimbabwe	Laos
		Mexico
		Mozambique
		North Vietnam
		Russia
		South Vietnam

Classifying the ideologies to which the leaders subscribe (our fourth independent variable) proved a most demanding task. Other scholars will no doubt adopt different postures, and an element of arbitrariness is virtually unavoidable in any such classification. Initially we identified some twenty separate ideological postures associated with our revolutionaries, including republican, democrat, constitutional monarchist, Puritan, Jacobin, deist, animist, an-

*In the earlier volume, it will be recalled, we did not use labor force in agriculture as a uniform and inflexible criterion. Thus, for reasons given therein, we classified England of the 1640s and France of the 1780s as developed, America of the 1770s as semideveloped. Needless to say, the new classification may change some of our findings. It is equally clear, however, that we cannot use *two* criteria for classifying the same phenomenon. Meanwhile, cognitive dissonance inevitably results when one finds America, France, and England in the same "undeveloped" category as Algeria, Kampuchea, and Mozambique. Such dissonance is an unavoidable outcome of the criterion we employ—labor force in agriculture—itself a relatively recent invention of Western social scientists.

archist, utopian socialist, democratic socialist, nationalist, Marxist, Marxist-anarchist, Marxist-Leninist, Maoist, Trotskyite, Castroite, and the like. Moreover, we found many permutations and combinations, most frequently involving varieties of nationalist and Marxist ideologies. All this being manifestly unwieldy, our final decision was to group the ideologies in the following fashion: (1) democratic, (2) Marxist-Leninist, (3) nationalist/Marxist-Leninist, (4) nationalist/Marxist-socialist, (5) nationalist/other, (6) leftist/other, (7) rightist/other, (8) other.

Collapsing these categories any further—for instance, in terms of a tripartite distinction between democratic, nationalist, and Marxist ideologies—would leave us open to the charge of oversimplification. Moreover, it is clear that we sharply distinguish socialism, Marxism, and Marxism-Leninism. Briefly, socialism is the genus of which Marxism and Marxism-Leninism (= communism) are specific expressions. It goes without saying that one can be a socialist without being a Marxist, or a Marxist without being a communist, and so on.

Having invested considerable time and effort in determining and defining our independent variables and in executing the appropriate data analyses, we came upon an understandable fact: two of our independent variables—region and country—overlap to such a great extent that it would be highly repetitious and wasteful of time to present both sets of findings. (A moment's reflection will clarify the reason: *in general,* Africa and Asia are undeveloped; Latin America, semideveloped; Europe and North America, developed.) Following careful examination of the results, we selected region over country for the simple reason that it yields a greater number of theoretically relevant findings. We should note, however, that the single most important independent variable is the time period in which the revolutions occurred, as reported in Chapter 3.

In the pages that follow, we present our findings relative to our two remaining independent variables. This chapter focuses on region; Chapter 5, on ideology. In these two chapters, the reader will note, some of our presentations cover both prewar and postwar groups, whereas others are limited to either one or the other. In all

latter instances, the reader may assume that the group not discussed is highly homogeneous with respect to the variable under
consideration.

All the bivariate tables found in these two chapters, as well as
in relevant portions of Chapter 3, carry a chi-square significance of
0.05 or less. As for measures of association, where the data are
organized into nominal/nominal or nominal/ordinal categories,
Cramer's V is employed. Where the data are grouped into ordinal/
ordinal categories, gamma is used.

FINDINGS

Using region as an independent variable, we initially ran our
data for all the 135 revolutionaries. Having found the results
blurred and inconclusive, we reran the data while controlling for a
distinction introduced in the previous chapter, between prewar
and postwar leaders. Since our 107 postwar elites come from all
four major regions, they tend to be a highly diverse group, marked
by many variations. By contrast, all the 28 prewar elites are from
the same region—Europe and North America—and are characterized by relatively few (and weak) differences. Accordingly, to keep
data presentations as uncluttered as possible, we limit the tables to
the postwar group while incorporating in the text appropriate references to prewar leaders.

Age, Birthplace, and Socioeconomic Status

In aggregate terms, surprisingly enough, postwar leaders tend
to be somewhat older than prewar elites at the time of their revolutions: 45 percent over the age of forty-five as compared to 29 percent. Regional variations occur with respect to the postwar revolutionaries, however, as illustrated in Table 4.1. Asian and African
leaders are older than their Latin American and European and
North American counterparts with, respectively, 84 percent and 71
percent being over the age of thirty-five at the time of their revolutions. By contrast, fully 50 percent of Latin American elites and 36

71

Table 4.1. Region by Age at Time of Revolution: Postwar Leaders

REGION	AGE										
	16–19		20–24		25–34		35–44		45–64		Total
	N	%	N	%	N	%	N	%	N	%	N	%
Africa	0	0.0	0	0.0	9	29.0	4	12.9	18	58.1	31	30.4
Asia	0	0.0	0	0.0	5	16.1	9	29.0	17	54.8	31	30.4
Latin America	1	5.6	0	0.0	8	44.4	7	38.9	2	11.1	18	17.6
Europe and North America	0	0.0	1	4.5	7	31.8	5	22.7	9	40.9	22	21.6
Total	1	1.0	1	1.0	29	28.4	25	24.5	46	45.1	102^a	100.0

Cramer's V = .27   Chi square = 21.68 $p < .04$

^{a}Totals do not correspond due to missing data.

percent of European and North American leaders are below this age. As can be seen, Asians are the oldest, Latin Americans the youngest.

A possible reason for this state of affairs may be the ages at which revolutionaries are first exposed to radical ideologies, as depicted in Table 4.2. Nearly 67 percent of Latin Americans and over 86 percent of Europeans and North Americans are introduced to revolutionary doctrines before the age of twenty, the correspond-

Table 4.2. Region by Age First Exposed to Revolutionary Ideology: Postwar Leaders

REGION	AGE										
	0–15		16–19		20–24		25–34		35–44		Total
	N	%	N	%	N	%	N	%	N	%	N	%
Africa	1	3.2	6	19.4	11	35.5	12	38.7	1	3.2	31	29.0
Asia	8	22.2	11	30.6	10	27.8	5	13.9	2	5.6	36	33.6
Latin America	6	33.3	6	33.3	3	16.7	3	16.7	0	0.0	18	16.8
Europe and North America	6	27.3	13	59.1	3	13.6	0	0.0	0	0.0	22	20.6
Total	21	19.6	36	33.6	27	25.2	20	18.7	3	2.8	107	100.0

Cramer's V = .30   Chi square = 29.40 $p < .003$

ing figures being 53 percent for the Asians and 23 percent for the Africans. These variations in age are likely due to radically differ-ent rates of modernization (for example, advances in transporta-tion, communication, literacy) in various regions of the world. And, to state the obvious, African and Asian countries were among the last to launch modernization efforts.

Moreover, given the general state of undevelopment and the firm grip of the imperialist powers, it takes longer for revolutionary elites of colonial countries to develop radical consciousness, spread this consciousness among their peoples, and gradually cultivate sufficient military strength openly to challenge the imperialist powers in revolutionary warfare. That the situation has been more fluid in Latin America is probably due to two reasons. First, on balance, Latin American countries are relatively more developed than African and Asian ones. Second, although most Latin Ameri-can societies are under the heavy influence of the United States, they are, at least nominally, independent rather than openly colo-nial.

In aggregate terms, there is virtually no variation in the ur-ban–rural birth pattern of prewar and postwar elites: both groups are about 46 percent urban, 54 percent rural. There are sharp varia-tions within the latter group, however, as seen in Table 4.3. Speci-

Table 4.3. Region by Birthplace: Postwar Leaders

REGION	BIRTHPLACE					
	Urban		Rural		Total	
	N	%	N	%	N	%
Africa	6	20.7	23	79.3	29	29.6
Asia	14	38.9	22	61.1	36	36.7
Latin America	12	75.0	4	25.0	16	16.3
Europe and North America	13	76.5	4	23.5	17	17.3
Total	45	45.9	53	54.1	98[a]	100.0

Cramer's V = .45   Chi square = 19.99 p < .0002

[a]Totals do not correspond due to missing data.

73

fically, considering the urban–rural distribution ratios of our regions as of the year 1920, an unexpectedly large proportion of postwar revolutionaries come from urban centers. (We use 1920 as the "base birth date" for postwar leaders, since, as suggested in Table 4.1, their median age at the time of their revolutions is approximately forty.) As of our base date, while Europe and North America were only about 50 percent urban,[3] these urban areas gave birth to over 76 percent of the revolutionaries. Similarly, with an urban population of slightly over 14 percent, fully 75 percent of Latin American revolutionaries come from urban centers. Asia, with an urban base of almost 7 percent, produces 39 percent of its revolutionaries from urban settings; and Africa, with an urban population of less than 5 percent, generates 21 percent of its elites from the cities. The urban–population–to–urban-birth ratio, then, is highest for Asia, followed by Latin America, Africa, Europe and North America. On the whole, the incidence of urban birth is beyond the realm of chance.

In aggregate terms, there is little variation between rural-born prewar and postwar elites as it concerns exposure to urban culture: nearly 79 percent of the former and over 70 percent of the latter are so exposed before the age of twenty. Of the postwar leaders born

Table 4.4. Region by Age Exposed to Urban Life if Nonurban Born: Postwar Leaders

REGION	AGE									
	0–15		16–19		20–24		25–29		Total	
	N	%	N	%	N	%	N	%	N	%
Africa	5	21.7	8	34.8	8	34.8	2	8.7	23	42.6
Asia	5	23.8	10	47.6	6	28.6	0	0.0	21	38.9
Latin America	4	100.0	0	0.0	0	0.0	0	0.0	4	7.4
Europe and North America	1	16.7	5	83.3	0	0.0	0	0.0	6	11.1
Total	15	27.8	23	42.6	14	25.9	2	3.7	54[a]	100.0

Cramer's V = .34   Chi square = 18.74 $p < .03$

[a]Totals do not correspond due to missing data.

74

in rural areas, however, exposure to urban life occurs earliest for the Latin Americans—100 percent before the age of *fifteen*—as indicated in Table 4.4. Similarly, all European and North American elites are exposed before the age of twenty, the corresponding figures being 71 percent for the Asians and nearly 57 percent for the Africans.

Important variations are found in the socioeconomic status of revolutionary elites. In aggregate terms, as reported in Chapter 3, while middle-class representation remains relatively constant, upper-class representation is more a characteristic of prewar leaders (36 percent) and lower-class representation more a mark of postwar elites (30 percent). As Table 4.5 documents, European and North American revolutionaries come exclusively from the middle and lower classes (59 percent and 41 percent, respectively), as do African elites (53 percent and 37 percent). In the Latin American context, the situation is different: while middle-class representation (57 percent) is almost identical to that of Europe and North America, there is also a relatively high proportion of upper-class leaders (28 percent) and a relatively low proportion of lower-class revolutionaries (17 percent). Asia has a lower representation from the middle class (44 percent), but the other two classes are nearly evenly divided (28 percent upper class, 25 percent lower class).

Table 4.5. Region by Socioeconomic Status: Postwar Leaders

REGION	Upper class		Middle class		Lower class		Other		Total	
	N	%	N	%	N	%	N	%	N	%
Africa	0	0.0	16	53.3	11	36.7	3	10.0	30	28.3
Asia	10	27.8	16	44.4	9	25.0	1	2.8	36	34.0
Latin America	5	27.8	10	55.6	3	16.7	0	0.0	18	17.0
Europe and North America	0	0.0	13	59.1	9	40.9	0	0.0	22	20.8
Total	15	14.2	55	51.9	32	30.2	4	3.8	106[a]	100.0

Cramer's V = .27   Chi square = 22.46 $p < .008$

[a]Totals do not correspond due to missing data.

Ethnicity and Religion

Whereas prewar revolutionary elites typically come from the main ethnic and religious groupings in their societies, the picture is different for postwar leaders, as demonstrated in Table 4.6. Asian leaders are largely from the main groups (82 percent), as are the Latin Americans (67 percent). By contrast, only 24 percent of European and North American elites and 37 percent of African leaders represent the main groupings, the remainder being members of minorities, large or small. These variations are likely due to the relative homogeneity of many Asian and Latin American populations and the relative heterogeneity of African and European and North American countries.

The same pattern holds, with lesser intensity, for religious affiliation (Table 4.7). All Latin American elites belong to the main religion of their region, as do almost 90 percent of Asian revolutionaries. On the other hand, over 83 percent of European and North American leaders emerge from religious minorities, as do 39 percent of African elites. (Needless to say, Catholicism and Protes-

Table 4.6. Region by Ethnicity: Postwar Leaders

	ETHNICITY							
REGION	Majority		Large minority		Small minority		Total	
	N	%	N	%	N	%	N	%
Africa	11	36.7	14	46.7	5	16.7	30	29.1
Asia	28	82.4	4	11.8	2	5.9	34	33.0
Latin America	12	66.7	2	11.1	4	22.2	18	17.5
Europe and North America	5	23.8	14	66.7	2	9.5	21	20.4
Total	56	54.4	34	33.0	13	12.6	103[a]	100.0
	Cramer's V = .38 Chi square = 29.99 p < .00001							

[a]Totals do not correspond due to missing data.

76

Table 4.7. Region by Religious Affiliation: Postwar Leaders

REGION	AFFILIATION					
	Main group		Minority group		Total	
	N	%	N	%	N	%
Africa	16	61.5	10	38.5	26	29.9
Asia	25	89.3	3	10.7	28	32.2
Latin America	15	100.0	0	0.0	15	17.2
Europe and North America	3	16.7	15	83.3	18	20.7
Total	59	67.8	28	32.2	87[a]	100.0
	Cramer's V = .63 Chi square = 35.08					
	$p < .00001$					

[a]Totals do not correspond due to missing data.

tantism can be either a majority or a minority religion, depending on the locale.) As with ethnicity, these differences are likely due to the more pluralistic nature of Africa and Europe and North America.

Table 4.8 exhibits the regional distribution of specific religious backgrounds of leaders for whom we have data. As can be seen, all Latin American leaders are Catholic, and 76 percent of European and North American elites share a Christian religious background, whether Catholic or Protestant. As may be expected, all Jewish leaders are from Europe and North America, all Buddhists from Asia, and all Muslims from Africa or Asia. We also note that Catholicism is the only religion to have some representation in all regions.

Whether or not a revolutionary retains his original religious affiliation varies with region, as seen in Table 4.9. None of the African revolutionaries abandons his religious convictions, whereas 94 percent of the Asians become atheists. Also turning to atheism are 82 percent of Latin Americans and 77 percent of Europeans and North Americans. In contrast to all this, only one-fourth of prewar leaders abandon their religious affiliation.

Table 4.8. Region by Religious Background: Postwar Leaders

REGION	Protestant		Catholic		Christian, other		Jewish		Muslim		Buddhist		Other		Total	
	N	%	N	%	N	%	N	%	N	%	N	%	N	%	N	%
Africa	13	48.1	4	14.8	0	0.0	0	0.0	10	37.0	0	0.0	0	0.0	27	29.7
Asia	0	0.0	2	7.1	1	3.6	0	0.0	5	17.9	19	67.9	1	3.6	28	30.8
Latin America	0	0.0	15	100.0	0	0.0	0	0.0	0	0.0	0	0.0	0	0.0	15	16.5
Europe and North America	2	9.5	14	66.7	0	0.0	4	19.0	0	0.0	0	0.0	1	4.8	21	23.1
Total	15	16.5	35	38.5	1	1.1	4	4.4	15	16.5	19	20.9	2	2.2	91[a]	100.0

Cramer's V = .68   Chi square = 127.32 $p < .00001$

[a]Totals do not correspond due to missing data.

Table 4.9. Region by Religious Orientation: Postwar Leaders

REGION	Atheist		Protestant		Catholic		Muslim		Total	
	N	%	N	%	N	%	N	%	N	%
Africa	0	0.0	13	54.2	2	8.3	9	37.5	24	28.2
Asia	31	93.9	0	0.0	0	0.0	2	6.1	33	38.8
Latin America	9	81.8	0	0.0	2	18.2	0	0.0	11	12.9
Europe and North America	13	76.5	0	0.0	4	23.5	0	0.0	17	20.0
Total	53	62.4	13	15.3	8	9.4	11	12.9	85[a]	100.0

Cramer's V = .55   Chi square = 78.15 $p < .00001$

[a]Totals do not correspond due to missing data.

Education and Occupation

Whereas prewar revolutionaries are typically educated in their home countries, postwar leaders constitute a highly diverse group. As Table 4.10 shows, revolutionary elites from Europe and North America are most likely to have attained their highest education in domestic institutions, whether private or public (84 percent). This also holds, to a lesser extent, for Latin American leaders (67 per-

Table 4.10. Region by Characteristics of Education: Postwar Leaders

	EDUCATION									
	Domestic				Foreign					
REGION	State		Private		State		Private		Total	
	N	%	N	%	N	%	N	%	N	%
Africa	11	40.7	1	3.7	12	44.4	3	11.1	27	27.6
Asia	12	34.3	1	2.9	19	54.3	3	8.6	35	35.7
Latin America	11	61.1	1	5.6	6	33.3	0	0.0	18	18.4
Europe and North America	11	61.1	4	22.4	2	11.1	1	5.6	18	18.4
Total	45	45.9	7	7.1	39	39.8	7	7.1	98[a]	100.0

Cramer's V = .25   Chi square = 18.09 $p < .03$

[a]Totals do not correspond due to missing data.

79

cent) as well. By contrast, Asian and African revolutionaries are likely to be educated in foreign institutions, private or public (63 percent and 56 percent, respectively). These findings are to be expected: the relatively high levels of education attained by revolutionary leaders are more readily available in European, North American, and Latin American societies; African and Asian leaders are typically educated in foreign lands.

Table 4.11 lends further credence to the finding reported in Chapter 3: the primary occupations of revolutionary elites are inconsistent with their educational attainments—most particularly for the postwar leaders. Specifically, the occupation of professional revolutionary characterizes 64 percent of the Asians, 63 percent of the Europeans and North Americans, 45 percent of the Africans, and 33 percent of the Latin Americans. The next most important category, the professions (law, medicine, teaching, priesthood), is embraced by 39 percent of the Latin Americans, 32 percent of the Africans, 16 percent of the European and North Americans, and 14 percent of the Asians.

Activities before and during Revolution

As reported in Chapter 3, revolutionary elites of all time periods and regions are, from an early age, heavily involved in illegal organization and agitation. This involvement, in turn, typically leads to arrest and imprisonment, which are more associated with postwar revolutionaries than with the prewar leaders of Europe and North America.

Similarly, prewar revolutionaries either have no foreign travel at all or travel only inside their own region and for relatively short periods of time. Postwar elites, by contrast, travel extensively before their revolutions. Almost without exception, African, Asian, and Latin American leaders spend long periods of time abroad, going to a variety of locales and developing a variety of foreign contacts.* These leaders tend to be more cosmopolitan than their

*Tables dealing with extent, location, and duration of foreign travel—and with foreign contacts—are available upon request. The commonsense nature of the topic does not demand their inclusion here.

Table 4.11. Region by Primary Occupation: Postwar Leaders

REGION	Professional		Professional revolutionary		Politician, business, landlord		Working class		Combination		Total	
	N	%	N	%	N	%	N	%	N	%	N	%
Africa	10	32.3	14	45.2	4	12.9	2	6.5	1	3.2	31	29.8
Asia	5	13.9	23	63.9	0	0.0	0	0.0	8	22.2	36	34.6
Latin America	7	38.9	6	33.3	0	0.0	0	0.0	5	27.8	18	17.3
Europe and North America	3	15.8	12	63.2	1	5.3	0	0.0	3	15.8	19	18.3
Total	25	24.0	55	52.9	5	4.8	2	1.9	17	16.3	104[a]	100.0

Cramer's V = .28   Chi square = 24.46 $p < .02$

[a]Totals do not correspond due to missing data.

Table 4.12. Region by Type of Ideology: Postwar Leaders

REGION	Marxist-Leninist		Nationalist/Marxist-Leninist		Nationalist/Marxist-socialist		Nationalist/other		Leftist/other		Total	
	N	%	N	%	N	%	N	%	N	%	N	%
Africa	0	0.0	15	48.4	5	16.1	11	35.5	0	0.0	31	29.0
Asia	0	0.0	34	94.4	0	0.0	2	5.6	0	0.0	36	33.6
Latin America	1	5.6	13	72.2	0	0.0	3	16.7	1	5.6	18	16.8
Europe and North America	4	18.2	4	18.2	4	18.2	5	22.7	5	22.7	22	20.6
Total	5	4.7	66	61.7	9	8.4	21	19.6	6	5.6	107	100.0

Cramer's $V = .43$ Chi square $= 58.26$ $p < .00001$

European and North American counterparts. This in turn is due, at least in part, to the fact that the former are typically educated abroad, whereas the latter are more likely to receive a domestic education.

Ideologies and Attitudes

The extensity and intensity of foreign exposure revolutionary elites experience accounts in part for the types and sources of ideologies they hold. Prewar leaders, as we have seen, are highly eclectic in their ideological postures, ranging from the left to the center to the right. Moreover, they divide about evenly concerning their reliance on indigenous and foreign ideologies.

Of the postwar elites, as seen in Table 4.12, Asians are the least varied in their ideological orientations, 100 percent accepting nationalist or nationalist/Marxist-Leninist beliefs. Similarly, nearly 90 percent of Latin Americans embrace the same two ideologies. Africans are somewhat more diverse: nearly half are nationalist/Marxist-Leninists, 16 percent nationalist/Marxist-socialists, and 36 percent nationalists of various persuasions, including Pan African. Once again, European and North American revolutionaries hold the most diverse set of ideologies, spanning the entire spectrum of political beliefs.

Table 4.13. Region by Origin of Ideology: Postwar Leaders

	IDEOLOGY							
REGION	Indigenous		Foreign		Foreign/ indigenous		Total	
	N	%	N	%	N	%	N	%
Africa	10	32.3	0	0.0	21	67.7	31	29.0
Asia	2	5.6	0	0.0	34	94.4	36	33.6
Latin America	2	11.1	0	0.0	16	88.9	18	16.8
Europe and North America	5	22.7	4	18.2	13	59.1	22	20.6
Total	19	17.8	4	3.7	84	78.5	107	100.0

Cramer's V = .35   Chi square = 25.82 $p < .0002$

Whereas prewar revolutionaries divide almost evenly on the issue, the origin of the ideologies postwar leaders hold varies by region, as shown in Table 4.13. Asian leaders are most likely to adapt foreign ideologies to local conditions (94 percent), as are Latin American revolutionaries (89 percent). African and European and North Amercian elites are more eclectic, some of them relying on exclusively indigenous political beliefs (32 percent and 23 percent, respectively). For the Africans, this ideological independence is probably a consequence of their prideful preoccupation with Pan Africanism; for the Eurpoeans and North Americans, it is probably due to the presence of a high degree of social and cultural diversity.

SUMMARY

Coming from the same region of the world, the twenty-eight prewar revolutionaries of Europe and North America constitute a relatively homogeneous group. On the other hand, the 107 leaders of the postwar period come from all four major regions and constitute a highly heterogeneous cluster of men marked by a series of significant variations. These variations occur in the following areas: age at the time of revolution, age first exposed to revolutionary ideology, urban birth (or age first exposed to urban culture), socio-economic status, ethnicity and religion, education and occupation, intensity and extensity of travel, type and source of ideologies.

5
Ideological & Attitudinal Patterns

In this chapter we focus in greater detail on the ideological and attitudinal differences that distinguish our revolutionary elites. As discussed in Chapter 4, ideology is one of the three independent variables associated with variations among our revolutionaries.

Two caveats are in order before proceeding. First, as an independent variable, ideology yields a more uneven set of meaningful variations among revolutionaries than either region or time period. This is to be expected. For one thing, nationalism, socialism, and Marxism do not span all four centuries covered by our thirty-one revolutionary movements. For another, leaders of varying age, birthplace, socioeconomic status, education, and ethnicity may well subscribe to quite similar ideologies.

Second, although we recognize that the prewar group is very small ($N = 28$) relative to the number of cells created by our ideology categories, we present our findings in the hope of shedding additional light on the beliefs of revolutionaries.

FINDINGS

Religion

When we consider the religious background of our revolutionaries, we find variations both among and between the prewar and postwar groups. As Table 5.1 illustrates, among prewar elites, 100 percent of the democrats have a Christian religious orientation, as compared to 40 percent of the Marxist-Leninists, of whom the other 60 percent are Jewish. Postwar leaders demonstrate greater variation (Table 5.2). Of the nationalist/Marxist-Leninists, 47 percent are Christians, 36 percent Buddhists, and 13 percent Muslims. The nationalist/Marxist-socialists are either Christian (44 percent) or

Table 5.1. Ideology by Religious Background: Prewar Leaders

IDEOLOGY	Protestant		Catholic		Christian, other		Jewish		Total	
	N	%	N	%	N	%	N	%	N	%
None	1	100.0	0	0.0	0	0.0	0	0.0	1	3.8
Democratic	8	72.7	3	27.3	0	0.0	0	0.0	11	42.3
Marxist-Leninist	0	0.0	0	0.0	2	40.0	3	60.0	5	19.2
Nationalist/other	0	0.0	2	100.0	0	0.0	0	0.0	2	7.7
Leftist	1	25.0	2	50.0	0	0.0	1	25.0	4	15.4
Rightist/other	1	100.0	0	0.0	0	0.0	0	0.0	1	3.8
Other	1	50.0	1	50.0	0	0.0	0	0.0	2	7.7
Total	12	46.2	8	30.8	2	7.7	4	15.4	26^a	100.0

Cramer's V = .62   Chi square = 30.32 p < .03

^{a}Totals do not correspond due to missing data.

Muslim (56 percent), as are the nationalists* (85 percent and 15 percent, respectively).

As might be expected, the religious orientations of revolutionary elites also vary by ideologies they adopt. As Table 5.3 suggests, of the prewar leaders, all the Marxist-Leninists turned atheists, whereas all the democrats remained steadfast in their religious convictions. As Table 5.4 documents, of the postwar elites, all the Marxist-Leninists and all the leftists** turned atheists, as did almost all (84 percent) of the nationalist/Marxist-Leninists. By contrast, regardless of ideology, a large proportion of Muslims (71 percent) retained their original religious affiliation.

Occupation

The ideologies to which postwar elites subscribe are almost uniformly compatible with their occupations as professional revolutionaries. There are variations among the prewar group, however.

*For stylistic convenience, we substitute "nationalist" for our "nationalist/other" data category.
**For stylistic convenience, we substitute "leftist" for "leftist/other."

Table 5.2. Ideology by Religious Background: Postwar Leaders

IDEOLOGY	Protestant		Catholic		Christian, other		Jewish		Muslim		Buddhist		Other		Total	
	N	%	N	%	N	%	N	%	N	%	N	%	N	%	N	%
Marxist-Leninist	0	0.0	3	60.0	0	0.0	2	40.0	0	0.0	0	0.0	0	0.0	5	5.5
Nationalist/ Marxist-Leninist	4	7.5	20	37.7	1	1.9	0	0.0	7	13.2	19	35.8	2	3.8	53	58.2
Nationalist/ Marxist-socialist	0	0.0	4	44.4	0	0.0	0	0.0	5	55.6	0	0.0	0	0.0	9	9.9
Nationalist/other	11	55.0	6	30.0	0	0.0	0	0.0	3	15.0	0	0.0	0	0.0	20	22.0
Leftist/other	0	0.0	2	50.0	0	0.0	2	50.0	0	0.0	0	0.0	0	0.0	4	4.4
Total	15	16.5	35	38.5	1	1.1	4	4.4	15	16.5	19	20.9	2	2.2	91[a]	100.0

Cramer's $V = .49$ Chi square $= 87.65$ $p < .00001$

[a] Totals do not correspond due to missing data.

Table 5.3. Ideology by Religious Orientation: Prewar Leaders

IDEOLOGY	Atheist		Protestant		Catholic		Christian, other		Other		Total	
	N	%	N	%	N	%	N	%	N	%	N	%
None	0	0.0	1	100.0	0	0.0	0	0.0	0	0.0	1	3.6
Democratic	0	0.0	6	54.5	3	27.3	1	9.1	1	9.1	11	39.3
Marxist-Leninist	5	100.0	0	0.0	0	0.0	0	0.0	0	0.0	5	17.9
Nationalist/other	0	0.0	0	0.0	0	0.0	0	0.0	2	100.0	2	7.1
Leftist/other	2	40.0	1	20.0	1	20.0	0	0.0	1	20.0	5	17.9
Rightist/other	0	0.0	1	50.0	0	0.0	0	0.0	1	50.0	2	7.1
Other	0	0.0	0	0.0	0	0.0	0	0.0	2	100.0	2	7.1
Total	7	25.0	9	32.1	4	14.3	1	3.6	7	25.0	28	100.0

Cramer's V = .59   Chi square = 39.51 $p < .02$

Table 5.4. Ideology by Religious Orientation: Postwar Leaders

IDEOLOGY	Atheist		Protestant		Catholic		Muslim		Total	
	N	%	N	%	N	%	N	%	N	%
Marxist-Leninist	5	100.0	0	0.0	0	0.0	0	0.0	5	5.9
Nationalist/Marxist-Leninist	43	84.3	3	5.9	2	3.9	3	5.9	51	60.0
Nationalist/Marxist-socialist	2	28.6	0	0.0	0	0.0	5	71.4	7	8.2
Nationalist/other	0	0.0	10	52.6	6	31.6	3	15.8	19	22.4
Leftist/other	3	100.0	0	0.0	0	0.0	0	0.0	3	3.5
Total	53	62.4	13	15.3	8	9.4	11	12.9	85'	100.0

Cramer's V = .55   Chi square = 76.04 $p < .00001$

[a]Totals do not correspond due to missing data.

Table 5.5. Ideology by Primary Occupation: Prewar Leaders

IDEOLOGY	Professional		Professional revolutionary		Politics, business, landlord		Combination		Total	
	N	%	N	%	N	%	N	%	N	%
None	1	100.0	0	0.0	0	0.0	0	0.0	1	3.7
Democratic	3	30.0	0	0.0	3	30.0	4	40.0	10	37.0
Marxist-Leninist	0	0.0	5	100.0	0	0.0	0	0.0	5	18.5
Nationalist/other	1	50.0	0	0.0	0	0.0	1	50.0	2	7.4
Leftist/other	1	20.0	1	20.0	0	0.0	3	60.0	5	18.5
Rightist/other	0	0.0	0	0.0	1	50.0	1	50.0	2	7.4
Other	2	100.0	0	0.0	0	0.0	0	0.0	2	7.4
Total	8	29.6	6	22.2	4	14.8	9	33.3	27[a]	100.0

Cramer's V = .65   Chi square = 34.57 $p < .01$

[a]Totals do not correspond due to missing data.

As documented in Table 5.5, all Marxist-Leninists are professional revolutionaries, whereas the democrats, being more eclectic, are found in the professions, business, and politics, or a combination of pursuits. Nationalists and leftists exhibit some variations as well.

Activities before and during Revolution

The early and sustained involvement of postwar leaders of all ideological colorations in revolutionary organization and agitation accounts for the heavy record of arrest and imprisonment they compile. As Table 5.6 demonstrates, on the whole, only less than 10 percent are never arrested. By contrast, all the Marxist-Leninists and nationalist/Marxist-socialists spend time in prison, as do 95 percent of the nationalists and 90 percent of the nationalist/Marxist-Leninists. Moreover, one-fourth each of nationalists and Marxist-Leninists are detained for ten or more years.

As a rule, as we know, revolutionaries are cosmopolitan, traveling far and wide, gaining exposure to a variety of cultures and traditions, and maintaining a host of foreign contacts. Not only, however, is the degree of cosmopolitanism stronger for the post-

Table 5.6. Ideology by Duration of Imprisonment: Postwar Leaders

IDEOLOGY	None		1 year or less		2–9 years		10+ years		Total	
	N	%	N	%	N	%	N	%	N	%
Marxist-Leninist	0	0.0	1	25.0	2	50.0	1	25.0	4	4.3
Nationalist/Marxist-Leninist	6	10.2	10	16.9	41	69.5	2	3.4	59	62.8
Nationalist/Marxist-socialist	0	0.0	2	28.6	4	57.1	1	14.3	7	7.4
Nationalist/other	1	5.0	6	30.0	8	40.0	5	25.0	20	21.3
Leftist/other	2	50.0	1	25.0	1	25.0	0	0.0	4	4.3
Total	9	9.6	20	21.3	56	59.6	9	9.6	94[a]	100.0

Cramer's V = .28   Chi square = 21.80 p < .04

[a]Totals do not correspond due to missing data.

Table 5.7. Ideology by Origin of Ideology: Postwar Leaders

IDEOLOGY	Indigenous		Foreign		Foreign/ indigenous		Total	
	N	%	N	%	N	%	N	%
Marxist-Leninist	0	0.0	2	40.0	3	60.0	5	4.7
Nationalist/Marxist-Leninist	0	0.0	2	3.0	64	97.0	66	61.7
Nationalist/Marxist-socialist	0	0.0	0	0.0	9	100.0	9	8.4
Nationalist/other	19	90.5	0	0.0	2	9.5	21	19.6
Leftist/other	0	0.0	0	0.0	6	100.0	6	5.6
Total	19	17.8	4	3.7	84	78.5	107	100.0

Cramer's V = .73   Chi square = 113.53 $p < .00001$

war elites; it further varies with the ideologies they hold. As might be expected (see Chapter 4), postwar nationalists and Marxists of various shades and persuasions are marked by intensity, extensity, and diversity of foreign experiences. This cosmopolitanism is in part due to their foreign education.

Ideologies and Attitudes

The origins of ideological postures that postwar leaders maintain vary by the type of ideology, as displayed in Table 5.7. All the Marxist-Leninists, nationalist/Marxist-Leninists, nationalist/Marxist-socialists, and leftists either borrow a foreign ideology wholesale or adapt one to local conditions. By contrast, almost 91 percent of nationalists develop indigenous ideologies.

Related to the ideologies of revolutionary elites are the personalities they admire. Table 5.8 summarizes the relevant available data. To keep the list meaningful and manageable, we exclude two kinds of personalities. First, we leave out members of the leaders' families, since virtually every leader admires *someone* in his own family. Second, we exclude contemporary revolutionaries in a leader's *own* country—that is, his colleagues, cohorts, or comrades-in-arms. Thus, for example, one can reasonably assume that most (if not all) Chinese leaders admire Mao. The same may be said of Lenin, Ho, Castro, and probably all other "charismatic" figures.

Table 5.8 is organized as it is because there is a definite "regional" flavor to the list of admired personalities, particularly for the Africans and Latin Americans. The Asians, Europeans, and North Americans are more eclectic in this respect. Beyond this, a simple count shows that, with a total of twelve "votes," Mao places first. In second place is Castro (nine "votes"), followed by Marx (eight). Then come Guevara, Lenin, and Nyerere (six each), Kaunda (five), Nkrumah and Marti (four each), Giap, Ho, and Trotsky (three each). All other admired personalities have only one or two "votes."

It is clear that some admired personalities (for instance, Marx, Lenin, Mao, Castro, Guevara) transcend time, country, and region, whereas others do not (for instance, Kaunda, Nkrumah, and Nyerere). That Mao and Castro somewhat outrank Marx and Lenin is not surprising, since the experiences of the former are more relevant to revolutionary conditions of contemporary times.

Looked at from another perspective, the group we label "national liberators" clearly dominates the list of admired personalities: Washington, Lincoln, Lenin, Tito, Mao, Ho, Castro, Nkrumah, and Nyerere, to name a few. A second (and partly overlapping) group of admired personalities consists of historic figures in the development of revolutionary theory and practice: Marx, Lenin, Mao, Giap, Castro, Guevara, Fanon. A third type embraces poets, philosophers, intellectuals, literati: Milton, Montesquieu, Neruda, Picasso, Rousseau, Sartre. A fourth category incorporates such military figures as Napoleon, Washington, and Giap. Finally, we note the presence of Jesus Christ and the Prophet Isaiah, representing the deep religious convictions of Torres and Sobukwe, respectively.

Reexamining our data by time and region, it can be seen that the postwar nationalists, Marxists, or Marxist-Leninists of Africa, Asia, and Latin America primarily favor national liberators, theorists and practitioners of revolution, and military figures. Being ideologically more eclectic, prewar revolutionaries of Europe and North America typically admire philosophers and poets.

Table 5.8. Personalities Leaders Admire: Prewar and Postwar

Leaders	*Personalities*
AFRICA	
Ahmed	Marx, Lenin, Mao
Ben Bella	Nasser
Boudiaf	Mao
Krim	Mao
Roberto	Fanon, Lumumba
Savimbi	Gandhi
Cabral	Guevara
Machel	Nyerere, Kaunda
Mondlane	Andrade, Neto, Cabral
Nujoma	Nyerere
Sobukwe	Prophet Isaiah
Chitepo	Nkrumah, Kaunda, Nyerere
Mugabe	Nkrumah, Kaunda, Nyerere
Nkomo	Nkrumah, Kaunda, Nyerere
Sithole	Nkrumah, Kaunda, Nyerere
ASIA AND THE MIDDLE EAST	
Chou En-lai	Ho
Chu Teh	Washington, Sun Yat-sen
Mao	Marx, Lenin, Napoleon, Washington
Kaysone Phomvihan	Ho, Giap
Souphanouvong	Giap
Ho	Lenin
Truong Chinh	Mao
Giap	Mao, Napoleon
Arafat	Lincoln
Habash	Mao, Giap
Shukairy	Mao
Buscayno	Marx, Lenin, Mao
Sison	Marx, Lenin, Mao
Vo Chi Cong	Phan Boi Chau, Phan Chu Trinh[a]
LATIN AMERICA	
Lechín	Trotsky
Marighella	Ho, Mao, Castro, Guevara
Torres	Jesus Christ
F. Castro	Marx, Lenin, José Martí[b]
R. Castro	José Martí
Cienfuegos	José Martí

94

Leaders	*Personalities*
Guevara	José Marti, Pablo Neruda,[c] Jacobo Arbenz Guzmán[d]
Turcios Lima	Augusto César Sandino,[e] Mao, Castro, Guevara
Yon Sosa	Castro, Guevara
Béjar	Picasso, Sartre,[f] César Vallejo,[g] Gabriel García Márquez[h]
Blanco	Túpac Amaru,[i] Trotsky, Castro
De la Puente	Castro
Sendic	Túpac Amaru,[i] Castro, Guevara

EUROPE AND NORTH AMERICA

Jefferson	Locke
Cromwell	John Milton
Vane	John Milton, Roger Williams[j]
Marat	Montesquieu, Rousseau
Mirabeau	Richelieu
Robespierre	Rousseau
Cohn-Bendit	Bakunin, Trotsky
Kadar	Josip Tito
Nagy	Josip Tito
Rakosi	Stalin
Mari Bras	Castro
Schoeters	Castro
Vallières	Marx, Mao, Guevara, Fanon
Villeneuve	Castro
Lenin	Marx
Trotsky	Marx

---

[a] National heroes.

[b] Great Cuban patriot in the war of independence against Spain.

[c] Chilean poet.

[d] Socialist president of Guatemala in the early 1950s.

[e] Nicaraguan patriot who fought the U.S. Marines sent to that country during the Coolidge and Hoover administrations. He was killed in 1934 by Anastasio Somoza Garcia, the first Somoza.

[f] In his role as a Marxist essayist.

[g] Peruvian poet.

[h] Peruvian novelist.

[i] A descendant of the Inca rulers who led a rebellion against the Spaniards and was beheaded in 1571. Also an Inca descendant who took the name Túpac Amaru and led an abortive rebellion against the Spanish, 1780 to 1783.

[j] Exponent of religious toleration (like Vane himself).

Table 5.9. Ideology by Attitude toward Own Country:
Prewar Leaders

IDEOLOGY	ATTITUDE									
	Strongly negative		Fluctu- ating		Mildly positive		Strongly positive		Total	
	N	%	N	%	N	%	N	%	N	%
Democratic	0	0.0	6	60.0	0	0.0	4	40.0	10	40.0
Marxist-Leninist	0	0.0	1	20.0	0	0.0	4	80.0	5	20.0
Nationalist/other	1	50.0	0	0.0	0	0.0	1	50.0	2	8.0
Leftist/other	0	0.0	1	25.0	0	0.0	3	75.0	4	16.0
Rightist/other	0	0.0	0	0.0	1	50.0	1	50.0	2	8.0
Other	1	50.0	1	50.0	0	0.0	0	0.0	2	8.0
Total	2	8.0	9	36.0	1	4.0	13	52.0	25"	100.0

Cramer's V = .61   Chi square = 28.12 $p < .02$

"Totals do not correspond due to missing data.

Although revolutionary leaders with divergent ideologies do not vary significantly in their attitudes toward human nature (tending to be generally positive), they do vary in attitudes toward their own countries and toward the international society. Specifically, as Table 5.9 indicates, among prewar elites, democrats either hold a positive attitude toward their own societies (40 percent) or fluctuate between the positive and the negative (60 percent). (Not much can be said about other distributions because of small numbers.) By contrast, as seen in Table 5.10, with the exception of the leftists, postwar elites of all ideological persuasions are almost uniformly positive.

As for attitudes toward the international community, postwar elites, it will be recalled, are uniformly dualistic, distinguishing sharply between friends and foes. Prewar elites, on the other hand, are more varied, as depicted in Table 5.11. Almost 56 percent of the democrats hold a negative view of the international society; 33 percent, a positive view; and 11 percent, a fluctuating one. Some degree of variation marks the Marxist-Leninists, nationalists, and leftists as well.

Table 5.10. Ideology by Attitude toward Own Country: Postwar Leaders

	ATTITUDE												
	Strongly negative		Mildly negative		Fluctuating		Mildly positive		Strongly positive		Total	
IDEOLOGY	N	%	N	%	N	%	N	%	N	%	N	%
Marxist-Leninist	0	0.0	0	0.0	0	0.0	0	0.0	1	100.0	1	1.0
Nationalist/Marxist-Leninist	0	0.0	0	0.0	1	1.6	2	3.2	60	95.2	63	64.3
Nationalist/Marxist-socialist	0	0.0	2	22.2	0	0.0	1	11.1	6	66.7	9	9.2
Nationalist/other	0	0.0	0	0.0	1	4.8	2	9.5	18	85.7	21	21.4
Leftist/other	1	25.0	1	25.0	0	0.0	1	25.0	1	25.0	4	4.1
Total	1	1.0	3	3.1	2	2.0	6	6.1	86	87.8	98[a]	100.0

Cramer's $V = .36$ Chi square $= 51.02$ $p < .00001$

[a]Totals do not correspond due to missing data.

Table 5.11. Ideology by Attitude toward International Community: Prewar Leaders

| | ATTITUDE | | | | | | | | | | | | |
| | Strongly negative | | Mildly negative | | Fluctuating | | Mildly positive | | Strongly positive | | Dualistic | | Total | |
IDEOLOGY	N	%	N	%	N	%	N	%	N	%	N	%	N	%
Democratic	0	0.0	5	55.6	1	11.1	1	11.1	2	22.2	0	0.0	9	40.9
Marxist-Leninist	0	0.0	0	0.0	1	20.0	0	0.0	0	0.0	4	80.0	5	22.7
Nationalist/other	0	0.0	0	0.0	1	50.0	0	0.0	1	50.0	0	0.0	2	9.1
Leftist/other	0	0.0	0	0.0	1	33.3	0	0.0	2	66.7	0	0.0	3	13.6
Rightist/other	0	0.0	0	0.0	0	0.0	1	100.0	0	0.0	0	0.0	1	4.5
Other	2	100.0	0	0.0	0	0.0	0	0.0	0	0.0	0	0.0	2	9.1
Total	2	9.1	5	22.7	4	18.2	2	9.1	5	22.7	4	18.2	22[a]	100.0

Cramer's V = .73   Chi square = 58.36 $p < .0002$

[a]Totals do not correspond due to missing data.

SUMMARY

Employing ideology as an independent variable, we arrive at further variations concerning characteristics of revolutionary elites: religion, occupation, arrest record, cosmopolitanism, type and source of ideology, admired personalities, attitudes toward own country and toward international society. These findings confirm and to some extent overlap those presented in the two foregoing chapters. Leaders with more moderate ideologies are found in the prewar societies of Europe and North America; those with more radical postures in the postwar countries of Africa, Asia, Latin America.

Finally, as we have seen in this and the preceding two chapters, revolutionary elites, regardless of temporal, regional, or doctrinal variations, persist from early on in cultivating and sharpening their ideological and organizational skills as means of mobilizing the people and channeling their energies toward the realization of revolutionary objectives. And they admire, for the most part, theorists and practitioners of revolution.

6
Personality Patterns

METHODOLOGICAL NOTE

The findings presented in the preceding chapters shed some light on the characteristics of our 135 revolutionary elites. These crosstabulations do not, however, permit us to classify our leaders into meaningful categories, either in terms of their attributes or of personalities. As noted in the Introduction, without data on a control group (for example, establishment elites), many multivariate statistical techniques are not available to us. On the other hand, the technique of factor analysis does provide, in principle, for grouping of both our leaders and their attributes.

In executing the factor analyses certain variables were discarded either because they lack appreciable variation or because of unacceptably high incidence of missing data: (1) exposure to urban life as well as age at which so exposed; (2) father's birthplace; (3) religious background as well as parents' religion; (4) legitimacy–illegitimacy status; (5) place and field of father's education; (6) such primary occupations as medicine, law, and journalism—for both the leader and the father; (7) participation in professional and revolutionary organization; and (8) attitude toward international society. For all remaining variables, mean values were substituted for missing data.

A factor, to refresh the reader's memory, is an artificially constructed composite variable to which several individual variables are correlated. R-factor analysis was performed in an effort to produce constellations of attributes our leaders may share; Q-factor analysis was intended to yield groupings of the leaders themselves.

When R-factor analysis was performed by principal component varimax rotation using all relevant variables, five principal factors emerged. These factors, however, explained only 7.4 to 22.6 percent of the variance in our data set, for a total of 61.7 percent. Individually, two of the five factors explained less than 10 percent of the variance. The top factor is best labeled Cosmopolitanism, a subject we have discussed in the foregoing pages and to which we shall return in other contexts. Given these limitations, we have chosen not to report the results of our R-factor analysis at all (copies of the findings are available upon request). We take note, however, of an important negative finding: the attributes of our revolutionary elites are so diverse that no small number of easily identifiable factors emerge.

Q-factor analyses were performed not only for the entire group of 135 revolutionaries but separately for prewar and postwar leaders as well. Factor analysis of the entire population did not prove particularly productive or enlightening. Specifically, the operation yielded four factors, explaining 66.6 percent of the variance in the data. One factor, however, explained only 4.8 percent of the variance, well below our acceptance criterion of around 10 percent. A second factor, best labeled the Founders, recurs in the discussion of prewar leaders below. The other two factors are so similar as to demand virtually identical labeling, differing principally on three variables: birthplace (urban–rural), education level (high–low), arrest record (frequent–infrequent). On the whole, these findings are not surprising: since postwar elites outnumber prewar leaders by nearly four to one, it follows that the former's characteristics overwhelm and drown out those of their earlier counterparts. In any event, and for obvious reasons, we forego reporting the results of this analysis as well (copies available upon request).

Q-factor analyses for the prewar and postwar groups turned out to be satisfactory. That the prewar group is embarrassingly small for factor analysis ($N = 28$) is compensated for by the fact that the operation yielded five distinctive factors explaining a compelling 100 percent of the variance in the data set. The results are more modest for the postwar group: four factors explain 65.8 percent of the variance. In both analyses, we should note, since all loadings greater than .40 are reported for each factor, an individual leader may appear in more than one factor.

Following the factor analyses, terminal scatterplots were produced using calculated factor scores on five sets of variables having the highest eigenvalues derived from the R-factor analysis, and the loading for every leader on each of the first four Q-factor dimensions. As might be anticipated, the scatterplots did not yield insights beyond those uncovered in the Q-factor analyses; hence they, too, go unreported (copies available upon request).[1]

Table 6.1. Q-factor Analysis by Principal Component Varimax Rotation: Prewar Leaders

Factor	Loading	Percentage variance
(1) THE FOUNDERS		33.5
Henry	.86	
Jefferson	.85	
Washington	.84	
Otis	.82	
S. Adams	.69	
Carranza	.69	
Madero	.67	
Vane	.64	
Zapata	.61	
Trotsky	.61	
Mirabeau	.57	
Obregón	.56	
Villa	.54	
Cromwell	.45	
Danton	.44	
J. Adams	.42	
Lenin	.40	
(2) THE PROFESSIONAL REVOLUTIONARIES		25.8
Stalin	.85	
Antonov-Ovseyenko	.80	
Lenin	.80	
Zinoviev	.80	
Sverdlov	.73	
Kamenev	.71	
Trotsky	.63	
Mirabeau	.56	
Madero	.45	
Zapata	.44	

Factor	Loading	Percentage variance
Marat	.44	
Danton	.40	
(3) THE PURISTS		20.6
Siéyès	.82	
Robespierre	.81	
Pym	.80	
J. Adams	.67	
Danton	.64	
Vane	.46	
Carranza	.44	
Cromwell	.41	
Kamenev	.40	
Obregón	.40	
(4) THE ARISTOCRATS		10.6
Hampden	.85	
Cromwell	.56	
Villa	.53	
(5) THE GENERALS		9.5
Devereux	.80	
Marat	.54	
Mirabeau	.41	
Total variance		100.0

FINDINGS

Prewar Elites

The results of Q-factor analysis for our prewar revolutionaries are displayed in Table 6.1. The first factor—the Founders—accounts for 33.5 percent of the variance in the data set and embraces seventeen leaders with factor loadings ranging from .40 to .86. Led by Patrick Henry (who is closely followed by Jefferson, Washington, and Otis), the list includes such seemingly disparate figures as Carranza, Cromwell, Danton, Lenin, Madero, Mirabeau, and Vane.

These men belong to diverse time periods, diverse countries, and diverse traditions. What unites them is that they represent a mature, solid, middle-class group—an image running counter to the popular stereotype of the revolutionary. These men are well educated, come from the professions, and subscribe (with obvious exceptions) to varieties of democratic ideologies. Typically members of the establishment in their own societies, most appear upon the revolutionary landscape in response to situations of national crisis or emergency. Though cultured and cosmopolitan, they experience little foreign travel and maintain few or no foreign contacts (again, with obvious exceptions). In this sense, they are homegrown revolutionaries.

Above all, we label this group the Founders because it comprises men who seek to capture or preserve the identity, integrity, or independence of their nations. They are the patriots, the nationalists, the patriarchs—"fathers" of their own countries, validating, justifying, and legitimizing the revolution for posterity.

Heading the list with a loading of .85—and closely followed by Antonov-Ovseyenko, Lenin, and Zinoviev—Stalin epitomizes our second factor, the Professional Revolutionaries, accounting for 25.8 percent of the variance. Though born in urban areas, these leaders are typically associated with underdeveloped lands. They come from middle or lower social strata, are radicalized quite early in life, and have extensive records of foreign travel. They have a long history of antiregime activity, are arrested with regularity, and spend long periods of time in prison, exile, or both. Giving up all other pursuits, they devote their entire lives to the vocation of revolution.

The third factor—the Purists—explains 20.6 percent of the variance in the data set. It incorporates ten men with factor loadings of .40 to .82. Led by Siéyès, Robespierre, and Pym—and including such other leaders as J. Adams and Cromwell—this factor describes a group of urban-born, professionally trained leaders. Pessimistic in outlook, seeing human nature as essentially evil and human society as thoroughly corrupt, they see themselves as instruments of purification through the "reign of virtue" (see Chapter 8). Alternatively, we could label this group the Moralists or the Incorruptibles.

Explaining 10.6 percent of the variance, the Aristocrats constitute a fourth distinctive factor, consisting, however, of only three leaders: Hampden (.85), Cromwell (.56), and Villa (.53). With this factor we tread on very thin intellectual ice, since, given the loadings, we must necessarily focus on the characteristics of Hampden. Therefore, we simply note that Hampden is an urban-born, middle-aged, upper-class, well-educated, lawyer/politician—altogether a member of the establishment in good standing.

Our fifth factor, the Generals, poses the same intellectual perils as the fourth—and it highlights the problems of factor analysis when applied to a small population. In any event, this factor explains 9.5 percent of the variance in the data set and embraces another three leaders: Devereux (.80), Marat (.54), Mirabeau (.41). Again, given the relative loadings, we simply refresh the reader's memory that Robert Devereux, the third earl of Essex, was a professional military man who also held high political office—in both respects mirroring the career of his father. Beyond this, he was urban born, middle aged, well educated, and held no apparent political ideology.

Postwar Elites

Q-factor analysis for the postwar elites unraveled four factors, explaining 65.8 percent of the variance in the data set, as seen in Table 6.2.

It will appear surprising, at first blush, that professional revolutionaries do not constitute a separate and distinct type among postwar leaders. This fact must be balanced against the realization that, on the whole, an overwhelming majority of our postwar elites *are* professional revolutionaries. Stated differently, given its ubiquity, "professional revolutionary" does not serve as a cutting edge for the postwar group. Accordingly, the factors identified in Table 6.2 represent four distinct constellations of variables *plus* that of the professional revolutionary.

The first factor—the Scholars—accounts for 28.8 percent of the variance in the data set and embraces an overwhelming seventy-five leaders with factor loadings ranging from .40 to .90. These men have a history of early involvement in revolutionary activity. They

Table 6.2. Q-factor Analysis by Principal Component Varimax Rotation: Postwar Leaders

Factor	Loading	Percentage variance
(1) THE SCHOLARS		28.8
Giap	.90	
Ahmed	.88	
Chitepo	.87	
Ho Thu	.85	
Vo Chi Cong	.85	
Bras	.85	
Blanco	.84	
Ch'en Yi	.83	
Béjar	.82	
Cabral	.82	
De la Puente	.81	
Montes	.80	
Khieu Samphan	.79	
De Andrade	.78	
Tran Buu Kiem	.77	
Torres	.75	
Neto	.75	
Shukairy	.74	
Habash	.71	
Geismar	.71	
Sithole	.70	
Lobatón	.69	
Krivine	.69	
Phung Van Cung	.67	
Ben M'Hidi	.67	
Dos Santos	.67	
Nguyên Van Hieu	.66	
Gerö	.66	
Huynh Tan Phat	.66	
Machel	.66	
Cienfuegos	.65	
Nguyên Huu Tho	.65	
Mandela	.64	
Ho Chi Minh	.63	
Sauvageot	.63	
Souphanouvong	.62	

Factor	Loading	Percentage variance
Tran Van Tra	.62	
Mugabe	.61	
Guevara	.61	
Sendic	.60	
Nagy	.60	
Turcios	.59	
Khalef	.59	
Kaysone Phomvihan	.59	
Yon Sosa	.58	
Pham Van Dong	.58	
Siles	.58	
F. Castro	.58	
El-Hwatmah	.57	
Tambo	.57	
Biko	.57	
Savimbi	.56	
Nkomo	.56	
Didouche	.55	
Mondlane	.54	
Paz Estenssoro	.54	
Ieng Sary	.54	
Truong Chinh	.52	
Ben Boulaid	.52	
Schoeters	.51	
Rakosi	.51	
Cohn-Bendit	.50	
El-Wazir	.50	
Pol Pot	.50	
Chou En-lai	.48	
Singkapo Chounramany	.47·	
Sison	.45	
Chu Teh	.44	
Lê Duân	.44	
Toivo	.43	
Phoumi Vongvichit	.42	
Lin Piao	.41	
Kadar	.40	
Arafat	.40	
Da Cruz	.40	

Factor	Loading	Percentage variance
(2) THE ELDERS		16.3
Sithon Kommadam	.91	
Bitat	.90	
Souk Vongsak	.90	
Khider	.86	
Boudiaf	.86	
Nouhak Phongsavan	.83	
Ben Bella	.76	
Phoumi Vongvichit	.75	
Ben M'Hidi	.74	
Da Cruz	.72	
Didouche	.71	
Ben Boulaid	.70	
Barbosa	.70	
Singkapo Chounramany	.69	
R. Castro	.66	
Cahill	.64	
Ho Chi Minh	.60	
Nujoma	.59	
Roberto	.56	
Maletér	.54	
Pol Pot	.54	
Machel	.52	
Dos Santos	.52	
Schirm	.52	
Lechín	.52	
Lê Duân	.50	
Lobatón	.49	
Nguyên Van Hieu	.49	
Chou En-lai	.46	
Khalef	.45	
Ahmed	.42	
El-Hwatmah	.41	
Souphanouvong	.41	
El-Wazir	.40	
(3) THE AGITATORS		11.7
Gagnon	.89	
Liu Shao-ch'i	.85	
Villeneuve	.79	
Mao Tse-tung	.78	
Lin Piao	.75	

Factor	Loading	Percentage variance
Hudon	.74	
Nujoma	.74	
Sobukwe	.74	
Arafat	.70	
Rakosi	.69	
Mondlane	.65	
F. Castro	.64	
Roberto	.63	
Chou En-lai	.62	
Souphanouvong	.62	
Ben Bella	.58	
R. Castro	.57	
Neto	.51	
Siles	.43	
Krivine	.41	
Chu Teh	.41	
(4) THE FAITHFUL		9.0
O'Connell	.76	
O'Bradaïgh	.75	
Sendic	.67	
Schoeters	.67	
Marighella	.64	
Sison	.61	
Gerö	.60	
Ieng Sary	.53	
Kaysone Phomvihan	.52	
Chikerema	.52	
El-Hwatmah	.50	
Huynh Tan Phat	.49	
El-Wazir	.47	
Shukairy	.46	
Khalef	.45	
Ch'en Yi	.45	
Khieu Samphan	.45	
Arafat	.44	
Savimbi	.43	
Paz Estenssoro	.43	
Phoumi Vongvichit	.41	
Nkomo	.40	
Total variance		65.8

come from predominantly middle social strata of major groupings in their societies. Not only do they typically come from professional families; they themselves are in the professions. Thus, among those with the highest loadings, Giap holds a doctorate and teaches history; Ahmed, Chitepo, and Bras are in the legal profession; Ho Thu has a doctorate in pharmacology, Vo Chi Cong in medicine.

This pattern repeats itself as we go further down the list. We find agronomists (Blanco and Cabral); lawyers (Ch'en Yi, Tran Buu Kiem, Shukairy); journalists/poets/intellectuals (Béjar, de Andrade, Neto); academics (Khieu Samphan and Geismar); clerics (Torres and Sithole); physicians (Neto and Habash). We have chosen the label "scholars" for this group of highly educated, professionals-turned-revolutionaries because, regardless of their specific professions, they write extensively on a variety of subjects and contribute heavily to the theory and practice of revolution.

The second factor—the Elders—explains a modest 16.3 percent of the variance, with factor loadings of .40 to .91. This factor describes a group of older leaders who begin early and continue lifetime involvement in revolutionary organization and agitation. The Elders are associated with underdeveloped countries, lower social strata, and ethnic or religious minorities in their societies. Although they have little formal education, they travel widely, thus gaining exposure to a variety of cultures and ideologies. Sithon, Bitat, Souk, Khider, and Boudiaf epitomize this factor.

Explaining 11.7 percent of the variance in the data set, the third factor—the Agitators—virtually mirrors the popular stereotype of the revolutionary: young, lower class, socially deprived, with extensive record of radical activity. The Agitators—whether Gagnon and Villeneuve or Liu Shao-ch'i and Mao Tse-tung—characteristically combine shades of leftist doctrines (socialism, Marxism, Marxism-Leninism) with strong nationalist commitments. The loadings for this group range from .41 to .89.

Our last factor—the Faithful—explains 9.0 percent of the variance with modest factor loadings of .40 to .76. The Faithful are from the middle class, relatively well educated, and extensively traveled. The top six leaders on the list are either practicing Catholics (O'Connell, O'Bradaïgh, Marighella) or Catholics-turned-athe-ists (Sendic, Schoeters, Sison). As with the Artistocrats and the Generals discussed above, however, in reality this factor is keyed to the top two personalities: O'Connell and O'Bradaïgh of North-ern Ireland, whose cause is first and foremost religious. They are the defenders of the faith.

SUMMARY

We have sought to use factor analysis as a means of identifying common traits revolutionary elites may share (R-factor analysis) or personality configurations into which they may fall (Q-factor analy-sis). R-factor analysis did not yield meaningful results because of the great diversity in the attributes of our leaders. Similarly, Q-fac-tor analysis for our entire population of 135 revolutionaries proved unsuccessful because characteristics of the 107 postwar elites over-whelm and neutralize those of the 28 prewar leaders. On the other hand, separate Q-factor analyses for prewar and postwar elites yielded, in effect, a nine-fold typology of revolutionary elites across time and space. As we have seen, however, three of these types (the Aristocrats, the Generals, the Faithful) have weaker em-pirical foundations than the other six. Taken together, our nine types of revolutionaries embody and personify (among other things) ideological and organizational skills of the highest order.

PART III

EMERGENCE OF REVOLUTIONARY LEADERS

7
Patterns of Radicalization

In the preceding chapters we have undertaken quantitative analyses of a large volume of data concerning our 135 revolutionary elites: their general characteristics; their similarities and differences relative to temporal, regional, and ideological patterns; their personality types. In this and the following chapter, we present qualitative analyses of the dynamics underlying the emergence of revolutionaries upon the landscape. Our central concern is conditions and motivations—political, social, psychological, situational—that impel men toward revolution.

As noted in the Introduction, in these two chapters we turn to the fifty revolutionary leaders—representing 37 percent of our entire group—for whom adequate autobiographical and biographical materials are available. In so doing, *we draw heavily on the experiences of revolutionaries new to this volume,* only occasionally referring to their "older" counterparts in the interest of balance or comprehensiveness. To refresh the reader's memory, the fifty leaders are:

AFRICA

Algeria

Ben Bella

Angola

Roberto

Guinea-Bissau

Cabral

Mozambique

Machel
Mondlane

South Africa

Biko

Zimbabwe

Nkomo
Sithole

ASIA AND THE MIDDLE EAST

China

Chou En-lai
Chu Teh
Lin Piao

Liu Shao-ch'i
Mao Tse-tung

Laos

Souphanouvong

115

North Vietnam
Ho
Giap

"Palestine"
Arafat
Habash

LATIN AMERICA

Bolivia
Paz Estenssoro

Colombia
Torres

Brazil
Marighella

Peru
Blanco
De la Puente

Cuba
F. Castro
Guevara

Uruguay
Sendic

EUROPE AND NORTH AMERICA

America
  J. Adams
  S. Adams
  Henry
  Jefferson
  Otis
  Washington

England
  Cromwell
  Devereux
  Hampden
  Pym
  Vane

France 1789
  Danton
  Marat
  Mirabeau
  Robespierre

Mexico
  Madero
  Villa
  Zapata

Quebec/Canada
  Schirm
  Schoeters
  Vallières

Russia
  Lenin
  Stalin
  Trotsky

We treat patterns of radicalization of our revolutionaries under four categories: (1) formative years and family socialization; (2) school socialization; (3) travel, foreign or domestic, and exposure to new experiences and cultures; (4) a variety of situational dynamics.*

FORMATIVE YEARS

As we have seen in Chapter 3, 59 percent of the revolutionaries for whom we have data lead tranquil family lives, whereas 41 percent either have stormy childhoods or come from broken homes. When we limit our analysis to the smaller group of forty-three elites for whom we have information on this subject, the variation shrinks even more, as seen in Table 7.1.

Fifty-one percent (twenty-two) of these leaders experience relatively tranquil lives, whereas 49 percent (twenty-one) have relatively stormy childhoods or come from broken homes. Thus, whereas such diverse leaders as Arafat, Mao, and Vallières are beset by long histories of childhood problems and conflicts, such others as Ben Bella, Guevara, and Sithole enjoy rather quiet lives. (The controversial topic of Oedipus complex is considered in Chapter 8.)

These findings change somewhat when we consider the distinction between prewar and postwar elites. As can be seen in Table 7.2, 58 percent (eleven) of the prewar leaders have tranquil lives, and 42 percent (eight) lead stormy childhoods. Similarly, 46 percent (eleven) of the postwar revolutionaries have tranquil lives, and 54 percent (thirteen) lead stormy ones. It appears, then, that formative years as a source of radicalization tend to be somewhat more characteristic of postwar elites than of prewar leaders.

On the whole, however, given the relatively minor differentiations depicted in Tables 7.1 and 7.2, we are forced to conclude that formative years are relatively unimportant as sources of radicalization: the tranquil or stormy nature of one's early life is not strongly associated with one's emergence as a revolutionary. This finding stands in sharp contrast to most socialization studies,

*Extensive references for each leader appear in the appropriate sections of the Bibliography; only direct quotations, little-known points, or controversial matters are documented here.

117

Table 7.1. Formative Years as a Source of Radicalization

Relatively tranquil (N = 22)	Relatively stormy (N = 21)	Unknown (N = 7)
J. Adams	Arafat	Habash
S. Adams	F. Castro	Hampden
Ben Bella	Chou En-lai	Machel
Biko	Chu Teh	Marighella
Blanco	Danton	De la Puente
Cabral	Devereux	Sendic
Cromwell	Ho	Vane
Giap	Lenin[a]	
Guevara	Lin Piao	
Henry	Liu Shao-ch'i	
Jefferson	Mao	
Madero	Mirabeau	
Marat	Mondlane	
Nkomo	Robespierre	
Otis	Schoeters	
Paz Estenssoro	Souphanouvong	
Pym	Stalin	
Roberto	Torres	
Schirm	Trotsky	
Sithole	Vallières	
Washington	Villa	
Zapata		

[a]"Lenin's youth lends itself to classification either as "relatively stormy" or "relatively tranquil." Although some sources note that he lived in a generally supportive environment, the former category was chosen here because of the oedipal problems he confronted (see Chapter 8), his father's frequent absences from home in his capacity as a tsarist school administrator, and the killing or death, in rapid succession, of his brother, father, and sister. In any event, placing Lenin in either category does not materially affect the analysis.

which stress the importance of formative years in the evolution of personality.

Two specific aspects of a leader's family life that do appear to have a bearing on his future radicalization are the number of siblings he has and his age ranking amongst the siblings. It is widely believed that both these factors decisively influence the evolution

Table 7.2. Formative Years as a Source of Radicalization: Prewar and Postwar Leaders

Relatively tranquil		Relatively stormy		Unknown	
Prewar (N = 11)	*Postwar (N = 11)*	*Prewar (N = 8)*	*Postwar (N = 13)*	*Prewar (N = 2)*	*Postwar (N = 5)*
J. Adams	Ben Bella	Danton	Arafat	Hampden	Habash
S. Adams	Biko	Devereux	F. Castro	Vane	Machel
Cromwell	Blanco	Lenin	Chou En-lai		Marighella
Henry	Cabral	Mirabeau	Chu Teh		De la Puente
Jefferson	Giap	Robespierre	Ho		Sendic
Madero	Guevara	Stalin	Lin Piao		
Marat	Nkomo	Trotsky	Liu Shao-ch'i		
Otis	Paz Estenssoro	Villa	Mao		
Pym	Roberto		Mondlane		
Washington	Schirm		Schoeters		
Zapata	Sithole		Souphanouvong		
			Torres		
			Vallières		

of personality. (Gender position is also considered important, but requisite data are virtually impossible to locate.)

As noted in Chapter 3, revolutionary elites come from large families, with over 65 percent having three or more siblings. Of the leaders for whom we have data, 26 percent (sixteen) are middle children; 37 percent (twenty-three), oldest children or oldest sons; 21 percent (thirteen), youngest children; and 11 percent (seven), only children. Given the relatively large number of the siblings, it is clear that middle children are underrepresented, oldest and youngest ones overrepresented.

As Table 7.3 demonstrates, our smaller group of forty-three leaders for whom we have this information also comes from large families, with over 74 percent (thirty-two) having three or more

Table 7.3. Age Ranking among Siblings as a Source of Radicalization

Leader	Number of siblings	Ranking
Arafat	4	Middle child
J. Adams	3	Oldest child
S. Adams	11	Oldest son
Ben Bella	6	Middle child
Biko	1	Youngest child
F. Castro	6–8[a]	Middle child
Chou En-lai	5	Middle child
Chu Teh	12	Middle child
Cromwell	10	Middle child
Danton	3	Youngest child
Devereux	3	Oldest child
Giap	0	Only child
Guevara	4	Oldest child
Henry	12	Middle child
Ho	3	Middle child
Jefferson	10	Oldest son
Lenin	5	Middle child
Lin Piao	4–9[a]	Middle child
Liu Shao-ch'i	9	Youngest child
Madero	15	Oldest child
Mao	4	Oldest child
Marat	5	Oldest child
Marighella	0	Only child

Leader	Number of siblings	Ranking
Mirabeau	10	Youngest child
Mondlane	14	Youngest child
Nkomo	1	Oldest child
Otis	13	Oldest child
Paz Estenssoro	0	Only child
Pym	2	Youngest child
Roberto	6	Oldest child
Robespierre	4	Oldest child
Schirm	0	Only child
Schoeters	0	Only child
Sithole	0	Only child
Souphanouvong	19	Youngest child
Stalin	0[b]	Only child
Torres	3	Youngest child
Trotsky	8	Middle child
Vallières	2	Oldest child
Vane	8	Oldest son
Villa	4	Oldest child
Washington	9	Oldest child
Zapata	4	Middle child

[a]Sources disagree on the exact number.
[b]Three older siblings had all died by the time Stalin was born.

siblings. Of this group, only 28 percent (twelve) are middle children 37 percent (sixteen), oldest children or oldest sons; 19 percent (eight), youngest children; and 16 percent (seven), only children. Comparing the larger group with our smaller sample of forty-three, we readily note remarkable consistencies: oldest children or sons remain constant at 37 percent; middle and youngest children are virtually identical; only children have changed by about 5 percent. On the whole, then, the two sets of results are the same: middle children remain underrepresented; oldest and youngest children, overrepresented.

Breaking down our forty-three leaders into prewar and post-war groups (Table 7.4) both reinforces some of these findings and adds a new dimension. In a set of twenty prewar leaders, oldest children constitute the largest single category, with 55 percent (eleven) being firstborn in families that range in size from four to sixteen offspring. Another 15 percent (three) are youngest children; one leader (Stalin) is an only child; and only 25 percent (five) are middle children.

The twenty-three postwar leaders are more evenly divided among the sibling categories: 30 percent (seven) middle children, 22 percent (five) oldest children, 22 percent (5) youngest children, and a surprisingly large 26 percent (six) only children. The presence of only children would not be unusual in contemporary advanced industrial societies, to be sure. But given the times these leaders were born (Giap, 1912; Marighella, 1911; Paz, 1907; Schirm, 1932; Schoeters, 1930; Sithole, 1920) and given the generally underdeveloped character of their countries, their status as only children seems outside the bounds of randomness.

Table 7.4. Age Ranking among Siblings as a Source of Radicalization: Prewar and Postwar Leaders

Leader	Number of siblings	Ranking
PREWAR		
J. Adams	3	Oldest child
S. Adams	11	Oldest son
Cromwell	10	Middle child
Danton	3	Youngest child
Devereux	3	Oldest child
Henry	12	Middle child
Jefferson	10	Oldest son
Lenin	5	Middle child
Madero	15	Oldest child
Marat	5	Oldest child
Mirabeau	10	Youngest child
Otis	13	Oldest child
Pym	2	Youngest child
Robespierre	4	Oldest child
Stalin	0'	Only child
Trotsky	8	Middle child
Vane	8	Oldest son
Villa	4	Oldest child
Washington	9	Oldest child
Zapata	4	Middle child

Leader	Number of siblings	Ranking
POSTWAR		
Arafat	4	Middle child
Ben Bella	6	Middle child
Biko	1	Youngest child
F. Castro	6–8[a]	Middle child
Chou En-lai	5	Middle child
Chu Teh	12	Middle child
Giap	0	Only child
Guevara	4	Oldest child
Ho	3	Middle child
Lin Piao	4–9[a]	Middle child
Liu Shao-ch'i	9	Youngest child
Mao	4	Oldest child
Marighella	0	Only child
Mondlane	14	Youngest child
Nkomo	1	Oldest child
Paz Estenssoro	0	Only child
Roberto	6	Oldest child
Schirm	0	Only child
Schoeters	0	Only child
Sithole	0	Only child
Souphanouvong	19	Youngest child
Torres	3	Youngest child
Vallières	2	Oldest child

[a]Three older siblings had all died by the time Stalin was born.
[b]Sources disagree on the exact number.

What accounts for this preponderance of oldest, youngest, and only children among revolutionaries? Generalizing and extrapolating from recent findings in the field of child development throw additional light on our data.[1] A degree of speculation is unavoidable, however, as these studies do not focus on revolutionaries as such. Moreover, they are culturally biased, dealing, as they do, with child development in the contemporary United States.

Oldest children or sons are typically held to strict and rigorous standards of performance, competence, and achievement. Inordinately high parental expectations generate acute anxiety, which requires reassurances that are (usually) freely given, which in turn

123

set the stage for success. The firstborns' achievement orientation, in other words, is likely to lead to eminence in their chosen endeavors, revolution included.

Typically viewed and treated as "princes," oldest or only sons gradually respond to parental and social expectations by developing an aura of power, command, authority. At the same time, since the firstborn are more idealistic and likely to have strong consciences, they are more sensitive to acts of oppression, exploitation, brutality, or injustice when these occur. Moreover, given the fact that parents are likely to be more attentive and patient toward the firstborn, oldest children are likely to experience an orderly and coherent world in their early years. Accordingly, once they are adults and on their own, revolution may become a way of introducing order in a chaotic universe.

Oldest children are also likely to experience intense feelings of anxiety over the loss of exclusive parental affection and attention once siblings begin to arrive. Coupled with this anxiety are intense feelings of guilt over the hostilities the firstborn exhibit toward their siblings. Externalizing and politicizing these feelings of guilt and hostility—even to the point of revolutionary action—may be a way of managing one's psychic balance.

The family experiences of *only* children are closer to those of the firstborn than to any other sibling rank. They differ from the oldest children, however, in that they occupy the center stage from beginning to end while at the same time being free from the anxiety and insecurity that the presence of siblings generates. Spending inordinate amounts of time with their parents, only children mature faster and are generally well informed and intelligent. Moreover, they are found to be independent personalities and to make strong leaders who can have difficulty following orders.

Youngest children are more striving and more defiant toward their siblings—and probably toward the world in general. They are more competitive and more vigilant in an effort to maintain their status and possessions in the cruel world that a large family may represent. They may resort to devious means in order to achieve their objectives. Bold and aggressive, they are typically seen as the "conquerors." Youngest children's sense of relative parental neglect and deprivation may generate repeated impulses toward rebellion. Moreover, being group oriented, youngest children may see revolutionary movements as a means of maintaining and enhancing their sense of identity and belongingness.

Middle children are underrepresented among revolutionaries because, as a group, they are not subjected to the same strict parental code and norms of behavior that are applied to the firstborn. Middle children are relatively neglected, and parental expectations are not as high. Being in relatively dependent and vulnerable positions, they tend to be pragmatic and conforming. They are likely to be "diplomats"—either as a means of working their way around older siblings or as a means of acting as mediators between older and younger siblings. On the whole, middle children are better adjusted and more content with their lives than either the firstborn or the last-born. Understandably, as a rule they do not seek radical change. There are times, however, when they may revolt against the dominance of the firstborn or imitate the rebelliousness of the firstborn and the last-born.

When we examine the overlap between Tables 7.3 and 7.1, it appears that the number of siblings has a bearing on the quality of one's family life. Of the twenty-two men who lead tranquil childhoods, eight (36 percent) have three or fewer siblings, and twelve (55 percent) have four or more (sibling data are missing for Blanco and Cabral). By contrast, of the twenty-one leaders who experience stormy lives, 33 percent (seven) have three or fewer siblings, and 67 percent (fourteen) have four or more. In other words, the greater the number of siblings, the more likely that one will have a turbulent childhood.

To summarize to this point, with the possible exception of some speculative generalizations relative to ordinal position amongst siblings, formative years appear to be relatively unimportant in the formation of revolutionary personality. For every revolutionary who has experienced a stormy childhood, we can identify one with the opposite set of experiences. We must locate the sources of radicalization elsewhere.

SCHOOL SOCIALIZATION

As will be recalled from Chapter 3, nearly all revolutionary elites have some form of education, with some 80 percent progressing beyond high school. Whether education uniformly serves as a source of radicalization requires qualifications, however. As Table 7.5 indicates, 57 percent (twenty-seven) of our leaders are radical-

Table 7.5. School Socialization as a Source of Radicalization

Yes (N = 27)	No (N = 20)	Unknown (N = 3)
Arafat	J. Adams	Nkomo
Ben Bella	S. Adams	Roberto
Biko	Chu Teh	Schirm
Blanco	Cromwell	
Cabral	Danton	
F. Castro	Devereux	
Chou En-lai	Hampden	
Giap	Henry	
Guevara	Jefferson	
Habash	Madero	
Ho	Marat	
Lenin	Mirabeau	
Lin Piao	Otis	
Liu Shao-ch'i	Paz Estenssoro	
Machel	Pym	
Mao	Robespierre	
Marighella	Vane	
Mondlane	Villa	
De la Puente	Washington	
Schoeters	Zapata	
Sendic		
Sithole		
Souphanouvong		
Stalin		
Torres		
Trotsky		
Vallières		

ized in school, whereas 43 percent (twenty) are not. Those who do not experience school radicalization are predominantly from Europe and North America and hold highly eclectic ideological beliefs. By contrast, leaders who are radicalized in school are predominantly from other regions of the world and subscribe almost exclusively to extremist ideologies.

When we divide our revolutionary elites into prewar and postwar groups, a much sharper picture emerges, as seen in Table 7.6. Specifically, radicalization in school is a characteristic of postwar leaders, not prewar ones. Virtually all leaders who are radicalized

Table 7.6. School Socialization as a Source of Radicalization: Prewar and Postwar Leaders

Yes		No	
Prewar (N = 3)	*Postwar (N = 24)*	*Prewar (N = 18)*	*Postwar (N = 2)*
Lenin	Arafat	J. Adams	Chu Teh
Stalin	Ben Bella	S. Adams	Paz Estenssoro
Trotsky	Biko	Cromwell	
	Blanco	Danton	
	Cabral	Devereux	
	F. Castro	Hampden	
	Chou En-lai	Henry	
	Giap	Jefferson	
	Guevara	Madero	
	Habash	Marat	
	Ho	Mirabeau	
	Lin Piao	Otis	
	Liu Shao-ch'i	Pym	
	Machel	Robespierre	
	Mao	Vane	
	Marighella	Villa	
	Mondlane	Washington	
	De la Puente	Zapata	
	Schoeters		
	Sendic		
	Sithole		
	Souphanouvong		
	Torres		
	Vallières		

in educational institutions are nationalists, communists, or nationalist/communists. Nearly all are from colonial or neocolonial societies, many being radicalized in the educational institutions of the metropolitan countries.

When we compare the findings of Table 7.5 with those of Table 7.1, it becomes clear that fifteen of the twenty-one revolutionaries (71 percent) who are radicalized in school also experience stormy childhoods. In other words, one is more likely to become radicalized in school if one comes from a turbulent home.

We conclude, then, that education as a source of radicalization has explanatory value for postwar leaders with stormy beginnings from colonial or neocolonial countries with nationalist, communist, or nationalist/communist ideologies. For elites who are not radicalized in educational institutions, we must investigate the sources of radicalization in other dynamics—social, psychological, situational.

NEW EXPERIENCES AND CULTURES

We have noted throughout this work that the vast majority of revolutionary elites travel widely outside their own countries and for relatively long periods of time. As far as our fifty leaders are concerned, exposure to new experiences and culture—whether obtained in foreign or domestic travel—has more explanatory value as a source of radicalization than either family or school socialization.

As Table 7.7 illustrates, less than one-fourth of our leaders do not travel abroad (or do so *after* their revolutions), whereas over three-fourths do, with 54 percent (twenty-seven) visiting four or more countries over long periods of time in various regions of the earth. With three exceptions (Mao, Villa, Zapata), those who do not travel are from the English, American, and French revolutions of the seventeenth and eighteenth centuries and expound generally democratic ideologies. (For Villa and Zapata, we discount as foreign travel border crossings or skirmishes along the Mexican-U.S. frontier.) Those who do travel abroad are men from different

Table 7.7. Foreign Travel as a Source of Radicalization

Extensive (4+ countries) (N = 27)	Moderate (2–3 countries) (N = 7)	Little (1 country) (N = 4)	None[a] (N = 12)
Arafat	Blanco	Biko	J. Adams
Ben Bella	Danton	Lin Piao	S. Adams
Cabral	Giap	Liu Shao-ch'i	Cromwell
F. Castro	Paz Estenssoro	Marighella	Hampden
Chou En-lai	Vallières		Henry
Chu Teh	Vane		Jefferson
Devereux	Washington		Mao
Guevara			Otis
Habash			Pym
Ho			Robespierre
Lenin			Villa
Machel			Zapata
Madero			
Marat			
Mirabeau			
Mondlane			
Nkomo			
De la Puente			
Roberto			
Schirm			
Schoeters			
Sendic			
Sithole			
Souphanouvong			
Stalin			
Torres			
Trotsky			

[a]Some of the individuals in this column traveled *after* their revolutions but not during or before.

times and different regions, and they hold a wide variety of political ideologies.

When we introduce the prewar–postwar distinction, the findings become clearer. As Table 7.8 shows, travel variations relative to the "moderate" and "little" categories are not appreciable, placing the focus on the "extensive" and "none" groups. Specifically,

Table 7.8. Foreign Travel as a Source of Radicalization: Prewar and Postwar Leaders

	Extensive		Moderate		Little		None[a]	
	Prewar (N = 7)	Postwar (N = 20)	Prewar (N = 3)	Postwar (N = 4)	Prewar (N = 0)	Postwar (N = 4)	Prewar (N = 11)	Postwar (N = 1)
	Devereux	Arafat	Danton	Blanco		Biko	J. Adams	Mao
	Lenin	Ben Bella	Vane	Giap		Lin Piao	S. Adams	
	Madero	Cabral	Washington	Paz Estenssoro		Liu Shao-ch'i	Cromwell	
	Marat	F. Castro		Vallières		Marighella	Hampden	
	Mirabeau	Chou En-lai					Henry	
	Stalin	Chu Teh					Jefferson	
	Trotsky	Guevara					Otis	
		Habash					Pym	
		Ho					Robespierre	
		Machel					Villa	
		Mondlane					Zapata	
		Nkomo						
		De la Puente						
		Roberto						
		Schirm						
		Schoeters						
		Sendic						
		Sithole						
		Souphanouvong						
		Torres						

[a] Some of these individuals traveled *after* their revolutions but not during or before.

only a solitary postwar leader (Mao) does not go to foreign lands, as compared to eleven (52 percent) of prewar elites. By contrast, only seven (33 percent) of prewar leaders travel to a variety of locales, as compared to twenty (69 percent) of postwar elites. In other words, foreign travel as a source of radicalization tends to be more characteristic of postwar elites.

Travel—especially of foreign variety—has a radicalizing influence in many ways. The traveller may witness oppression, exploitation, and brutality of unimaginable proportions. He may see privation, misery, hunger, disease, and death. He may observe— or even personally experience—cruelty, torture, imprisonment, and exile. If he is a colonial, not only will the traveller witness discrimination, harassment, and humiliation—he is likely to experience them personally as well. Moreover, the colonial traveller will see stark differences between (1) the conditions of the colony and those of the metropolitan country and (2) the way the colonists treat one another (with courtesy and civility) and the way they treat the colonized (with derision and contempt). The conclusion becomes unavoidable: only revolutionary change can alter the existing state of affairs.

Foreign travel has a cosmopolitanizing effect as well. Those who travel gain exposure to a variety of cultures, values, institutions, practices, and ideologies. They develop a set of standards against which to measure their own societies. They develop foreign contacts, share experiences of other revolutionaries, and cultivate potential sources of international support.

When we examine the overlap between Tables 7.7 and 7.1, we find that fourteen of the twenty-seven revolutionaries (52 percent) with records of extensive travel have stormy childhoods, whereas nine (33 percent) do not. (As can be seen in Table 7.1, data relative to formative years are missing for Habash, Machel, de la Puente, and Sendic.) In other words, travel is more likely to be a source of radicalization if one experiences turbulent beginnings. Alternatively, one is more likely to travel if one has had a stormy childhood and hence little or no sense of roots.

Similarly, a comparison of the findings of Table 7.7 with those of 7.5 makes clear that nineteen of the twenty-seven revolution-

131

aries (70 percent) who travel extensively are also radicalized in school. The five exceptions (Chu Teh, Devereux, Madero, Marat, and Mirabeau) are radicalized as a result of foreign travel but not of education. (School-radicalization data are missing for Nkomo, Roberto, and Schirm.) In other words, travel is very likely to intensify radicalization experienced in school.

SITUATIONAL DYNAMICS

Some revolutionaries appear upon the scene, not necessarily as a result of radicalization in family, school, or exposure to new experiences and cultures, but simply as a response to situations of national crisis, trauma, or emergency. Whatever their source and nature, national crises catapult into prominence—at times willy-nilly—men who possess and demonstrate the appropriate competencies and skills.

Revolutions are "times of trouble," to be sure; and they all occur under identifiable conditions, whether political, military, economic, social, or psychological.[2] A real distinction is to be drawn, however, between (1) revolutions that are systematically thought out, planned, organized, and executed by elite groups over relatively long periods of time and (2) revolutions that explode upon the scene as a consequence of sharp escalation of systemic conflicts between major social groups, taking relatively short periods of time. Accordingly, at first glance, of our thirty-one revolutionary movements, twenty-six fall in the first group, and five—the English, American, French 1789, French 1968, and Hungarian—in the second.

In one way or another, the five "situational" revolutions are characterized by the swift exacerbation of conflicts among internal forces and groups. A variety of political, social, economic, and religious issues coalesce to produce revolutionary explosions. The sluggish and frequently ill-conceived responses of the established regimes serve only to aggravate the situation and mobilize the masses. To the extent to which they exist, revolutionary ideology and organization are ad hoc and homespun. Groups of leaders are propelled into roles other people are unwilling or unable to play.

In addition to these five distinctive cases, however, it can be argued that all colonial and neocolonial revolutions—which incorporate nearly all our twenty-six remaining cases—are, virtually by definition, situational: these movements would likely not have occurred were it not for the sheer presence of the outsider. The only "real" exception here is Russia. From the standpoint of the French Canadians—or at least those who are not co-opted—even Quebec may be said to represent a colonial situation. Given the perennial environment of discrimination, oppression, and humiliation, it would be very difficult for the nonco-opted persons to avoid radicalization.[3]

In the foregoing context, as we have seen, World War II played a pivotal role in awakening the colonial peoples and accelerating the revolutionary process in their societies. This theme recurs in the thought of many colonial leaders. Reverend Sithole of Zimbabwe, who is most explicit on this point, deserves quotation at length:

> World War II . . . had a great deal to do with the awakening of the peoples of Africa. During the war the African came into contact with practically all the peoples of the earth. He met them on a life-and-death struggle basis. He saw the so-called civilized and peaceful and orderly white people mercilessly butchering one another just as his so-called savage ancestors had done in tribal wars. He saw no difference between the so-called primitive and so-called civilized man. . . .
>
> But more than this, World War II taught the African most powerful ideas. During the war, the Allied Powers taught their subject peoples . . . that it was not right for Germany to dominate other nations. They taught the subject people to fight and die for freedom. . . .
>
> The big lesson that the African learned during the last war was that he fought and suffered to preserve the freedom he did not have back home. . .
>
> The hatred against Hitler was transferred to European colonialism. . . . An Asiatic once told me, "We owe our independence to Adolf Hitler!"[4]

A related consideration in this regard is that once a colonial revolutionary movement succeeds—once a colony attains independence—a contagion effect sets in: other countries' expectations heighten, and the process of consciousness accelerates. Thus, for instance, the attainment of independence by Ghana in 1957 and the success of the Algerian Revolution in 1962 served as inspirations to revolutionary or potentially revolutionary leaders throughout much of Africa. Similarly, the success of the Chinese Revolution set an example for Asia; the Cuban Revolution, for Latin America.

There is another type of situation—much different from the ones mentioned heretofore—that may incline men toward revolution. The turbulent political histories of such countries as China, Colombia, Cuba, Guatemala, Mexico, Northern Ireland, "Palestine," Peru, and Vietnam set the stage for and facilitate the emergence of revolutionary elites. Thus, for example, given the continued presence of the Irish Republican Army since 1916 (albeit with ebbs and flows), or the perennial fact of *la violencia* in Colombia, it would be virtually impossible not to become radicalized.

The Palestinian situation is also instructive. Since the formation of Israel in 1947 and the Arab-Israeli War if 1948, the area has been racked by uninterrupted violence. Thus, George Habash readily acknowledges that these events constituted personal as well as national traumas, setting him on a revolutionary course:

> I have no personal motive (to participate in the political struggle in the area) except that which every Palestinian citizen has. Before 1948 I was . . . far from politics. . . . [In view of the circumstances, however,] you cannot but become a revolutionary and fight for the cause. Your own cause as well as that of your people.[5]

For Yasir Arafat, these two events were exacerbated by a third: the unilateral diversion by Israel of the upper waters of the Jordan River in 1963. He told his biographer in the mid-1970s:

> The timing could not have been more perfect. . . . [I]t was precisely [Israeli] arrogance that blinded them to the true consequences of their action. It would be accurate to say that everything that has happened in the Middle East in the last twelve years stems from

the Jordan diversion. The Israeli action gave us in the liberation movement a specific focus around which to build our cause. It put flesh on the skeleton of our ideology. It gave us the power and influence we had been struggling to achieve. It gave us a specific strategy and tactical approach that we could shape to our needs. But most important, it settled the issue once and for all—that is, that there would never be peace in the Middle East until the Palestinian people were given their rights, as individuals and as a nation.[6]

Potential situational sources of radicalization can also be found in some personal traits or characteristics of revolutionaries over which they have little or no control. We have seen, for example, that exposure to urban culture can have radicalizing consequences, as can number of siblings and age ranking among them. As we shall see in Chapter 8, marginality—whether physical, social, or psychological—can also lead to radicalization. (Provisionally we define *marginality* as deviation from established norms.) Social class can also have an impact; it is a variable that has been painfully detailed by Pierre Vallières, for instance.

A child of Montreal slums, "tough neighborhoods," and gang fights, Vallières identifies the poverty associated with his lower-class status as an intrinsic source of radicalization. He writes:

Money [or lack thereof] had turned all of us into perpetual rebels who rebelled in vain. Protesting victims, how could we seriously believe in our freedom when we knew that freedom was based on money? And how could we not protest, when we knew that money was being stolen from us every day? But our protest changed absolutely nothing. . . . We had to act, not protest. And in order to act effectively, we had to unite, to confront the systematic organization of exploitation with an even stronger organization.[7]

Vallières proceeds to depict the working-class family as the working class writ small: the "working-class family was only the product of the condition of the working class, which was itself the product of centuries of exploitation of man by man." He continues:

The terrible thing about the working-class family is the function, imposed on it by the present system, of renewing and perpetuating the supply of slaves, of niggers, of cheap labor to be exploited, alienated, and oppressed. . . . The proletarian child . . . revolts against his parents, but very early his revolt turns against the condition of his class and those who are responsible for that condition. . . . Of course the system crushes a great number of them. . . .

It is an understatement to say that the working-class family is a double or quadruple monstrosity. This "possessing unit"—as Engels calls it—is a hell, a room with no exit, in which the self-destruction of human beings is accomplished mechanically.[8]

A final situational dynamic we must consider is, simply, the role of chance. Thus it happens that at age twelve Georges Schoeters—an illegitimate child who was abandoned by both parents—joined and worked for Belgian partisans in the forests of Ardennes during the German occupation. Examining his condition, a Canadian psychoanalyst writes:

He observed the Belgians defending themselves against the Nazis with lies, deceit, fraud, civil disobedience, underground bombs, and murder. It is not surprising, therefore, that a young man brought up in these circumstances . . . would have a difficult time after the war in adapting himself to an orderly life in which fraud, sabotage, violence, and insurrection were no longer acceptable.[9]

Similarly, Joshua Nkomo was propelled into the limelight, not as a result of determination and hard work, but of fortuitous circumstances. Having returned to Zimbabwe following training as a social worker in South Africa, Nkomo was appointed as Rhodesia Railways' first African welfare worker.

African employees liked Nkomo well enough to select him in 1951 as the first full-time general secretary of the Rhodesia Railways African Employees' Association, then the best situated, if not the most powerful, of Central Africa's fledgling unions. He was not a particularly energetic or successful union organizer, but very soon Nkomo found himself, unexpectedly, a national political figure.[10]

As can be seen, then, a variety of situations may thrust men toward revolutionary leadership. These men have the requisite qualities and skills, but in an important sense—and in one way or another—they are children of circumstances.

SUMMARY

We have examined the patterns of radicalization of our fifty revolutionary elites in terms of four major topics. We find family socialization to have the least explanatory or predictive value. School socialization is of some importance, particularly in the radicalization of postwar elites from colonial countries. Exposure to new experiences and cultures is a most compelling consideration in the radicalization of many revolutionary leaders. Situational dynamics of one sort or another would seem to affect virtually all revolutionary elites.

Nonetheless, we do not anticipate a single pattern in the radicalization of all revolutionaries. Since each person is likely to encounter a different set of life experiences, the radicalization process is likely to vary from revolutionary to revolutionary.

8
Psychological Dynamics

The personality development of revolutionary elites is conditioned not only by their social, cultural, political, and situational experiences discussed in the preceding chapter but also by the interaction of a series of psychological dynamics they share in varying combinations and degrees. Among these dynamics we include: (1) vanity, egotism, narcissism, (2) asceticism, puritanism, virtue, (3) relative deprivation and status inconsistency, (4) marginality, inferiority complex, compulsion to excel, (5) oedipal conflict writ large, (6) estheticism and the romantic streak.

Two characteristics are so universally descriptive of revolutionary elites—and so pervasively discussed in the literature—as to render elaboration unnecessary. All revolutionaries are driven by a sense of justice–injustice and a corresponding commitment to right the wrongs. This sense of justice–injustice may be personally rooted, or it may be perceived in societal conditions (oppression and humiliation at home and abroad, for example). Whatever its source, and whatever form it may take, the sense of justice–injustice is ubiquitous among revolutionaries—so much so, in fact, that in his seminal work *Injustice* Barrington Moore, Jr., sets out to give the subject a biological foundation. Specifically, he proposes "a conception of innate human nature" to which all instances of injustice (defined as any act injurious to physical or psychological wants and needs of human beings) are noxious and hence unacceptable. This conception, he argues, "implies the existence of a 'natural morality.' " And to Moore, "the main value of any conception of natural morality lies in the implication that moral codes, moral anger, and hence a sense of social injustice have some very important roots in human biology."[1] Controversial though it is, Moore's position highlights the centrality and universality of justice–injustice as a motivating force among revolutionary elites.

A second characteristic all revolutionaries share is an unalterable commitment to varieties of nationalism and patriotism. Revolutionary leaders uniformly express devotion to the fatherland. They seek to maintain the independence and integrity of their countries. They set out to free their nations from the oppression and exploitation of other nations. They act to improve the status, power, and prestige of their homelands. Put differently, as we can see, nationalism may serve as another means of pursuing justice. In this sense, the two are interrelated.

To keep the discussion manageable, and to avoid repetition, we limit the treatment of each of the other psychological dynamics to a relatively few—but we hope representative and instructive— instances of their manifestations among revolutionaries new to this work, *only occasionally* referring to their "older" counterparts for balance and comprehensiveness.* The entire picture is summarized in Table 8.1.

VANITY, EGOTISM, NARCISSISM

In varying forms and degrees, vanity, egotism, and narcissism are present among twenty-seven (54 percent) of our fifty revolutionaries.

John Adams candidly considers vanity "my cardinal vice and cardinal folly."[2] Leon Trotsky is given to monumental self-aggrandizement, particularly in the intellectual field. Joshua Nkomo basks in recognition and adulation. Souphanouvong's vanity and egotism have been noted by any number of scholars and journalists. Pierre Vallières's narcissism repeatedly surfaces in his autobiographical work, *White Niggers of America*. Instructive in this regard is his recounting of his feelings as a budding writer in his late teens:

> Every evening, every night, I spent long hours writing—or rather, describing myself. During these hours of silence and solitude I lived out my narcissism to the full. . . .

*Extensive references for each leader appear in the appropriate sections of the Bibliography; only direct quotations, little-known points, or controversial matters are documented here.

Table 8.1. Psychological Dynamics of Revolutionary Behavior

LEADER	Vanity, egotism, narcissism	Asceticism, puritanism, virtue	Relative deprivation and status inconsistency	Marginality, inferiority complex, compulsion to excel	Oedipal conflict	Estheticism and romanticism
J. Adams	X	X				X
S. Adams	X		X	X		
Arafat	X	X	X	X		X
Ben Bella	X	X	X	X		X
Biko				X		X
Blanco		X	X	X		
Cabral			X	X		
F. Castro	X	X	X	X	X	X
Chou En-lai		X			X	X
Chu Teh					X	X
Cromwell	X	X		X		
Danton	X	X		X		
Devereux	X	X	X			
Giap	X	X				
Guevara		X		X		X
Habash		X	X			
Hampden	X	X				
Henry	X	X				X
Ho	X	X	X	X		X
Jefferson	X					X
Lenin		X		X		X
Lin Piao	X	X		X	X	X

Liu Shao-ch'i	×				×	
Machel	×			×	×	
Madero			×	×		
Mao	×	×	×		×	
Marat	×		×	×		×
Marighella			×		×	
Mirabeau			×		×	
Mondlane			×	×	×	
Nkomo				×		×
Otis				×		×
Paz Estenssoro				×	×	×
De la Puente	×				×	
Pym			×	×	×	×
Roberto			×		×	×
Robespierre			×		×	
Stalin			×		×	×
Schirm	×		×	×	×	
Schoeters			×	×	×	
Sendic			×		×	
Sithole	×		×	×	×	
Souphanouvong			×	×	×	×
Torres	×		×	×	×	×
Trotsky	×	×	×	×	×	×
Vallières	×		×	×	×	×
Vane	×			×	×	×
Villa				×		×
Washington			×	×		×
Zapata			×	×		
Total	23	6	31	25	37	27

Noces obscures [*Dark Weddings*, his first novel] was a book filled with my narcissism. [And I learned] to take responsibility for that narcissism without being ashamed of it.[3]

From early in his formative years Yasir Arafat's influential mentor and granduncle Yusuf el-Akbar sought to convince the child that he possessed divine powers and was entrusted with a supernatural mission. As he grew up, Arafat became increasingly arrogant and ruthless. A fellow activist and student at the University of Cairo recalls:

In my opinion, winning the presidency of PSF [Palestine Student Federation, in 1952] turned Yasir into a power maniac. . . . [H]e suddenly began to thrive on his position. He learned what it is to be president of something, to be able to issue orders, form committees, handle money, push people around who disagreed with him. He became arrogant. He became pretentious. He used to say that he could no longer have close friends because there might be times when he had to discipline or dismiss or even punish [them][4].

Excessive vanity has a variety of attendant consequences. In some (for example, Nkomo, Trotsky), it alternates with self-doubt. (Self-doubt, in fact, may be so strong as to drive a revolutionary to the verge of suicide, as was the case with Vallières—at least twice.) In others (Souphanouvong, Vallières), it generates a compulsion to excel. In still others (Arafat, Stalin), it produces persecution complex and the need to purge all of one's "enemies."

While strong-willed, self-confident, and self-assured, some revolutionary personalities are noted for the *absence* of vanity, egotism, or narcissism. Thus, among the "seven sins of the urban guerrilla," Carlos Marighella specifies the third as "vanity."[5] According to one biographer, Stephen Biko remained a most modest man throughout his life:

Biko's was a new style of leadership. It was not an obvious style. He never ever proclaimed himself a leader, and in fact he generally discouraged the cult of personality and often tried to play a backroom role. He preferred to think that the struggle for black liberation was led by many rather than few, and that Black Consciousness was a mass movement of which he was only one of many articulators.[6]

In a similar vein, Sithole insists on maintaining his Christian humility. Father Camilo Torres writes: "I chose Christianity because I found in it the best way to serve my neighbor. I was chosen by Christ to be a priest forever, motivated by the desire to devote myself completely to the love of my brothers."[7] For him,

> The Revolution is the means of obtaining a government that will feed the hungry, clothe the naked, teach the uneducated, perform works of charity, [teach the people to] love their neighbors not only in a transitory and occasional way, not just a few but the majority of their neighbors. For this reason the Revolution is not only permissible but obligatory for Christians who see in it the one effective and complete way to create love for all.[8]

Among other revolutionary leaders without pronounced ego problems, we may include Cabral, Fidel Castro, Guevara, Habash, Machel, Madero, and de la Puente.

ASCETICISM, PURITANISM, VIRTUE

Asceticism, puritanism, and a corresponding demand for virtue are rather common attributes of revolutionary elites, applying, as they do, to thirty-seven (74 percent) of our leaders. Some of the specific manifestations of these qualities warrant elaboration.

Father Torres, as we have seen, is the very personification of Christian virtue, love, and charity. Even before he formally enters the priesthood, this man of aristocratic background practices the values he was later to preach. Thus, according to his mother, while studying sociology at the University of Louvain, "He lived . . . in a very humble little village where he had to prepare his own meals and wash his own clothes."[9] Similarly, having become disillusioned with church hierarchy, and having determined to leave the comforts of Bogotá for the life of the guerrilla fighter in October 1965, he announces: "I have to take a long and painful trip. I don't know if I will return to Bogotá. We revolutionaries must be prepared to give all—even our lives."[10] The statement proved prophetic: Torres was killed in combat in February 1966.

Carlos Marighella identifies among the essential qualities of the revolutionary: "to be able to stand up against fatigue, hunger, rain, heat. To. . . be vigilant. To conquer the art of dissembling. Never to fear danger. To behave the same by day as by night. Not to act impetuously. To have unlimited patience. . . . Not to get discouraged." It follows, then, according to Marighella, that the revolutionary enjoys "moral superiority."[11]

According to one scholar, George Habash "adhered to a personal code of conduct which was strict, rigid, and uncompromising." He stressed

> the necessity of individual sacrifice in the course of the struggle. . . . [Moreover] no one could be more qualified than George to speak about sacrifice. Since the mid-fifties Habash had put aside his medical degree and with it a most promising career, left his family and lived the life of a permanent political refugee, always on the run, harassed by the security agents of several Arab countries (not to mention Israel) . . . all this for the sake of his political convictions.[12]

Arafat is said to have manifested asceticism in his childhood (preschool) years: an older brother attributes Arafat's subdued and withdrawn behavior at this time to "a deep instinctive asceticism."[13] More to the point: "His single-mindedness impressed the Palestinians he came in contact with. His disdain for comfort and luxury and his abstinence from wine and sex were elements in a legend that soon grew up around him."[14] Arafat himself sums up the matter succinctly: "But I was a *fedayeen*,* so sacrifice meant nothing. . . . To die at the hands of the real enemy, that would make me proud."[15]

Souphanouvong declares:

> The patriot who consciously sacrifices himself for the sake of national liberation is sure to encounter at the end one of these three things: death, prison (or exile), or victory. If you wish only for a riskless victory, then you have embarked on a "gondola of dreams. . . ."[T]he political arena . . . demands men of action and of self-denial. As for me, I decided at the age of thirteen to rid myself, whatever the cost . . . of this inclination toward letting things drift . . . of indolence, of this "resting on big words," all so

*Literally, those who are prepared to sacrifice themselves (for a cause).

characteristic of our country and of declining races destined to
serve as sheep to the hungry wolves.[16]

Samora Machel relentlessly stresses the importance of hard
work and self-sacrifice, on the one hand, and service to the people,
on the other. Revolutionary leaders, he asserts, must "live mod-
estly and with the people, not turning the task entrusted to them
into a privilege." He is outraged at "material, moral, and ideological corruption, bribery, seeking comforts, string pulling, nepo-
tism," and the like.[17] Indeed, the purification of a decadent society
and its tranformation into a righteous one is a recurrent theme in
all revolutionary thought.

Just as in the previous section we discovered revolutionaries
who lack vanity and egotism, so also we find leaders who are not
given to asceticism. Thus it is said of Biko: "He was no ascetic—he
loved life and its good things and imparted this relish."[18] Similarly,
Nkomo is known for his "love of comfort and good living, his easy,
affable way with whites, . . . [his knowledge] of joys of world travel and the mental and physical comforts of life abroad."[19] Indeed, a
black-and-white photograph in the *Newsweek* of July 9, 1979, shows
Nkomo an overweight man, cleanly shaven, with silvery hair neat-
ly trimmed and brushed back. He wears what appears to be an
expensive print shirt with solid dark cuffs. A fancy bracelet casu-
ally dangles from the right wrist. Altogether, the photograph depicts a gentleman of leisure—a far cry from the boots and fatigues
of Castro and Guevara.

RELATIVE DEPRIVATION
AND STATUS INCONSISTENCY

Relative deprivation and status inconsistency have been in-
strumental in shaping the motivation of a variety of revolutionaries. Briefly, relative deprivation refers to one's *perception* of discrepancy between one's value expectations (aspiration) and one's
value capabilities (achievement). Status inconsistency denotes a
perceived discrepancy between one's economic status and one's
political power (or more generally, social position).

Relative deprivation and status inconsistency may be said to characterize most (if not all) lower-class revolutionaries and to be *inherent* in the very nature of colonial contexts and hence of colonial personalities. We limit our discussion, however, to the twenty-five leaders (exactly half of our group) for whom we have direct and persuasive evidence.

François Schirm and Georges Schoeters of the Front de libération québecois (FLQ) have a great deal in common. Both are foreigners, Schirm having been born in Budapest, Schoeters in Antwerp. Men without countries, both travel widely (but separately) in Europe and elsewhere in search of material security and self-respect, but all in vain. Both immigrate to Canada and end up in Montreal, only to confront menial job after menial job and to experience further discrimination and humiliation. Both are drawn to revolution as a means, at least in part, of redressing personal grievances and injustices.

Vallières is acutely and obsessively aware of his lower-class status and the continued futility of trying to improve his condition in English-dominated Quebec. Brutally candid, he writes: "My itinerary from lower-class slums to the FLQ was long and tortuous." His childhood was anything but peaceful, secure, or happy. As for school, "the only thing" he learned "was to be ashamed of my—of our—condition." On the whole, he finds, his "entire existence was nothing but a daily obscenity." Yet, he continues to strive: "I wanted to *do* something, to become someone." Failing on all fronts, he ends up seeing himself as a "white nigger":

> To be a "nigger" in America is to be not a man but someone's slave. For the rich white man of Yankee America, the nigger is a sub-man. Even the poor whites consider the nigger their inferior. They say: "to work as hard as a nigger," "to smell like a nigger," "as dangerous as a nigger," "as ignorant as a nigger." Very often they do not even suspect that they too are niggers, slaves, "white niggers." White racism hides the reality from them by giving them the opportunity to despise an inferior, to crush him mentally or to pity him.[20]

Sithole and Souphanouvong experience status inconsistency as well as relative deprivation. Within a year after entering missionary school at age fifteen, Sithole's poverty is driven home to him:

> In 1936 my little savings were exhausted and I was compelled to remain on the Mission Station, working holiday after holiday. It was not an easy thing to remain on the Mission Station every holiday. It was a great stigma as it revealed the poor financial circumstances of my parents. Youthful pride . . . made me feel sharply what it meant to be born of poor parents. Like all others who were in the same boat with me, I was held in great contempt but I soon got used to the game.[21]

Following nearly four years of education in a theological school in the United States, Sithole returns to Zimbabwe to be appointed a teacher and primary school principal in 1959. His economic condition having relatively improved, he comes to a new realization:

> But no African teacher was allowed by the African Education Department to participate actively in politics. That is to say, no teacher was allowed to hold an executive position in any political party. The effect of this was to deprive the African nationalist movement of really educated people. It would appear that the African Education Department used the question of relatively high salary to frighten African teachers off politics, since if any one of them actively participated in politics he would lose his teaching post and thus his high salary.[22]

By all accounts, Souphanouvong established an exceptional record at the University of Paris while obtaining an engineering degree. Having returned to Laos in 1938, he was greatly disillusioned by the inferior post he was offered in French colonial administration. "Thus, his mind was especially receptive to revolutionary doctrines."[23] Written in the third-person singular, a statement identified as "autobiographical," reveals Souphanouvong's state of mind:

> His heart was so full of enthusiasm . . . he felt so happy with the idea of "serving." . . .
> He was astonished to see the piteous positions which the Indochinese administration was offering its most gifted children. . . . Was this how the country welcomed the best of its children, those who had exiled themselves and had devoted their years of youth to austerity and study?

Bitterness, rebellion, and discouragement disabled this young man.[24]

What made matters particularly unbearable was that: (1) the treatment Souphanouvong received was wholly inconsistent with his position as a member of the Laotian royal family, and (2) his status in no way approached that of three older brothers who were playing prominent political roles in Laos.

Far from being phenomena limited to the experience of contemporary revolutionaries, relative deprivation and status inconsistency affect earlier, European and North American elites as well. The case of Washington, for instance, is quite instructive. His compulsion to expand his landholdings brings him into conflict with English law: by a 1767 proclamation, the king had forbidden further invasion of Indian territory by settlers. But Washington's thirst for more land remains unsatiated. Similarly, his interest in the Stamp and Navigation acts is more than that of an interested member of the Virginia House of Burgesses. He is personally affected: he owns nearly ten thousand acres and is a heavy exporter to England.[25]

Having failed, in a series of acts of protest and official correspondence, to reform the system, Washington concludes that more potent action is called for. Having been deprived of his rights, having failed to obtain redress in a peaceful manner, Washington's only alternative is to embrace the radicalism that the situation thrusts upon him.

The case of Washington is illustrative of a whole genre of revolutionaries around the globe who begin as reformers and seek to work within the system. Finding the system unresponsive, running into constant frustration and intimidation, they become disillusioned, reject establishment politics, and turn to revolutionary politics. Cases in point include Madero of Mexico, F. Castro of Cuba, Paz Estenssoro of Bolivia, Torres of Colombia, Habash of "Palestine," Nkomo and Sithole of Zimbabwe, Biko of South Africa. For instance, were it not for the Batista coup of March 1952, which effectively suspended the Cuban constitution and political processes, Fidel Castro, who at the time was campaigning for a parliamentary seat in the upcoming June elections, might have turned out to be a regular politician.

MARGINALITY, INFERIORITY COMPLEX, COMPULSION TO EXCEL

It is a recurrent theme in the literature on revolutionaries that they tend to be marginal men in their societies—that is, they deviate in significant and perceptible ways from accepted norms, whether social, psychological, or physical. As we have seen in Chapter 1, for example, Harold D. Lasswell maintains that all forms of power seeking represent compensatory mechanisms growing out of inferiority complex, low self-esteem, and a corresponding compulsion to excel.

As with relative deprivation and status inconsistency, one can argue that all colonial revolutionaries are almost by definition marginal, since the colonizers systematically and consciously infuse them with a deep sense of inferiority. (It is a truism, for instance, that the colonizer typically views and treats the colonial as subhuman.) Nonetheless, we again limit discussion to the thirty-one revolutionaries (62 percent)—colonial or otherwise—for whom we have compelling evidence.

We return to the case of Prince Souphanouvong, the twentieth and youngest son of the viceroy, a hereditary position of a collateral branch of the Laotian royal family. His mother was a commoner, perhaps even a concubine. His father "apparently paid little attention to him and even was rumored not to be his real father." His inferiority vis-à-vis his three older illustrious brothers continued to plague him. Accordingly, "his remarkable vigor, combative, adventurous, and romantic spirit, his strong desire to excel . . . may not be unrelated to the pressures he felt to make up for [his marginal status] . . . in a royal household."[26]

At the opposite end of the social spectrum stands Vallières, whose inferiority complex is just as real and just as intense. His lower-class background haunts him as he fails at everything he touches. Following the collapse of his third love affair, he feels "humiliated and half mad." At the peak of an identity crisis, he turns to religion and feels content as he begins "to dream about God." Finding the church hypocritical, he abandons religion and travels to France in search of roots and identity. Disillusioned by his experiences in France, he reaches the point of contemplating suicide. He concludes: "There was nothing for me to do here [in France]. I could be of no use to anyone. As in Quebec. . . . No one needed me or my services. . . . I am certainly a man who has been flayed alive."[27]

Colonial revolutionaries typically experience bitter personal degradation and humiliation as a result of the treatment they receive at the hands of the colonizers. Whether in the colony or while traveling in the metropolitan country, they are typically subjected to racial discrimination, harassment, police searches, and imprisonment. Having experienced one such incident, Mondlane reports:

> One of the last questions I was asked before I was released concerned my own conception of the moral, intellectual, and cultural capabilities of people of my own race. The question was phrased generally this way, "Do you think that the black man has evolved morally, intellectually, and culturally enough to be able to govern himself?" Since my answer was obviously a strong "Yes," while I was shivering in my boots, the gentleman who had been investigating me . . . asked further why then only purely African independent states were in his view so backward and primitive. Then he gave me a stern lecture concerning what I had said.[28]

Our revolutionaries experience other forms of marginality and humiliation as well. F. Castro is an illegitimate child whose parents subsequently married. In addition to being illegitimate, Schoeters never knew his father and was abandoned by his mother, who branded him a "savage."[29] Schirm and Schoeters are foreigners, it will be recalled, who, hard as they try, never adjust to their social environment and never find acceptance. Blanco and Zapata are mestizos who take pride in their descent. Cabral, Marighella, and Sendic are born to immigrant parents—Cape Verdian, Italian/African, and Serbian/Sicilian, respectively. (Marighella is nicknamed *O Preto*, the Negro.)

Physical disfigurement seems to function as a source of marginality and inferiority complex for a number of revolutionaries. Mirabeau "is said to have been born with two teeth, to have beaten his nurse at the age of three, and to have shown in early childhood that excess of vitality which drove most of his family to the extremes of either virtue or vice. It was so to the end."[30] His facial disfigurement by smallpox at age three led his father to consider him "ugly as Satan."[31] And when he went to school, "the boy was not allowed to bear his family name, but was registered in the institution, at his father's request, as Pierre Buffiere, a slight, an ignominy put upon him, that must have irritated his proud nature."[32]

According to an older brother, from early childhood, Arafat "was fat, soft, ungainly, and completely unimpressive. He had a very high voice, and was beginning to suffer from comparison to girls. . . . Even my father . . . blamed my mother for much of what he thought was wrong with Rahman [Arafat's given name], saying that her dreaming of a girl had caused Rahman to be born more like a girl than a boy."[33] In a male-dominated culture, this could be psychologically debilitating, setting in motion any number of compensatory mechanisms aimed at power seeking.

OEDIPAL CONFLICT WRIT LARGE

As we have seen in Chapter 1, E. Victor Wolfenstein has developed a theory of the revolutionary personality based on the Oedipus complex. According to this theory, the revolutionary externalizes and projects onto the political arena the private conflict with the father, thus moderating his feelings of ambivalence and guilt.

In our group of fifty revolutionaries, we can identify situations of parental conflict and possible oedipal problems in only six cases (12 percent). For three of these (Lenin, Trotsky, Mao), our information is relatively adequate; for the other three (Chou En-lai, Chu Teh, F. Castro), our knowledge is extremely sketchy. Having presented the available information for the six individuals in our earlier work, here we merely sample the case of Trotsky.

"Trotsky's life," as Wolfenstein writes, "is a study in discontinuities—between city and country, farmer father and intellectual son, dutiful schoolboy and lifelong revolutionary."[34] Conflict and tension between son and father were routine. On the farm, when disagreements developed between the father and his workers, Trotsky regularly sided with the latter. The father's attempt to persuade him to become an engineer ignited an acute crisis. Above all, Trotsky deeply resented his father's monopolization of his mother's time and affection. A feeling of being unloved and uncared for haunted him through much of his childhood.

Trotsky left his father at age ten to go to school in Odessa, leaving the oedipal problems unresolved. His later determination to stay away from the farm was an open defiance of paternal authority and an open affirmation of the self. His arrest and imprisonment shortly thereafter were the catalysts in his radicalization. According to Wolfenstein, "it was this imprisonment that transformed Trotsky's rebellion against parental authority into a long-term commitment to the overthrow of tsarism. . . . [It] served to convince him that there was a malevolent authority against which revolt was justified."[35]

ESTHETICISM AND ROMANTICISM

Throughout the foregoing pages we have depicted revolutionary elites as vain and egotistical; ascetic and puritanical; and racked by a variety of social, political, economic, and psychological tensions. Twenty-three of our revolutionaries (46 percent), we should note, have a gentler side as well: they exhibit estheticism and romanticism of various forms. Although strictly speaking not all expressions of estheticism and romanticism function as "psychological dynamics," they help provide a more balanced picture of revolutionary personalities.

To begin with, some revolutionaries are well steeped in literature, poetry, philosophy, and the arts. Such diverse figures as Jefferson, Trotsky, Mao, and Vallières are voracious consumers of literature, philosophy, and poetry—Western as well as Eastern,

Marxist as well as non-Marxist. Even a highly selective list of their favorites would amount to a who's who of world literature and philosophy: Baudelaire, Camus, Dostoyevsky, Einstein, Hegel, Heidegger, Hugo, Kafka, Kierkegaard, Locke, Malraux, Marx, J. S. Mill, Proust, Rousseau, Sartre, Shakespeare, Adam Smith, Tolstoy, Zola. Moreover, such an unlikely figure as Vallières writes three novels before age eighteen and destroys them because he is not satisfied with any.

Some of our revolutionaries are poets in their own right. The best known and most prolific is Mao, of course. Less well known are Ch'en Yi, Chu Teh, Ho Chi Minh, Liu Shao-ch'i, Torres, and Vallières.

Some revolutionaries are infatuated by music. Jefferson called music "the favorite passion of my soul"[36] and played the violin in a string quartet. Biko and Torres compose and perform their own music. Not only is Vallières a lover of art, music, and the theater, he also expounds on the role of the artist in liberation: "They [the artists] express through their poetry, songs, and plays the aspirations of the Québecois. Their work has a political direction, and at the same time, a taste of the kind of personal freedom we all desire. They bring hope to the people just like the FLQ does in its own way."[37]

Some revolutionaries are nature lovers. Mao's poetry, for example, frequently depicts the sky, clouds, storm, snow, rain, wind, mountains, rivers, fish, birds, trees, flowers, blossoms, and the like. Father Torres loves all things Colombian: rivers, mountains, flowers, cornfields. He is particularly struck by Los Llanos— the vast sunburnt plains lying on the other side of the mountains from Bogotá. Visiting the place, in fact, transforms his life:

> The immensity of that place, the silence, the tropical explosion of life, of sun, impressed me very much. I began to be disturbed. I wanted to be alone. I realized that life as I understood it, as I was living it, lacked meaning. I thought I could be more useful socially. . . . I analyzed the professions one by one: medicine, law, engineering, chemistry. . . ? None of those. What about the seminary? I told myself that the immensity of [Los Llanos] had helped me find God. It was the solution. It seemed to me a total solution. The most logical.[38]

Therein lies the genesis of Torres's motivation to devote himself to an endless quest for the betterment of humanity: "I have resolved to dedicate myself, fulfilling in this way part of my task of leading men through mutual love to the love of God. I consider this an essential duty of my Christian and priestly life as a Colombian."[39]

In fact, Torres counts himself among "a handful of [Don] Quixotes"[40]—a condition that afflicts other revolutionaries as well. Blanco's version, for example, reads:

> The revolutionary loves life. For, though he suffers intensely his own affliction and the affliction of all his brothers, he lives in order to destroy affliction. So, despite the suffering, he is happy.
>
> The revolutionary loves the world. For, though he lives in a world of misery, injustice, and hatred. . . , he exists in order to change that world. So, the revolutionary loves the world; for though he lives in an earthly hell, he exists in order to transform it into an earthly paradise. . . .
>
> To be a revolutionary is to love the world, to love life, to be happy. So, he doesn't flee from life, he understands that it is his duty to live for the fight, and he enjoys life.
>
> But neither must he flee from death![41]

PREWAR AND POSTWAR ELITES

Ranking our psychological dynamics in order of frequency of appearance (see Table 8.1), it is apparent that asceticism is at the top (74 percent), followed closely by marginality (62 percent), vanity (54 percent), relative deprivation and status inconsistency (50 percent), and estheticism and romanticism (46 percent). Quite some distance away (12 percent) is oedipal conflict writ large. Individually considered, asceticism and marginality have greater explanatory potential than vanity, relative deprivation and status inconsistency, or estheticism and romanticism. The latter three, in turn, have far greater explanatory value than oedipal conflict. Not surprisingly, however, the particular *mix* of psychological dynamics varies from revolutionary to revolutionary.

Introducing the distinction between prewar and postwar elites, a different set of results emerges. Setting aside oedipal conflict, Table 8.2 demonstrates that vanity is an overwhelming characteristic of prewar revolutionaries, affecting, as it does, seventeen of twenty-one elites (81 percent), the corresponding figures for the postwar group being eleven of twenty-nine leaders (38 percent). Beyond this, postwar revolutionaries tend to rank higher than prewar elites on asceticism (83 percent as compared to 62 percent), relative deprivation and status inconsistency (55 percent and 38 percent, respectively), and estheticism and romanticism (52 percent and 38 percent). As for marginality, it applies to twelve of twenty-one prewar leaders (57 percent) as compared to nineteen of twenty-nine postwar elites (66 percent).

In other words, the prewar and postwar groups are least alike in terms of vanity and most alike in terms of marginality. In fact, given our findings, next to justice–injustice and nationalism/patriotism, marginality must be rated as the most consistent and the most enduring characteristic of revolutionary elites, impervious to time, place, and conditions.

SUMMARY

We have examined our fifty revolutionary elites in the light of a series of psychological dynamics, some of them closely interrelated. We noted at the outset the centrality and universality of two characteristics all revolutionaries seem to share: a sense of justice–injustice and a commitment to nationalism/patriotism.

Ranking our psychological dynamics in order of frequency of appearance among all fifty leaders, asceticism emerges at the top, followed closely by marginality, vanity, relative deprivation and status inconsistency, and estheticism and romanticism—and quite distantly by the Oedipus complex. Considering the prewar and postwar groups, we find the two least alike in terms of vanity and most alike in terms of marginality.

Table 8.2. Psychological Dynamics of Revolutionary Behavior: Prewar and Postwar Leaders

LEADER	Vanity, egotism, narcissism	Asceticism, puritanism, virtue	Relative deprivation and status inconsistency	Marginality, inferiority complex, compulsion to excel	Oedipal conflict	Estheticism and romanticism
Prewar (N = 21)						
J. Adams	×	×		×		×
S. Adams	×		×	×		
Cromwell	×	×		×		×
Danton	×			×		
Devereux	×	×	×			
Hampden	×	×				
Henry	×	×				×
Jefferson	×	×				×
Lenin		×		×	×	×
Madero	×		×	×		
Marat			×	×		×
Mirabeau		×		×		
Otis	×		×			
Pym	×	×				
Robespierre	×	×		×		
Stalin	×	×		×		
Trotsky	×	×		×	×	×
Vane	×	×				×
Villa	×		×			
Washington	×		×			
Zapata			×	×		
Total	17	13	8	12	2	8

Postwar (N = 29)

Arafat	×	×	×	×		×
Ben Bella	×	×	×	×		×
Biko		×	×	×		×
Blanco		×	×	×		×
Cabral		×		×	×	
F. Castro	×	×	×	×		×
Chou En-lai		×		×	×	×
Chu Teh					×	×
Giap	×	×				
Guevara		×	×	×		×
Habash		×				
Ho	×	×	×	×		×
Lin Piao	×	×		×		×
Liu Shao-ch'i		×				×
Machel		×	×			×
Mao		×		×	×	×
Marighella		×	×	×		
Mondlane		×	×	×		
Nkomo	×					
Paz Estenssoro	×	×	×			
De la Puente		×				
Roberto	×	×				
Schirm			×	×		
Schoeters			×	×		
Sendic		×	×	×		
Sithole		×	×	×		×
Souphanouvong	×			×		
Torres	×	×	×	×		×
Vallières		×		×		×
Total	11	24	16	19	4	15

Though marginality appears to be a most enduring attribute of our revolutionaries, we conclude, as we did in Chapter 7, that there is no single pattern in the emergence of revolutionary elites, the particular mix varying from leader to leader. Oedipal conflict has a particularly weak explanatory value among the leaders we have studied.

PART IV

SYNTHESIS

9
Revolutionary Leaders: Theory and Research

In this volume, we have presented the results of our continued search for answers to two interrelated sets of questions about revolutionary elites across time and space: their characteristics (What are they like?), their emergence upon the scene (Why and how do they become revolutionaries?). We have cast this search in the light of a situational theory of revolutionary leadership, stressing the interplay between three principal variables: situation, psychology, skills. It is now time to take stock of a decade* of continuous research by synthesizing our major findings and indicating their bearing on our theoretical concerns.

CHARACTERISTICS OF REVOLUTIONARY ELITES

Beyond the most general characteristics of our 135 revolutionary elites, it will be recalled, our more specialized findings are framed by a central distinction between two groups of leaders: (1) the 28 revolutionaries who were involved in five revolutions that took place before World War II and (2) the 107 elites who were active in twenty-six revolutionary movements that unfolded (or climaxed) after that watershed event. Although we had initially postulated time as an independent variable, our temporal contrast was between twentieth-century revolutionaries and all their earlier counterparts. The prewar–postwar distinction—a much sharper dichotomy than the one we had postulated—was fortuitous and unanticipated, having come to light as a result of close scrutiny

*A decade and a half, in fact, if one takes into account both authors' time.

(and alternative handling) of our data. For reasons discussed in Chapter 3, the war gave rise to a new breed of revolutionaries significantly different in many ways from their earlier counterparts. To avoid repetition, we combined the two sets of findings (general characteristics, prewar–postwar variations) into a single presentation in Chapter 3.

In addition to the temporal distinction, we successfully employed two other independent variables in order to highlight further heterogeneity among revolutionary leaders: the region of the world from which they come and the ideologies they hold. As is readily apparent, some overlap between our three independent variables is unavoidable: prewar elites come from Europe and North America and subscribe to an eclectic array of (moderate and radical) ideologies; postwar leaders come from Africa, Asia, and Latin America as well and hold a more limited set of (radical) political beliefs. We have made every effort, however, to minimize repetition and duplication.

General and Temporal Patterns

Revolutionary elites turn out to be somewhat older at the time of their revolutions than we had anticipated. On the other hand, as far as exposure to radical ideologies and actual participation in radical activities are concerned, our leaders tend to be quite young, particularly the postwar group.

Either revolutionary leaders are urban born or, if born and raised in rural locales, they acquire early and sustained exposure to urban cultures. Not surprisingly, in other words, "revolutionariness" is an urban phenomenon.

Revolutionary elites come from all social strata, with a distinct concentration in the middle class. In the postwar period, however, whereas the middle-class proportion remains constant, upper-class representation is down and lower-class representation up.

Contrary to our expectations, revolutionary leaders tend to have "normal" or "tranquil" family lives. They are typically of legitimate birth and typically come from large families. Whereas postwar leaders tend to have relatively fewer siblings than prewar ones, revolutionary elites as a whole tend to be the oldest child (or son) or the youngest child or the only child.

Revolutionary leaders are of mainstream variety with respect to ethnicity and religion in their societies. The religious background of our revolutionaries tends to be heterogeneous, more so for the postwar group than the prewar one. Their religious orientation, on the other hand, is characterized by considerable uniformity: with the exception of most Muslim leaders, revolutionary elites take a sharp turn to atheism.

Revolutionary leaders are well educated, a preponderant majority having had college, university, or professional training. Although very few revolutionaries have formal military education (Ben Bella, Chou En-lai, and Devereux come to mind), virtually all acquire military experience in informal ways. Postwar elites tend to be more broadly and professionally educated than their prewar counterparts. Regardless of their education, revolutionary elites are prolific publishers, chiefly (though not exclusively) on matters of revolutionary theory and practice. As such, they can be called intellectuals.

The occupations of our leaders are inconsistent with their education, a large number becoming professional revolutionaries pure and simple. When compared with the occupations of their fathers, which tend to be rather diverse, it appears that "like father, not necessarily like son."

Almost by definition, revolutionary elites are intensely involved in radical organization and agitation (though some participate in legal institutions as well). Accordingly, they tend to have substantial records of imprisonment and exile, postwar elites far more so than prewar ones.

Revolutionary leaders—especially postwar ones—are cosmopolitan in many senses: they speak foreign languages, travel far and long, and develop foreign contacts. Accordingly, their ideologies tend to have a foreign source. In fact, postwar leaders typically adapt foreign ideologies to local conditions, whereas many prewar elites work with exclusively indigenous ideologies. Similarly, reflecting the times in which they live, prewar leaders draw upon a variety of rightist, leftist, and centrist ideologies; postwar elites typically turn to shades of Marxism, nationalism, or a combination of the two. Related to these ideologies are historic figures our leaders admire: national liberators, theorists and practitioners of revolution, poets and philosophers.

Revolutionary elites are typically indigenous to the country in which they operate. The only exceptions are Guevara (an Argentine), Schirm (a Hungarian), and Schoeters (a Belgian).

The attitudes of revolutionary leaders toward man, society, and the international community are shaped by the ideologies they hold. Specifically, they tend to have an optimistic view of human nature and a positive view of their own countries. On the other hand, their attitude toward international society is dualistic; they see it as composed of friends and foes—this being far more the case for postwar elites than prewar ones.

Regional Patterns

Using region as an independent variable, we find the prewar leaders of Europe and North America a relatively homogeneous group and the postwar revolutionaries of Africa, Asia, Latin America, Europe and North America a highly heterogeneous one.

Asian and African leaders are older at the time of their revolutions than their Latin American and European and North American counterparts—and they are exposed to revolutionary ideologies at older ages as well. This is not surprising, since the colonial situations in which they find themselves (a general state of underdevelopment and in the firm grip of imperialism) make it more difficult—and require longer periods of time—to become sensitized to societal issues and, in turn, to sensitize and mobilize the masses into revolutionary action. The Latin American context is somewhat more propitious in this respect, since Latin American countries are relatively more developed and since they have been (at least nominally) independent.

The incidence of urban birth among postwar elites well outstrips the urban–rural compositions of their regions. In this context, the highest urban–population–to–urban–births ratio occurs in Asia, followed closely by Latin America and Africa, and distantly by Europe and North America. As for rural-born elites, the earliest exposure to urban life occurs for the Latin Americans, followed by the Europeans and North Americans, the Asians, and the Africans. Once again, in short, urban centers emerge as the cradles of revolutionary learning in all regions of the world.

The socioeconomic status of postwar revolutionary elites varies sharply with region. African and European and North American revolutionaries come exclusively from the middle and lower classes; Asian and Latin American leaders draw upon the upper class as well. Asian revolutionaries appear to be most evenly distributed across the social strata: about half (in round figures) from the middle class, about one-quarter each from the upper and lower classes.

Regional variations are found when revolutionary leaders are grouped by their ethnic backgrounds, relative to the populations of their homelands. Asian and Latin American leaders tend to be from the main ethnic groups; African and European and North American revolutionaries represent a variety of minorities, large and small. These variations are attributed to the relative homogeneity of the Asian and Latin American populations in contrast to the relative heterogeneity of African and European and North American ones.

Latin American and Asian revolutionaries belong to the main religions of their respective regions, whereas significant proportions of African and European and North American leaders represent minority religions. These variations, too, are associated with the more pluralistic character of Africa, Europe, and North America.

As for religious orientation, Asian leaders are most likely to turn to atheism, followed by the Latin Americans, and the Europeans and North Americans. African revolutionaries remain steadfast in their religious beliefs, whether Protestant, Catholic, or Muslim.

European, North American, and Latin American leaders are likely to have been educated in domestic institutions, Asian and African revolutionaries in foreign ones. This is not surprising: the relatively high levels of education attained by Western and Latin

American revolutionaries are readily available in their own home-lands; Asian and African revolutionaries typically acquire education abroad.

The educational attainment of revolutionary elites is at variance with their occupations. Asian and European and North American leaders tend to become professional revolutionaries pure and simple. Latin American and African elites are more likely to remain in such professions as law, medicine, teaching, and the priesthood.

African and Asian revolutionaries are more likely to have traveled to foreign lands—and to have acquired cosmopolitanism—than their Latin American and European and North American counterparts. Some of this travel is for educational purposes, some an effort to develop and maintain contacts with other revolutionaries throughout the world.

The type of ideology to which revolutionary elites subscribe varies by region of the world. Asian and Latin American leaders are least varied in their political orientations, combining as they do shades of Marxist and nationalist ideologies. African revolutionaries are only slightly more varied, since their Pan Africanism is nothing more than nationalism writ region. European and North American elites are most diverse, subscribing to a spectrum of radical ideologies. Accordingly, Europeans and North Americans and, to a lesser extent, Africans are more likely to work with both indigenous and foreign doctrines; Asians and Latin Americans tend to adapt foreign ideologies to local needs.

Ideological and Attitudinal Patterns

Employing ideology as an independent variable, we arrive at further variations concerning characteristics of revolutionary elites. Prewar leaders of virtually all ideological orientations have Judaeo-Christian religious backgrounds. Postwar elites are less diverse in terms of specific ideologies but more heterogeneous in religious affiliation, incorporating Buddhists, Muslims, and others as well. Among the prewar leaders, only the Marxist-Leninists turn atheists; among the postwar elites, atheism is a common phenomenon

166

affecting all ideological groupings, except for those who have a Muslim religion.

Ideologically more moderate leaders of the prewar period are likely to hold a variety of primary occupations. Ideologically more radical elites of the postwar era typically become professional revolutionaries. The more moderate prewar leaders are seldom arrested. The more radical postwar elites are arrested with regularity and spend long periods of time in prison.

Radical postwar leaders tend to be more cosmopolitan in all respects than their moderate prewar counterparts: they travel extensively, accumulating new experiences of various kinds. The former either borrow a foreign ideology or adapt one to local needs; the latter work with indigenous ideologies. Ideological inclinations of all revolutionaries are related to the personalities they admire: radical postwar leaders of Africa, Asia, and Latin America favor national liberators and theorists/practitioners of revolution; moderate prewar elites of Europe and North America typically admire the philosophers and the poets.

Radical postwar elites hold a highly positive attitude toward their own countries; moderate prewar leaders range between the positive and the negative. The former are dualistic toward the international society; the latter are more eclectic.

Finally, needless to say, much of the ideological radicalism of postwar elites is rooted in their proclaimed belief in various shades of Marxism. What may not be immediately apparent is that they define Marxism in a loose, fluid, and highly protean fashion. Thus, given the context, Marxism may mean anti-imperialism, antiestablishment, or even simply antiwhite. In short, for many postwar leaders, Marxism is more a badge of radicalism and a symbol of credibility than a coherent system of politicoeconomic analysis. Stated differently—and with apologies to Karl Marx—Marxism has become the opiate of postwar revolutionary elites.

Situational Patterns

Many of the characteristics identified with revolutionary elites are situational in nature: they are functions of time, place, and specific conditions from which the leaders emerge. Thus, for instance, among "situational" traits over which elites have no control we may note birthplace, socioeconomic status, legitimacy status, character of family life, number of siblings, age ranking among siblings, ethnicity, religion, and the like.

Overarching—and overlapping—situational considerations are provided by our independent variables as well. Prewar revolutionaries come from Europe and North America, and they subscribe to a range of ideologies, moderate as well as radical; postwar revolutionaries come from Africa, Asia, and Latin America as well and typically subscribe to radical political beliefs.

Thus, for instance, any number of variations associated with prewar and postwar elites are due to the colonial nature of the regions in which the latter emerge. This is as true of age at the time of revolution (note the older age of African and Asian revolutionaries), as it is of socioeconomic status (note the increasing number of lower-class leaders), or the diversity of ethnic and religious backgrounds (note the marked presence of minorities of all sorts).

The radical ideologies of postwar elites dictate an abandonment of religion and a turn to atheism. The only exception is provided by a large proportion of Muslim leaders of Africa and Asia, whose religious convictions reinforce their ideological beliefs: they see their adversaries not only as aliens but as infidels as well.

Similarly, it is in the nature of the contemporary world that postwar revolutionaries of Africa and Asia come to acquire broad education and training in the mother countries. In the process, they come into contact with radical ideologies, internalizing and "exporting" them to the colonies.

The relatively high educational levels of postwar colonial elites, combined with their extensive travels and foreign associations, make for a cosmopolitanism simply not within the realm of possibility in the prewar period. Having become thoroughly conversant with the life styles of the mother countries, and having compared these life styles with their own, it is almost inevitable that postwar colonial leaders would break with old customs and traditions, shun conventional occupations (however prestigious), and become professional revolutionaries. Nor is it surprising that in their attempt to overturn the status quo, postwar colonial elites would appeal to foreign as well as indigenous symbols and values, nor that they should see their own countries in a highly positive light while viewing the world in dualistic terms.

In general, the relative diversity of ideological and attitudinal orientations among European and North American elites in contrast to their relative uniformity among African, Asian, and Latin American leaders is most likely a result of our temporal variable: revolutions in the Western world span four centuries; revolutions in the other three regions are postwar phenomena. And the postwar period, as we know, has been dominated by variants of Marxist and nationalist ideologies.

In broader terms, regardless of temporal, regional, or doctrinal orientations, revolutionary elites are routinely and heavily involved in developing and honing the requisite skills by fashioning (or adapting) appropriate ideologies and organizations as indispensable components of their revolutionary programs.

Personality Patterns

We use Q-factor analysis as a means of identifying personality configurations into which revolutionary elites may fall. Specifically, separate Q-factor analyses for prewar and postwar leaders yield, in effect, a nine-fold typology of revolutionary elites across time and space.

Of the five factors associated with prewar elites, the Founders constitute the largest group: mature, middle-class, well-educated members of the establishment—"fathers" of their respective countries who legitimize and institutionalize the revolution. The Professional Revolutionaries come from middle or lower social strata, are radicalized in their youths, and devote their entire lives to revolution. The Purists consist of an educated group who see man and society as corrupt and evil and who seek to bring about a new age of innocence and virtue. The Aristocrats and the Generals are, needless to say, well-educated men from upper social strata. Like the Founders, they are catapulted into revolution in response to situations of crisis or emergency.

169

Of the four factors pertaining to postwar leaders—a commanding majority of whom are simultaneously professional revolutionaries as well—the Scholars constitute the most important group. They are a highly educated set of professionals-turned-revolutionaries, who write extensively, particularly on matters of revolutionary theory and practice. Coming from underdeveloped lands and lower social strata, the Elders become radicalized in their youths and continue lifelong involvement in revolutionary activity. The Agitators, by contrast, are much younger and combine shades of nationalist and Marxist ideologies. The Faithful are middle class, relatively well educated, and committed to revolutionary action rooted in primordial religious conflict.

On the whole, whereas such revolutionary types as the Founders and the Scholars are as far removed as possible from the popular stereotype of the revolutionary, the Professional Revolutionaries and the Agitators are as close to it as one can come.

As will be recalled from Chapter 6 (Tables 6.1 and 6.2), each revolutionary leader may load on more than one factor, and each factor (revolutionary type) is present in more than one revolution. Thus, for instance, it can be seen that the Founders and the Purists are present in all five prewar revolutions; the Professional Revolutionaries, in three; the Aristocrats and the Generals each, in two. Similarly, the Professional Revolutionaries are found in all twenty-six postwar movements; the Scholars, in twenty-four; the Elders, in sixteen; the Faithful, in fourteen; the Agitators, in thirteen.

These findings lend additional credence to some propositions advanced in our earlier work, *Leaders of Revolution.* The nine groups of revolutionaries we have identified are ideal types, historically and analytically considered. As such, although revolutionary leadership is a collective enterprise, not all revolutionary types are necessarily present in all revolutions. Rather, we anticipate finding a mix of revolutionary personalities, varying from revolution to revolution, from the prewar to the postwar period. Decisive factors in this context are the sociohistorical context and the particular needs of the revolutionary process.

Finally, of the nine types of revolutionaries we have identified, four are new to this volume, whereas five duplicate findings in our earlier book. The latter are, in descending order of significance, the Founders, the Agitators, the Generals, the Scholars, and the Professional Revolutionaries. This replication, though only partial, is gratifying nonetheless, since it suggests a degree of social science accuracy, denoting perhaps that we have not been far off the mark in either study.

EMERGENCE OF REVOLUTIONARY ELITES

In an effort to integrate social, cultural, situational, and psychological variables into our theory of revolutionary leadership, we have examined the patterns of radicalization of fifty revolutionaries (for whom adequate data are available) as they go through life: family socialization, school socialization, exposure to new experiences and cultures, purely situational dynamics. We have also analyzed the psychological dynamics that in various degrees and combinations may motivate them toward revolutionary action.

Patterns of Radicalization

We find, in contrast to most socialization studies, that formative years are of little explanatory or predictive value in the emergence of revolutionary personality. Nearly half the leaders for whom we have data experience tranquil beginnings; the other half, stormy childhoods. When we divide our leaders into prewar and postwar categories, however, we find that formative years as a source of radicalization is slightly more characteristic of the latter group.

Among early experiences, number of siblings and age ranking among siblings turn out to be consequential agents of radicalization: even in relatively large families, oldest and youngest children are overrepresented among revolutionary elites, whereas middle children are underrepresented. We further find that the greater the number of siblings, the more likely that one will experience a turbulent childhood.

171

Introducing the prewar–postwar distinction, we find the over-representation–underrepresentation pattern holding for the prewar group. Postwar leaders turn out to be more evenly divided among siblings categories, except that a surprisingly large number (over one-fourth) are *only* children born between 1907 and 1932 in relatively underdeveloped countries (where ordinarily one would expect the family size to be large). Exploring the implication or meaning of these findings in recent literature on child development, we conclude that oldest or only children are treated—and are expected to behave—as "princes," youngest children as "conquerors," and middle children as "diplomats." Princes and conquerors, needless to say, have a greater potential for emerging as revolutionaries than do diplomats.

School socialization as a source of radicalization has somewhat more explanatory value than formative years. In general, we find no striking differences in the number of leaders who are and are not radicalized in school. Those who are not radicalized in school, however, are typically from European and North American countries and hold eclectic ideologies, whereas those who are radicalized are typically from other regions of the earth and hold almost exclusively extremist political beliefs. We also note that one is more likely to become radicalized in school if one experiences a stormy childhood.

When we distinguish the prewar and postwar groups, we find that education as a source of radicalization tends to be associated with postwar elites who come from colonial or neocolonial lands and who hold ideologies of nationalism, communism, or nationalism/communism.

Exposure to new experiences and cultures—particularly in foreign contexts—is an important source of radicalization, especially for postwar leaders. Traveling far and wide, and for relatively long periods of time, revolutionary elites may witness (or personally experience) oppression and exploitation, misery and hunger, cruelty and torture, discrimination and humiliation. At the same time, they become cosmopolitan by learning about a variety of cultures and values, sharing the experiences of other revolutionaries, cultivating potential sources of international support, and developing standards against which to measure the conditions of their own societies. On the whole, their experiences point to an inescapable conclusion: the necessity of mounting revolution as a means of changing the existing state of affairs. Finally, we note, exposure to new experiences and cultures is more likely to serve as an agent of radicalization if one experiences turbulent beginnings or school radicalization.

Situational dynamics are important sources of radicalization, in one way or another, it would seem, for virtually all revolutionary elites. Some leaders, as we have seen, are propelled into revolutionary roles in response to situations of national crisis, trauma, or emergency. Possessing the necessary qualities and skills, these individuals find themselves, at times unexpectedly, playing leadership roles others are unwilling or unable to play.

Leaders from colonial or neocolonial countries are also catapulted into revolutionary roles by the sheer presence of the outsider and the oppression, exploitation, and humiliation attendant thereto—once consciousness of these conditions begins to emerge. In this context, World War II played a key role in awakening the colonial peoples and accelerating the revolutionary process in their countries. Moreover, the attainment of independence by (or the success of revolution in) one country sets off a contagion effect, heightening revolutionary expectations in other societies.

Another type of situational dynamic is to be found in the particularly violent political histories of such countries as China, Colombia, Cuba, Guatemala, Mexico, Northern Ireland, "Palestine," and Peru. Having become a "routine" matter over a period of time, violence sets the stage for and facilitates the emergence of revolutionary elites.

Psychological Dynamics

We have examined our fifty revolutionaries in the light of a series of psychological dynamics, some of them closely interrelated. We noted at the outset the apparent universality of two traits all revolutionaries seem to share: a sense of justice–injustice and a commitment to nationalism/patriotism.

Vanity, egotism, and narcissism are found among twenty-seven (54 percent) of our leaders. At times, vanity may alternate with humility and self-doubt. At times, it produces a compulsion to excel. At times, it generates a persecution complex and the drive to purge one's "enemies."

While strong-willed and self-confident, some revolutionary personalities are remarkably free of vanity, at least prior to the seizure of power. Among them: Biko, Cabral, F. Castro, Guevara, Habash, Lenin, Machel, Madero, Mao, Marighella, de la Puente, Sithole, Torres.

Asceticism, puritanism, and a corresponding demand for virtue define thirty-seven (74 percent) of our revolutionary elites. Self-discipline, self-denial, disdain for luxury and comfort, a commitment to hard work and a spartan life, being prepared to give even one's life—these, of course, lie at the heart of asceticism and puritanism. Asceticism is designed, at least in part, as a means of driving out societal evil and bringing about a new age of purity and virtue. The reign of purity and virtue, in turn, is frequently impossible without coercion and terror. The drive for purity and virtue may also serve as rationalizations for vanity and egotism.

Relative deprivation and status inconsistency characterize exactly half of the revolutionaries for whom we have data. Relative deprivation—a perceived disjunction between achievement and aspiration—may be rooted in personal experiences or it may be observed in societal conditions. Whatever the source, the resulting bitterness and humiliation serve as powerful motivating forces in radicalization. Status inconsistency—a perceived disjunction between socioeconomic status and political power—marks a distinctive genre of revolutionaries who begin as reformers, are consistently frustrated and disillusioned, come to reject the system as beyond repair, and turn to radical politics. In a sense, then, there are times when the system itself creates the conditions for its own destruction.

Marginality, inferiority complex, and a compulsion to excel describe thirty-one (62 percent) of our leaders. These men possess characteristics—social, psychological, physical—that represent serious deviations from accepted norms and expectations. Failure in one's profession or occupation, traumatic personal experiences, feelings of anxiety and despair, being haunted by an inferior social background—all these have the effect of producing combativeness, a compulsion to excel, a determination to prove oneself, a resolve for revenge. Moreover, involvement in revolutionary movements becomes a search for comfort, acceptance, and belongingness, for a revolutionary is judged, not by his marginality or inferiority complex, but by the capabilities and skills at his command.

Of our fifty revolutionaries, oedipal conflict writ large pertains to only six, for three of whom data are inadequate. Conflict with the father—and the concomitant attachment to the mother—produces feelings of ambivalence and guilt. The politicization of the conflict—the substitution of governmental authority for the father—assuages these feelings and makes the world more manageable. This politicization is usually triggered by a traumatic experience.

Estheticism and romanticism of various forms distinguish twenty-three (46 percent) of our revolutionary elites. Whether expressed in love of philosophy, literature, poetry and the arts, or demonstrated in love of music or nature, or depicted in a Don Quixote complex—however expressed—estheticism and romanticism suggest that our rugged and ruthless revolutionaries are gentle and human in many ways as well.

Ranking our psychological dynamics in order of frequency of appearance among the fifty leaders, asceticism emerges on top, followed by marginality, vanity, relative deprivation and status inconsistency, and estheticism and romanticism. Individually, asceticism has the highest explanatory value, Oedipus complex the lowest.

Introducing the prewar–postwar distinction, we find the two groups least alike in terms of vanity (an overwhelming attribute of prewar revolutionaries) and most alike in terms of marginality (a characteristic of both groups, though somewhat more of postwar leaders). Thus, next to justice–injustice and nationalism/patriotism, marginality emerges as the most consistent and the most enduring feature of the fifty revolutionaries for whom we have detailed data.

In an effort to determine the distribution of psychological dynamics among our nine types of revolutionaries, we compared the findings of Table 6.1 (Q-factor analysis) with those of Table 8.1 (psychological dynamics). Each leader was counted only once, on the Q factor on which he has the highest loading.

The results show that, although the nine types of elites partly overlap in membership (within the prewar and postwar groups), each type is marked by a particular set of psychological dynamics. Specifically, in aggregate terms: (1) vanity is a prime trait of the Founders, the Professional Revolutionaries, the Purists, the Aristocrats, and the Generals; (2) asceticism is a principal mark of the Professional Revolutionaries, the Scholars, the Elders, and the Agitators; (3) relative deprivation and status inconsistency apply to the Founders, the Generals, the Scholars, the Elders, and the Faithful; (4) marginality is found among the Professional Revolutionaries, the Elders, the Agitators, and the Faithful; (5) oedipal conflict is an attribute of only the Agitators and the Professional Revolutionaries; (6) estheticism is a primary trait of the Scholars. No single psychological dynamic defines all revolutionaries, nor does any single revolutionary possess all psychological dynamics. It is apparent, moreover, that there is no such thing as *a* or *the* "revolutionary personality"—only revolutionary personalities.

THE SITUATIONAL THEORY: AN ASSESSMENT

What, in the light of the foregoing, can we conclude about our situational theory of revolutionary leadership? How well has it held up under the rigors of "hard" and "soft" data?

To begin with, the situational theory has drawn on the strong points of rival theories we criticize, and it has sought to integrate social and psychological considerations toward explaining the emergence of revolutionary elites. It has further stressed the interplay between psychology, skills, and situation in the rise of revolutionaries: without a revolutionary situation, psychology and skills are likely to remain dormant; without psychology and skills, the situation is to no avail. The three must coincide before a revolutionary leader can emerge.

We have examined the patterns of radicalization of our revolutionary elites, together with a variety of psychological dynamics that may impel them. There is no invariant pattern, we find, in the radicalization of revolutionary leaders. Since each revolutionary encounters a different constellation of experiences, the particular mix of social and psychological factors will vary from leader to leader. We do find, however, that some variables have greater explanatory (and predictive?) value than others. Among the former we include exposure to new cultures and asceticism; among the latter, family socialization and the Oedipus complex. Moreover, some factors are more associated with prewar elites, others with postwar leaders. Among the former we include vanity; among the latter, school socialization. One variable defines both groups with almost equal force: marginality.

Our revolutionaries, we have seen, uniformly possess some degree of verbal and organizational skills, as demonstrated in their activities, writings, speeches, platforms, programs, and the like. The mere possession of skills, in turn, suggests certain social/experiential backgrounds from which leaders come.

Verbal and organizational skills are essential for undermining regime morale, for cultivating revolutionary respectability and legitimacy, for articulating and implementing a revolutionary program revolving around leaders, cadres, and masses. Among other things, as is readily apparent, verbal and organizational skills serve as key bases for leader–follower interaction.

Moreover, our nine-fold typology of revolutionary elites demonstrates that revolution requires a certain specialization of skills and talents. In this context, the Scholars and the Faithful undermine the regime and provide ideological justification for the revolution. The Agitators, the Professional Revolutionaries, the Purists, and the Elders provoke the regime, create an atmosphere of popular unrest, mobilize the masses, formulate a revolutionary program, and coordinate revolutionary action. The Generals perform a military function, directing and fighting the battles that need to be fought. The Founders and the Aristocrats institutionalize the revolution and give it respectability and legitimacy.

These functions and skills are found in all revolutions, but to a lesser or greater extent, depending on the particular needs of the environment. In other words, although different revolutionary types interact to produce a revolution, different historical requirements intervene to produce different mixes of revolutionary personalities. Moreover, the functions the nine types perform overlap to some extent. Thus, for example, the Professional Revolutionaries may well discharge some of the functions performed by the Generals and the Founders. The Founders and the Aristocrats may perform a variety of functions other than institutionalizing and legitimizing the revolution.

Where verbal and organizational skills remain uncultivated, where they are prematurely or improperly deployed, where they are undermined by internal fragmentation and strife, where pragmatism is lost sight of—under any of these circumstances a revolution is likely to fail or, minimally, experience great difficulties. Thus, for instance, premature and uncoordinated action led to defeat in France, Quebec, and Uruguay in the 1960s and 1970s. Internal factionalism has created serious problems in "Palestine," Peru, and Zimbabwe. The deployment of a flawed *foco* theory (*foquismo*), developed by Régis Debray and Che Guevara to stress the primacy of military action over political mobilization, produced a chronicle of failures (or major setbacks) in a host of Latin American countries in the last couple of decades: Argentina, Bolivia, Brazil, Colombia, Guatemala, Paraguay, Peru, Venezuela.

Purely situational dynamics of various sorts, we have seen, interact with psychology and skills to account, in one way or another, for the emergence of all revolutionary elites we have studied in this volume. "Situation" may take the form of a national crisis or emergency. Or it may be set off by a momentous world event such as the Second World War. Or it may be found in the colonial context and the sheer presence of the outsider. Or it may be shaped by education and travel in the metropolitan countries. Or it may be located in the violent political histories of many lands. Or it may take the form of pure chance casting a person into a revolutionary mold.

We also identified some personal traits or characteristics over which one has little or no control and which may act as situational dynamics. Specifically, urban birth and exposure to urban culture, number of siblings and ordinal position among them, socioeconomic status, and ethnicity and religion act as potential sources of radicalization.

On the whole, then, we conclude, our situational theory of revolutionary leadership has held up quite well when confronted with the available data. Indeed, with the exception of a few qualifications and modifications noted in Chapter 3, we have been pleasantly surprised at the fit between theory and data throughout this volume.

AFTERTHOUGHTS

Afterthoughts

Throughout the preparation of this study, some recurrent thoughts have either disturbed our intellectual peace or provided intellectual nourishment or both.

First, we are concerned that we have no way of conclusively demonstrating a direct link between the psychodynamics we have identified and the actual radicalization of revolutionary elites. Surely, if human experience is any guide, vanity, asceticism, relative deprivation and status inconsistency, marginality, and the Oedipus complex must affect any number of people; yet only a few emerge as revolutionaries. Ponder the dilemma as we have, there is no alternative but to take seriously the best of the autobiographical and biographical materials available to us.

Second, we are concerned that, of our psychodynamics, estheticism is generally considered a desirable or positive trait, asceticism may be categorized as either positive or neutral (depending on the context), and the other four are generally deemed undesirable or negative. The issue arises, in other words, as to whether we have inadvertently sided with that group of writers who views revolutionaries as pathological in some way(s). And the issue becomes more pressing when a glance at Chapter 8 (Table 8.1) reveals that only three leaders—Liu Shao-ch'i, de la Puente, and Torres—possess none of the negative traits. We insist on our neutrality, however, by reminding the reader that two other highly desirable psychodynamics—a sense of justice–injustice and nationalism/patriotism—describe all revolutionary elites we have studied. Moreover, the psychodynamics of revolutionary behavior cannot be considered in isolation from the patterns of radicalization (Chapter 7), particularly situational variables.

We should note specifically that, persistent and recurring though it is, we find marginality a most troublesome concept. On reflection, it seems, the notion is so broadly defined as to apply to virtually the entire population of any given country at any given point in time. Thus, it will be recalled, in the foregoing pages—and in our earlier work—we use marginality in a *social* sense (for example, immigrant status), a *psychological* sense (for instance, parental rejection), an *economic* sense (poverty), a *physical* sense (facial or bodily disfigurement), a *medical* sense (poor health), and a *historical* sense (colonial context). Given this all-encompassing approach—and remembering Lasswell's attribution of inferiority complex to all politicians—it may be that marginality is a *human* characteristic and not an attribute of revolutionaries or politicians alone. Should this be the case, needless to say, all "findings" concerning marginality, our own included, are no findings at all.

Third, we are concerned that our situational theory of revolutionary leadership may appear to have used "situation" in a broad and preemptive fashion. Put differently, we may appear to have stretched the concept to the breaking point in an effort to accommodate our theoretical posture. This has not been our intention, however. On the contrary, at every turn we have been careful to define and document our situational dynamics, whether at societal or individual levels. Moreover, we have repeatedly noted the insufficiency of situation by itself, stressing its interplay with psychodynamics and verbal and organizational skills. Most important, far from claiming exclusivity for our theory, we are prepared to assign partial validity to rival theoretical stances. We do claim superiority for our theory, needless to say, insofar as it appears to be of far greater applicability to a far greater number of circumstances and contexts.

Nonetheless, we are fully aware that our situational theory of revolutionary leadership does not enjoy the rigor, precision, and comprehensiveness of, say, a mathematical theory. Not every link can be clearly and undisputably established, and direct demonstration of causality remains a goal toward which social science can only continue to strive. Accordingly, our situational theory remains suggestive and indicative, not definitive or absolute; and we shall strive to improve upon it in our future work.

Finally, it will be recalled, a sizable group of revolutionaries begin as reformers, participate in the legal political processes of their societies (even to the point of running for office), find the system unresponsive, and turn to revolutionary politics. In other words, had it not been for the unresponsiveness of the system, these revolutionaries might well have become members of the establishment elites. (Conversely, at least one revolutionary—Béjar of Peru—became a member of the parliament in the 1970s, following the decline of the revolutionary movement in 1966. Similarly, Krivine became involved in the French presidential election of 1981 but did not attract much support.) Moreover, another group of "situational" leaders *are* members of the establishment in good standing, being catapulted into revolutionary roles as a consequence of national crises or emergencies. In other words, we have hints and clues—if not some tentative evidence—that revolutionary and establishment elites may be much alike in terms of social characteristics if not motivation.[1] This of course is the subject of a separate work, to be undertaken some time in the future.

NOTES
AND
BIBLIOGRAPHY

Notes

[These notes follow an abbreviated format. For full citations, see appropriate sections of the bibliography.]

INTRODUCTION

1. M. Rejai and K. Phillips, *Leaders of Revolution.*
2. For elaboration, see M. Rejai, *The Comparative Study of Revolutionary Strategy,* chap. 1.
3. For relevant population data see, for example, A. S. Banks, *Political Handbook of the World 1979,* pp. 96–97, 612–14.
4. See, for example, Banks, *Political Handbook of the World 1979,* pp. 474–75; Banks, *Political Handbook of the World 1977,* p. 433; C. L. Taylor and M. C. Hudson, *World Handbook of Political and Social Indicators,* p. 429.
5. R. Segal, *Political Africa,* p. 162.

CHAPTER 1

1. Freud, *Group Psychology and the Analysis of the Ego,* p. 14.
2. Ibid., p. 71.
3. H. D. Lasswell, *Psychopathology and Politics,* p. 17.
4. H. D. Lasswell, *Power and Personality,* p. 38; cf. Lasswell, *Psychopathology and Politics,* passim.
5. Lasswell, *Psychopathology and Politics,* pp. 175, 263–64.
6. Ibid., p. 264.
7. E. V. Wolfenstein, *The Revolutionary Personality.*
8. Ibid., pp. 308–309.
9. E. H. Erikson, *Young Man Luther;* idem, *Gandhi's Truth.*
10. Erikson, *Young Man Luther,* p. 67.
11. Erikson, *Gandhi's Truth,* passim.
12. B. Mazlish, *The Revolutionary Ascetic,* p. 23.
13. Ibid., p. 5.
14. Ibid., p. 34.

15. P. Roazen, *Erik H. Erikson,* p. 129.
16. Quoted in A. Schweitzer, "Theory and Political Charisma," 151–52.
17. M. Weber, *From Max Weber,* p. 246.
18. M. Weber, *The Theory of Social and Economic Organization,* pp. 358–59.
19. Ibid., p. 359.
20. Ibid., pp. 361–63.
21. A. R. Willner, *Charismatic Political Leadership,* p. 44.
22. R. C. Tucker, "The Theory of Charismatic Leadership," pp. 732, 735.
23. Ibid., pp. 737–38 (emphasis in original).
24. Ibid., p. 740.
25. Ibid., pp. 742–43 (emphasis in original).
26. J. V. Downton, *Rebel Leadership.*
27. Ibid., pp. 78, 230.
28. Ibid., p. 283.
29. K. J. Ratnam, "Charisma and Political Leadership," p. 341.
30. R. M. Stogdill, *Handbook of Leadership,* p. viii.

CHAPTER 2

1. Although some recent studies have attempted to incorporate "situation" (variously defined) in the study of political—though not revolutionary—leadership, no coherent or systematic theory has yet evolved. See, for example, the following papers in M. G. Hermann, *A Psychological Examination of Political Leaders:* (1) Crow and Noel, "An Experiment in Simulated Historical Decision Making"; (2) Driver, "Individual Differences as Determinants of Aggression in the Inter-Nation Simulation"; (3) Druckman, "The Person, Role, and Situation in International Negotiations"; (4) Hermann, "Some Personal Characteristics Related to Foreign Aid Voting of Congressmen." See also R. C. Tucker, "Personality and Political Leadership."

2. D. Katz, "Patterns of Leadership," p. 222. For a parallel formulation, see J. C. Davies, *Human Nature in Politics,* chap. 9.

3. As discussed in R. C. Tucker, "The Theory of Charismatic Leadership," 745; cf. Davies, *Human Nature in Politics,* esp. pp. 289–90.

4. For a more elaborate discussion of revolutionary ideology, see M. Rejai, *The Comparative Study of Revolutionary Strategy,* chap. 3 et passim.

5. P. Selznick, *The Organizational Weapon,* p. 10.

6. S. P. Huntington, *Political Order in Changing Societies*, p. 461.

7. For a more elaborate discussion of revolutionary organization, see Rejai, *Comparative Study of Revolutionary Strategy*, chap. 3 et passim.

CHAPTER 4

1. See, for example, A. S. Banks and R. B. Textor, *A Cross-Polity Survey*, p. 61.

2. Labor-force data for countries engulfed in postwar revolutions will be found in B. M. Russett et al., *World Handbook of Political and Social Indicators*, pp. 177–79; C. L. Taylor and M. C. Hudson, *World Handbook of Political and Social Indicators*, pp. 332–34. Labor forces in the five countries experiencing revolution in the prewar period were up to 90 percent agricultural.

3. All data are calculated from United Nations, Department of Economic and Social Affairs, *Growth of the World's Urban and Rural Populations, 1920–2000*, pp. 23–28. *Urban* is defined as cities of 20,000 or more population.

CHAPTER 6

1. All factor analyses and scatterplots were performed using Norman H. Nie et al., *Statistical Package for the Social Sciences*, 2nd ed. (New York: McGraw-Hill, 1975); *SAS User's Guide: 1979 Edition* (Raleigh, N.C.: SAS Institute, 1979).

CHAPTER 7

1. See, for example, the following works and the sources cited therein: L. Forer and H. Still, *The Birth Order Factor*; B. Sutton-Smith and B. G. Rosenberg, *The Sibling*; L. H. Stewart, "Birth Order and Political Leadership"; C. A. Broh, "Adler on the Influence of Siblings in Political Socialization." See also Didi Moore, "The Only-Child Phenomenon," *New York Times Magazine*, January 18, 1981, pp. 26, 45–48.

2. For a convenient summary of the conditions of revolution, see M. Rejai, *The Comparative Study of Revolutionary Strategy*, chap. 3 and the sources cited therein.

3. For a graphic documentation of this point, see P. Vallières, *White Niggers of America*, passim.

4. N. Sithole, *African Nationalism*, pp. 47–49, 53.
5. Quoted in W. W. Kazziha, *Revolutionary Transformation in the Arab World: Habash and His Comrades from Nationalism to Marxism*, pp. 17–18.
6. Quoted in T. Kiernan, *Arafat*, p. 229.
7. Vallières, *White Niggers of America*, p. 122.
8. Ibid., pp. 85–86, 87.
9. G. Morf, *Terror in Quebec*, pp. 20–21.
10. R. Rotberg, "From Moderate to Militant: The Rise of Joshua Nkomo and Southern Rhodesian Nationalism," p. 3.

CHAPTER 8

1. B. Moore, Jr., *Injustice*, p. 7 et passim.
2. L. H. Butterfield, *Diary and Autobiography of John Adams*, 1: 25.
3. P. Vallières, *White Niggers of America*, pp. 145, 152.
4. Quoted in T. Kiernan, *Arafat*, p. 184.
5. C. Marighella, "Minimanual of the Urban Guerrilla," p. 110.
6. D. Woods, *Biko*, p. 30.
7. Quoted in G. Guzmán, *Camilo Torres*, p. 12.
8. C. Torres, "The United Front," in idem, *Revolutionary Writings*, p. 172.
9. Quoted in Guzmán, *Camilo Torres*, p. 5.
10. Quoted in ibid., p. 239.
11. Marighella, "Minimanual of the Urban Guerrilla," pp. 72, 73.
12. W. W. Kazziha, *Revolutionary Transformation in the Arab World*, pp. 23–24.
13. T. Kiernan, *Arafat*, p. 38.
14. Z. Schiff and R. Rothstein, *Fedayeen*, p. 59.
15. Quoted in Kiernan, *Arafat*, pp. 231–32.
16. Quoted in P. F. Langer and J. J. Zasloff, *North Vietnam and the Pathet Lao: Partners in Struggle for Laos*, pp. 39–40.
17. S. Machel, *Mozambique: Revolution or Reaction*, p. 9. Cf. idem, *Establishing People's Power to Serve the Masses;* idem, *The Tasks Ahead*.
18. Woods, *Biko*, p. 66.
19. R. Rotberg, "From Moderate to Militant: The Rise of Joshua Nkomo and Southern Rhodesian Nationalism," pp. 3, 4.
20. Vallières, *White Niggers of America*, pp. 21, 62, 103, 111, 122.
21. N. Sithole, *African Nationalism*, p. 15.
22. Ibid., p. 30.
23. S. N. Champassak, *Storm Over Laos*, p. 25.

24. Ibid., p. 25. Cf. Langer and Zasloff, *North Vietnam and the Pathet Lao*, p. 30.

25. See, for example, F. R. Bellamy, *The Private Life of George Washington*, pp. 152 ff.

26. Langer and Zasloff, *North Vietnam and the Pathet Lao*, pp. 29, 230.

27. Vallières, *White Niggers of America*, pp. 164, 169, 194, 196.

28. Quoted in R. H. Chicote, *Emerging Nationalism in Portuguese Africa: Documents*, p. 412.

29. G. Morf, *Terror in Quebec*, p. 21.

30. J. M. Thompson, *Leaders of the French Revolution*, p. 19.

31. L. Madelin, *Figures of the Revolution*, p. 33.

32. C. F. Warwick, *Mirabeau and the French Revolution*, p. 152.

33. Quoted in Kiernan, *Arafat*, p. 56.

34. E. V. Wolfenstein, *The Revolutionary Personality*, p. 99.

35. Ibid., pp. 135–36.

36. Quoted in R. B. Morris, *Seven Who Shaped Our Destiny*, p. 119.

37. Quoted in N. M. Regush, *Pierre Vallières*, p. 27.

38. Quoted in Guzmán. *Camilo Torres*, p. 14.

39. C. Torres, "Laicization," in idem, *Revolutionary Writings*, p. 164.

40. See Guzmán, *Camilo Torres*, p. 244.

41. H. Blanco, *Land or Death: The Peasant Struggle in Peru*, p. 97.

AFTERTHOUGHTS

1. Some concrete evidence concerning such characteristics has been recently provided by Jean Blondel. In his study of 1,028 heads of governments in the 1945 to 1976 period, he finds, for example: (1) the almost total absence of women—only five to be exact, (2) mean age of about fifty upon assuming office, (3) high level of education, and (4) predominance of such occupational backgrounds as law, teaching, and civil service generally—and of the military in the third world. See J. Blondel, *World Leaders*, especially pp. 115–34.

In a pathbreaking work, James Kirby Martin finds a series of intriguing similarities and differences between a set of 134 loyalist leaders and a group of 308 revolutionary elites in America of the 1770s. Specifically, he finds both groups consisting exclusively of men, mostly in their forties and fifties, sharing a Protestant religion of one form or another, and engaged in professional, mercantile, and agricultural occupations.

As for differences, he finds the loyalists to have been wealthier on the whole, though not a single member of either group fell in the "below average" category. Moreover, whereas the loyalists either came from "old families" (46 percent) or were immigrants (41 percent), the revolutionaries tended to be from old families (73 percent). On the other hand, some 60 percent of the loyalists came from distinguished families whose reputation transcended their own specific colony, as compared to 31 percent of the revolutionaries. And loyalists tended to have a higher proportion of men with college and professional training than the revolutionaries—52 percent and 44 percent, respectively. See J. K. Martin, *Men in Rebellion.*

To what extent these findings are generally applicable is a matter that stands in need of further investigation.

Bibliography

As noted in the Introduction, this bibliography is in four parts: theoretical literature, general data sources, regional studies, country studies.

THEORETICAL LITERATURE

Bell, David V. J., *Resistance and Revolution*. Boston: Houghton Mifflin, 1973.

Bendix, Reinhard. *Max Weber: An Intellectual Portrait*. New York: Doubleday, Anchor, 1962.

Bensman, Joseph, and Michael Givant. "Charisma and Modernity: The Use and Abuse of a Concept." *Social Research* 42 (Winter 1975): 570–614.

Berman, Paul. *Revolutionary Organization*.Lexington, Mass.: Lexington Books, 1974.

Bianchi, Eugene C. *The Religious Experience of Revolutionaries*. New York: Doubleday, 1972.

Billington, James H. *Fire in the Minds of Men: Origins of Revolutionary Faith*. New York: Basic Books, 1980.

Blau, Peter M. "Critical Remarks on Weber's Theory of Authority." *American Political Science Review* 57 (June 1963): 305–16.

Blondel, Jean. *World Leaders: Heads of Government in the Postwar Period*. Beverly Hills, Calif.: Sage, 1980.

Brinton, Crane. *The Anatomy of Revolution*. New York: Random House, Vintage, 1956.

———. *The Jacobins: An Essay in the New History*. New York: Macmillan, 1930.

Broh, C. Anthony. "Adler on the Influence of Siblings in Political Socialization." *Political Behavior* 1 (Summer 1979): 175–200.

Burns, James M. *Leadership*. New York: Harper & Row, 1978.

Bychowski, Gustav. *Dictators and Disciples: From Caesar to Stalin*. New York: International Universities, 1948.

Camus, Albert. *The Rebel: An Essay on Man in Revolt*. New York: Random House, Vintage, 1956.

Clague, Monique. "Conceptions of Leadership: Charles de Gaulle and Max Weber." *Political Theory* 3 (November 1975): 423–40.

Cohen, D. C. "The Concept of Charisma and the Analysis of Leadership." *Political Studies* 20 (September 1972): 299–305.

Coles, Robert. *Erik H. Erikson: The Growth of His Work*. Boston: Little, Brown, 1970.

Crozier, Brian. *The Study of Conflict*. London: Institute for the Study of Conflict, 1970.

Daly, William T. *The Revolutionary: A Review and Synthesis*. Beverly Hills, Calif.: Sage, 1972.

BIBLIOGRAPHY

Davies, James C. *Human Nature in Politics.* New York: Wiley, 1963.

Davis, Jerome. "A Study of 163 Outstanding [Russian] Communist Leaders." *American Sociological Review* 24 (1929): 42–55.

Debray, Régis. *Revolution in the Revolution? Armed Struggle and Political Struggle in Latin America.* New York: Grove, 1967.

Downton, James V., Jr. *Rebel Leadership: Commitment and Charisma in the Revolutionary Process.* New York: Free Press, 1973.

Edinger, Lewis J. "The Comparative Study of Political Leadership." *Comparative Politics* 7 (January 1975): 253–69.

Eichler, Margrit. "Leadership in Social Movements." *Sociological Inquiry* 47 (1977): 99–107.

Eisenstadt, S. N., ed. *Max Weber on Charisma and Institution Building.* Chicago: University of Chicago Press, 1968.

Erikson, Erik H. *Childhood and Society.* 2nd ed. New York: Norton, 1963.

——. *Gandhi's Truth: On the Origins of Militant Nonviolence.* New York: Norton, 1969.

——. *Identity: Youth and Crisis.* New York: Norton, 1968.

——. *Young Man Luther: A Study in Psychoanalysis and History.* New York: Norton, 1962.

Force, George T., and Jack R. Van Der Slik. *Theory and Research in the Study of Political Leadership.* Rev. ed. Carbondale: Southern Illinois University, Public Affairs Research Bureau, 1972.

Forer, Lucille, and Henry Still. *The Birth Order Factor.* New York: McKay, 1976.

Freud, Sigmund. *Group Psychology and the Analysis of the Ego.* 1921. Reprint. New York: Bantam, 1960.

Friedrich, Carl J. "Political Leadership and the Problem of Charismatic Power." *Journal of Politics* 23 (February 1961): 3–24.

Glassman, Ronald. "Legitimacy and Manufactured Charisma." *Social Research* 42 (Winter 1975): 615–36.

Gurr, Ted Robert. *Why Men Rebel.* Princeton, N.J.: Princeton University Press, 1970.

——, ed. *Handbook of Political Conflict: Theory and Research.* New York: Free Press, 1980.

Hermann, Margaret G., ed. *A Psychological Examination of Political Leaders.* New York: Free Press, 1977.

Huntington, Samuel P. *Political Order in Changing Societies.* New Haven, Conn.: Yale University Press, 1968.

Katz, Daniel. "Patterns of Leadership." In *Handbook of Political Psychology,* edited by Jeanne N. Knutson. San Francisco: Jossey-Bass, 1973.

Kautsky, John H. "Revolutionary and Managerial Elites in Modernizing Regimes." *Comparative Politics* 1 (July 1969): 441Ø67.

Korten, D. C. "Situational Determinants of Leadership Structure." *Journal of Conflict Resolution.* 6 (1962): 222–35.

Lacouture, Jean. *The Demigods: Charismatic Leadership in the Third World.* New York: Knopf, 1970.

Lasky, Melvin J. *Utopia and Revolution.* Chicago: University of Chicago Press, 1976.

Lasswell, Harold D. *Power and Personality.* 1948. Reprint. New York: Viking, 1962.

——. *Psychopathology and Politics.* 1930. Reprint. New York: Viking, 1960.

Lasswell, Harold D., and Daniel Lerner, eds. *World Revolutionary Elites.* Cambridge: MIT Press, 1965.

THEORETICAL LITERATURE

Lasswell, Harold D., Daniel Lerner, and C. Easton Rothwell. *The Comparative Study of Elites*. Stanford, Calif.: Stanford University Press, 1952.

Le Bon, Gustave. *The Psychology of Revolution*. New York: Putnam's, 1913.

Lee, Ming T. "The Founders of the Chinese Communist Party: A Study in Revolutionaries." *Civilisations* 13 (1968): 113Ø27.

Lewin, Kurt. *Field Theory in the Social Sciences: Selected Theoretical Papers*. Edited by Dorwin Cartwright. New York: Harper, 1951.

Lewy, Guenter. *Religion and Revolution*. New York: Oxford University Press, 1974.

Lifton, Robert J. *Boundaries: Psychological Man in Revolution*. New York: Random House, 1969.

Loewenstein, Karl. *Max Weber's Political Ideas in the Perspective of Our Time*. Boston: Univeristy of Massachusetts Press, 1966.

Martin, James Kirby. *Men in Rebellion*. New Brunswick, N.J.: Rutgers University Press, 1973.

Mazlish, Bruce. *The Revolutionary Ascetic*. New York: Basic Books, 1976.

Moore, Barrington, Jr. *Injustice: The Social Bases of Obedience and Revolt*. White Plains, N.Y.: Sharpe, 1978.

Paige, Glenn D., ed. *Political Leadership*. New York: Free Press, 1972.

————. *The Scientific Study of Political Leadership*. New York: Free Press, 1977.

Putnam, Robert D. *The Comparative Study of Political Elites*. Englewood Cliffs, N.J.: Prentice-Hall, 1976.

Quandt, William B. *The Comparative Study of Political Elites*. Beverly Hills, Calif.: Sage, 1970.

Ratnam, K. J. "Charisma and Political Leadership." *Political Studies* 12 (October 1964): 341–54.

Rejai, Mostafa. *The Comparative Study of Revolutionary Strategy*. New York: McKay, 1977.

————. *The Strategy of Political Revolution*. New York: Doubleday, Anchor, 1973.

Rejai, Mostafa, and Kay Phillips. *Leaders of Revolution*. Beverly Hills, Calif.: Sage, 1979.

Riezler, Kurt. "On the Psychology of Modern Revolution." *Social Research* 10 (1943): 320–66.

Roazen, Paul. *Erik H. Erikson: The Power and Limits of a Vision*. New York: Free Press, 1976.

Robins, Robert S., ed. *Psychopathology and Political Leadership*. New Orleans: Tulane University, 1977.

Sanders, Joseph. "Beauty and Charisma: A Comment on A. Schweitzer's 'Theory of Political Charisma.'" *Comparative Studies in Society and History* 16 (March 1974): 182Ø86.

San Juan, E., Jr. "Orientation of Max Weber's Concept of Charisma." *Centennial Review* 11 (Spring 1967): 270Ø85.

Scalapino, Robert A., ed. *The Communist Revolution in Asia*. 2nd ed. Englewood Cliffs, N.J.: Prentice-Hall, 1969.

Schiffer, Irving. *Charisma: A Psychoanalyst Looks at Mass Society*. Toronto: University of Toronto Press, 1973.

Schwartz, David C. *Political Alienation and Political Behavior*. Chicago: Aldine, 1973.

Schweitzer, Arthur. "Theory of Political Charisma." *Comparative Studies in Society and History* 16 (March 1974): 150Ø81.

197

Searing, Donald D. "Models and Images of Man and Society in Leadership Theory." *Journal of Politics* 31 (February 1969): 3Ø31.

Selznick, Phillip. *The Organizational Weapon: A Study of Bolshevik Strategy and Tactics.* New York: McGraw-Hill, 1952.

Shils, Edward. "Charisma, Order, and Status." *American Sociological Review.* 30 (1965): 199–213.

————. "The Concentration and Dispersion of Charisma: Their Bearing on Economic Policy in Underdeveloped Countries." *World Politics* 11 (October 1958): 1–19.

Stewart, Louis H. "Birth Order and Political Leadership." In *A Psychological Examination of Political Leaders,* edited by M. G. Hermann. New York: Free Press, 1977.

Stogdill, Ralph M. *Handbook of Leadership: A Survey of Theory and Research.* New York: Free Press, 1974.

Stone, Lawrence. "Prosopography." *Daedalus* 106 (Winter 1971): 46–79.

Strauss, Harlan J. "Revolutionary Types: Russia in 1905." *Journal of Conflict Resolution* 17 (1973): 297–316.

Sutton-Smith, Brian, and B. G. Rosenberg. *The Sibling.* New York: Holt, Rinehart & Winston, 1970.

Taintor, Zebulon C. "Asserting the Revolutionary Personality." In *Revolution and Political Change,* edited by Claude E. Welch, Jr., and Mavis Bunker Taintor. North Scituate, Mass.: Duxbury, 1972.

Tilly, Charles. *From Mobilization to Revolution.* Reading, Mass.: Addison-Wesley, 1978.

Tucker, Robert C. "Personality and Political Leadership." *Political Science Quarterly* 92 (Fall 1977): 383–93.

————. "The Theory of Charismatic Leadership." *Daedalus* 97 (Summer 1968): 731–56.

Wada, George, and James C. Davies. "Riots and Rioters." *Western Political Quarterly* 10 (1957): 864–74.

Weber, Max. *From Max Weber: Essays in Sociology.* Translated, edited, and with an introduction by H. H. Gerth and C. Wright Mills. New York: Oxford University Press, 1958.

————. *The Theory of Social and Economic Organization.* Edited with an Introduction by Talcott Parsons. New York: Free Press, 1964.

Willner, Ann Ruth. *Charismatic Political Leadership: A Theory.* Princeton, N.J.: Center of International Studies, 1968.

Willner, Ann Ruth, and Dorothy Willner. "The Rise and Roles of Charismatic Leaders." *Annals* 358 (March 1965): 77–88.

Wistrich, Robert S. *Revolutionary Jews: From Marx to Trotsky.* London: Harrap, 1976.

Wolfenstein, E. Victor, *The Revolutionary Personality: Lenin, Trotsky, Gandhi.* Princeton, N.J.: Princeton University Press, 1967.

GENERAL DATA SOURCES

Ali, Tariq. *The New Revolutionaries: A Handbook of the International Radical Left.* New York: Morrow, 1969.

Banks, Arthur S., ed. *Political Handbook of the World 1977.* New York: McGraw-Hill, 1977.

———, ed. *Political Handbook of the World 1979.* New York: McGraw-Hill, 1979.

Banks, Arthur S., and Robert B. Textor. *A Cross-polity Survey.* Cambridge: MIT Press, 1963.

Banks, Arthur S., et al. *Cross Polity Time Series Data.* Cambridge: MIT Press, 1971.

Beal, Carleton. *Great Guerrilla Warriors.* Englewood Cliffs, N.J.: Prentice-Hall, 1970.

Beck, Carl, and J. T. McKechnie. *Political Elites: A Select and Computerized Bibliography.* Cambridge: MIT Press, 1968.

Biography Index. 10 vols. New York: Wilson, 1946–1976.

Blackey, Robert. *Modern Revolutions and the Revolutionists: A Bibliography.* Santa Barbara, Calif.: ABC-Clio, 1976.

Chaliand, Gérard. *Revolution in the Third World.* New York: Viking, 1978.

Clark, Barrett H. *Great Short Biographies of the World.* New York: McBride, 1928.

Conflict Studies. Nos. 1–103. London: Institute for the Study of Conflict, 1970–1979.

Crozier, Brian. *The Rebels: A Study of Post-war Insurrections.* London: Chatto & Windus, 1960.

Current Biography. New York: Wilson, 1940–1977.

Current Biography Yearbook. New York: Wilson, 1940–1976.

Current World Leaders: Almanac. Pasadena, Calif.: Current World Leaders, 1957–1976.

Current World Leaders: Biography and News. Pasadena, Calif.: Current World Leaders, 1957–1976.

Deadline Data on World Affairs. New York: McGraw-Hill, 1955–1979.

Dictionary of International Biography. London: Rowman, 1963–1977.

Encyclopedia of World Biography. 12 vols. New York: McGraw-Hill, 1973.

Facts on File. New York: Facts on File, 1942–1977.

Fairbairn, Geoffrey. *Revolutionary Guerrilla Warfare: The Countryside Version.* Harmondsworth: Penguin, 1974.

Fishman, W. J. *The Insurrectionists.* London: Methuen, 1970.

Hodges, Donald C., and A. E. Abu Shanab. *National Liberation Fronts, 1960–1970.* New York: Morrow, 1972.

Hoover Institution. *Yearbook on International Communist Affairs.* Stanford, Calif.: Hoover Institution Press, 1966–1978.

Institute for Research in Biography. *World Biography.* 5th ed. Bethgage, N.Y.: Institute for Research in Biography, 1954.

International Labour Organization. *Yearbook of Labour Statistics 1977.* Geneva: International Labour Organization, 1977.

International Who's Who. London: Europa and Allen & Unwin, 1935–1978.

International Yearbook and Statesmen's Who's Who. London: Burke's Peerage, 1953–1978.

Lartéguy, Jean. *The Guerrillas.* New York: World, 1970.

Mallin, Jay, ed. *Terror and Urban Guerrillas.* Coral Gables, Fla.: University of Miami Press, 1971.

Men in the News: 1958. Edited by Robert H. Phelps. Philadelphia: Lippincott, 1958.

Men in the News: 1959. Edited by Robert H. Phelps. Philadelphia: Lippincott, 1959.

Moss, Robert. *Urban Guerrillas.* London: Temple Smith, 1972.

Newsweek, selected issues.

New York Times, selected issues.

BIBLIOGRAPHY

Robinson, Donald. *The 100 Most Important People in the World Today.* New York: Putnam's, 1970.
Rummel, R. J. *The Dimensions of Nations.* Beverly Hills, Calif.: Sage, 1972.
Russett, Bruce M., et al. *World Handbook of Political and Social Indicators.* New Haven, Conn.: Yale University Press, 1964.
Smith, Godfrey, ed. *1000 Makers of the Twentieth Century.* Newton Abbot: David & Charles, 1971.
Swearingen, Roger, ed. *Leaders of the Communist World.* New York: Free Press, 1971.
Taylor, Charles L., and Michael C. Hudson. *World Handbook of Political and Social Indicators.* 2nd ed. New Haven, Conn.: Yale University Press, 1972.
Time Magazine, selected issues.
United Nations, Department of Economic and Social Affairs. *Demographic Yearbook 1976.* New York: United Nations, 1977.
————. *Growth of the World's Urban and Rural Population, 1920–2000.* New York: United Nations, 1969.
————. *Statistical Yearbook 1977.* New York: United Nations, 1978.
Webster's Biographical Dictionary. 14 eds. Springfield, Mass.: Merriam, 1943–1976.

REGIONAL STUDIES

Africa

Abshire, David M., and Michael A. Samuels. *Portuguese Africa: A Handbook.* New York: Praeger, 1969.
Africa Encyclopedia. London: Oxford University Press. 1974.
Africa Yearbook and Who's Who. London: Africa Journal, 1976.
Bretton, Henry L. *Power and Politics in Africa.* Chicago: Aldine, 1973.
Burchett, Wilfred. *Southern Africa Stands Up: The Revolutions in Angola, Mozambique, Zimbabwe, Namibia, and South Africa.* New York: Urizen, 1978.
Chaliand, Gérard. *Armed Struggle in Africa.* New York: Monthly Review Press, 1969.
Chilcote, Ronald H. *Emerging Nationalism in Portuguese Africa: A Bibliography of Documentary Ephemera through 1965.* Stanford, Calif.: Hoover Institution Press, 1969.
————. *Emerging Nationalism in Portuguese Africa: Documents.* Stanford, Calif.: Hoover Institution Press, 1972.
————. *Portuguese Africa.* Englewood Cliffs, N.J.: Prentice-Hall, 1967.
Cornwall, Barbara. *The Bush Rebels: A Personal Account of Black Revolt in Africa.* New York: Holt, Rinehart & Winston, 1972.
Davidson, Basil, et al. *Southern Africa.* Bungay: Chaucer, 1976.
Davis, John A., and James K. Baker, eds. *Southern Africa in Transition.* New York: Praeger, 1966.
De Figueiredo, Antonio. *Portugal and Its Empire: The Truth.* London: Gollancz, 1961.
Dickie, John, and Alan Rake. *Who's Who in Africa.* London: African Buyer and Trader, 1973.
Dictionary of African Biography. London: Melrose, 1971.
Duffy, James. *Portugal in Africa.* Cambridge: Harvard University Press, 1962.
Evans, L. O. *Emerging African Nations and Their Leaders.* 2 vols. Yonkers, N.Y.: Educational Heritage, 1964.

First, Ruth. *Portugal's Wars in Africa.* London: Anti-Apartheid Committee, 1971.

Gibson, Richard. *African Liberation Movements: Contemporary Struggles against White Minority Rule.* London: Oxford University Press, 1972.

Grundy, Kenneth W. *Guerrilla Struggle in Africa.* New York: Grossman, 1971.

Junod, Violaire I., and Idrian N. Resnick. *The Handbook of Africa.* New York: New York University Press, 1963.

Legum, Colin. "Africa's Contending Revolutionaries." *Problems of Communism* 30 (March–April 1972): 2–15.

————. *Africa: A Handbook of the Continent,* New York: Praeger, 1966.

————, ed. *Africa Contemporary Record.* London: [publisher varies], 1968–1979.

Legum, Colin, and Tony Hodges. *After Angola: The War Over Southern Africa.* New York: Americana, 1976.

Marcum, John A. "Three Revolutions." *Africa Report* 12 (November 1967): 8–22.

Metrowich, F. R., ed. *African Freedom Annual 1977.* Sandton: Southern African Freedom Foundation, 1977.

Minter, William. *Portuguese Africa and the West.* Baltimore: Penguin, 1972.

O'Brien, Jay. "Portugal and Africa: A Dying Imperialism." *Monthly Review* 26 (May 1974): 19–36.

Pothlom, Christian, and R. Dale, eds. *Southern Africa in Perspective.* New York: Free Press, 1972.

Roder, Wolf, ed. *Voices of Liberation in Southern Africa.* Waltham, Mass.: African Studies Association, 1972.

Rotberg, Robert I. *Rebellion in Black Africa.* London: Oxford University Press, 1971.

Rotberg, Robert I., and Ali A. Mazrui, eds. *Protest and Power in Black Africa.* New York: Oxford University Press, 1970.

Segal, Ronald. *Political Africa: A Who's Who of Personalities and Parties,* New York: Praeger, 1961.

Sharma, B. S., "African Nationalism: An Unfinished Revolution." *Africa Quarterly* 13 (April–June 1973): 66–79.

Venter, A. J. *Portugal's Guerrilla War.* Cape Town: Malherbe, 1973.

Whitaker, Paul M. "The Revolutions of 'Portuguese' Africa." *Journal of Modern African Studies* 8 (April 1970): 15–35.

Asia and the Middle East

Burchett, Wilfred G. *The Furtive War: The United States in Laos and Vietnam.* New York: International Publishers, 1963.

————. *The Second Indochina War: Cambodia and Laos.* New York: International Publishers, 1970.

Gettleman, Marvin, et al., eds. *Conflict in Indochina: A Reader in the Widening War in Laos and Cambodia.* New York: Random House, 1970.

Haddad, George M. *Revolutions and Military Rule in the Middle East: The Arab States.* New York: Speller, 1971.

Hammond, Paul Y., ed. *Political Dynamics in the Middle East.* New York: American Elsevier, 1972.

Ismael, Tareq. *Government and Politics of the Contemporary Middle East.* Homewood, Ill.: Dorsey, 1970.

Kahin, George, ed. *Government and Politics of Southeast Asia.* Ithaca, N.Y.: Cornell University Press, 1964.

BIBLIOGRAPHY

Kimche, Jon. *The Second Arab Awakening.* New York: Holt, Rinehart & Winston, 1970.

Laqueur, Walter, ed. *The Israeli-Arab Reader.* New York: Bantam, 1970.

Little, Tom. *The Arab Extremists: A View From the Arab World.* Conflict Studies No. 4. London: Institute for the Study of Conflict, 1970.

The Middle East and North Africa [Yearbook]. London: Europa, 1948–1978.

O'Ballance, Edgar. *Arab Guerrilla Power, 1967–1972.* London: Faber & Faber, 1974.

Perlmutter, Amos. "Sources of Instability in the Middle East: Two Decades of Nationalism and Revolution," *Orbis* 12 (Fall 1968): 718–53.

Scalapino, Robert A., ed. *The Communist Revolution in Asia.* 2nd ed. Englewood Cliffs, N.J.: Prentice-Hall, 1969.

Shaplen, Robert. *Time Out of Hand: Revolution and Reaction in Southeast Asia.* New York: Harper & Row, 1969.

Sharabi, H. B. *Nationalism and Revolution in the Arab World.* Princeton, N.J.: Van Nostrand, 1966.

Vatikiotis, P. J., ed. *Revolution in the Middle East.* Totowa, N.J.: Rowman & Littlefield, 1972.

Zasloff, Joseph J., and Alan E. Goodman, eds. *Indochina in Conflict: A Political Assessment.* Lexington, Mass.: Heath, 1972.

Latin America

Adie, Robert F., and Guy E. Poitras. *Latin America: The Politics of Immobility.* Englewood Cliffs, N.J.: Prentice-Hall, 1974.

Alexander, Robert J. *Prophets of Revolution: Profiles of Latin American Leaders.* New York: Macmillan, 1962.

Alphonse, Max. *Guerrillas in Latin America.* The Hague: International Documentation and Information Center, 1971.

Bambirra, Vanie, et al. *Diez años de insurrección en América latina.* Santiago: Prensa latinoamericana, 1971.

Blackburn, Robin, ed. *Strategy for Revolution: Essays on Latin America by Régis Debray.* New York: Monthly Review Press, 1969.

Fals Borga, Orlando. "Marginality and Revolutions in Latin America." *Studies in Comparative International Development* 6 (1970–1971): 63–89.

Frank, André G. *Latin America: Underdevelopment or Revolution.* New York: Monthly Review Press, 1969.

————. *Lumpenbourgeoisie/Lumpendevelopment: Dependence, Class, and Parties in Latin America.* New York: Monthly Review Press, 1972.

Gott, Richard. *Guerrilla Movements in Latin America.* New York: Doubleday, 1972.

Halperin, Ernst. *Terrorism in Latin America.* Beverly Hills, Calif.: Sage, 1976.

Horowitz, Irving Louis, et al., eds. *Latin American Radicalism.* New York: Random House, Vintage, 1969.

Huberman, Leo, and Paul M. Sweezy, eds. *Régis Debray and the Latin American Revolution.* New York: Monthly Review Press, 1968.

Kohl, James, and John Litt. *Urban Guerrilla Warfare in Latin America.* Cambridge, MIT Press, 1974.

Landsberger, Henry, ed. *Latin American Peasant Movements.* Ithaca, N.Y.: Cornell University Press, 1969.

ALGERIA

McCamant, John F. *Violence and Repression in Latin America: A Quantitative and Historical Analysis.* New York: Free Press, 1976.
Mercier Vega, Luis. *Guerrillas in Latin America.* New York: Praeger, 1969.
Petras, James. "Guerrilla Movements in Latin America: I." *New Politics* 6 (Winter 1967): 80–94.
———. "Guerrilla Movements in Latin America: II." *New Politics* 6 (Spring 1967): 58–72.
———. *Politics and Social Structure in Latin America.* New York: Monthly Review Press, 1970.
Petras, James, and Maurice Zeitlin, eds. *Latin America: Reform or Revolution?* New York: Fawcett, 1968.
Pollack, David, and R. M. Ritter, eds. *Latin America: Prospects for the 1970s.* New York: Praeger, 1973.

COUNTRY STUDIES

Country bibliographies are uneven—some rather lengthy, others rather brief. They are arranged alphabetically and should be consulted in conjunction with regional studies and general data sources.

Algeria

Behr, Edward. *The Algerian Problem.* New York: Norton, 1961.
Brace, Richard, and Joan Brace. *Algerian Voices.* Princeton, N.J.: Van Nostrand, 1965.
———. *Ordeal in Algeria.* Princeton, N.J.: Van Nostrand, 1960.
Bromberger, Serge. *Les rebelles algériens.* Paris: Plon, 1958.
Clark, Michael K. *Algeria in Turmoil: A History of the Rebellion.* New York: Praeger, 1959.
Courrière, Yves. *Les fils de la Toussaint.* Paris: Fayard, 1968.
Estier, Claude. *Pour l'Algérie,* Paris: Maspero, 1964.
Gallagher, Charles F. "The Algerian Year." Pts. 1, 2, 3. *AUFS Reports: North Africa Series* IX: 6, 7, 8. New York: American Universities Field Service, 1963.
Gillespie, Joan. *Algeria: Rebellion and Revolution.* London: Benn, 1960.
Gordon, David C. *The Passing of French Algeria.* London: Oxford University Press, 1966.
Heggoy, Alf Andrew. *Insurgency and Counterinsurgency in Algeria.* Bloomington: Indiana University Press, 1972.
Humbaraci, Arslan. *Algeria: A Revolution That Failed.* New York: Praeger, 1966.
Joesten, Joachim. *The New Algeria,* Chicago: Follett, 1964.
Jureidini, Paul A. *Case Studies in Insurgency and Revolutionary Warfare: Algeria, 1954–1962.* Washington, D.C.: American University, Special Operations Research Office, 1963.
Kraft, Joseph. *The Struggle for Algeria.* New York: Doubleday, 1961.
Mansell, Gerard. *Tragedy in Algeria.* London: Oxford University Press, 1961.
Matthews, Tanya. *War in Algeria: Background for Crisis.* New York: Fordham University Press, 1961.
Merle, Robert. *Ahmed Ben Bella.* New York: Walker, 1967.

BIBLIOGRAPHY

O'Ballance, Edgar. *The Algerian Insurrection, 1954–1962.* Hamden, Conn.: Shoe String, Archon, 1967.
Ottaway, David, and Marina Ottaway. *Algeria: The Politics of a Socialist Revolution.* Berkeley and Los Angeles: University of California Press, 1970.
Quandt, William B. *Berbers in the Algerian Political Elite.* Santa Monica, Calif.: RAND Corporation, 1970.
―――. *Revolution and Political Leadership: Algeria, 1954–68.* Cambridge: MIT Press, 1969.

America

Appleton's Cyclopaedia of American Biography. Edited by James C. Wilson and John Fiske. New York: Free Association Compilers, 1915.
Bailyn, Bernard. *The Ideological Origins of the American Revolution.* Cambridge: Harvard University Press, 1967.
Becker, Carl L. *The Declaration of Independence.* New York: Harcourt, Brace, 1922.
Beeman, Richard R. *Partick Henry: A Biography.* New York: McGraw-Hill, 1974.
Bellamy, Francis R. *The Private Life of George Washington.* New York: Crowell, 1951.
Boorstein, Daniel J. *The Lost World of Thomas Jefferson.* Boston: Beacon, 1963.
Borden, Morton. *George Washington.* Englewood Cliffs., N.J.: Prentice-Hall, 1969.
Bowen, Catherine D. *John Adams and the American Revolution.* Boston: Little, Brown, 1950.
Brodie, Fawn M. *Thomas Jefferson: An Intimate History.* New York: Norton, 1974.
Butterfield, L. H., ed. *Diary and Autobiography of John Adams.* 3 vols. Cambridge: Harvard University Press, 1961.
―――, ed. *The Earliest Diary of John Adams.* Cambridge: Harvard University Press, 1966.
Canfield, Cass. *Samuel Adam's Revolution 1765–1776.* New York: Harper & Row, 1976.
Chinard, Gilbert. *Honest John Adams.* Boston: Little, Brown, 1933.
Corbin, John. *The Unknown Washington.* New York: Scribner's, 1930.
Dictionary of American Biography. Edited by Allen Johnson. New York: Scribner's, 1928.
Dictionary of National Biography. 22 vols. Edited by Leslie Stephen and Sidney Lee. London: Oxford University Press, 1921–1922.
Fallows, Samuel. *Sam Adams: A Character Sketch.* New York: Instructor, 1958.
Flexner, James T. *George Washington in the American Revolution, 1775–1783.* Boston: Little, Brown, 1968.
Graves, J. T., et al., eds. *Eloquent Sons of the South.* Vol. 1. Boston: Chapple, 1909.
Guedalla, Phillip. *Fathers of the Revolution.* New York: Putnam's, 1926.
Haraszti, Zoltan. *John Adams and the Prophets of Progress.* Cambridge: Harvard University Press, 1952.
Harlow, Ralph V. *Samuel Adams: Promotor of the American Revolution.* New York: Henry Holt, 1923.
Hosmer, James K. *Samuel Adams.* Baltimore: Johns Hopkins University Press, 1884.
Jameson, J. Franklin. *The American Revolution Considered as a Social Movement.* Princeton, N.J.: Princeton University Press, 1967.

Jensen, Merrill. *The Founding of a Nation.* New York: Oxford University Press, 1968.
Knollenberg, Bernhard. *George Washington: The Virginia Period, 1732–1775.* Durham, N.C.: Duke University Press, 1964.
———. *Origins of the American Revolution.* New York: Macmillan, 1960.
———. *Washington and the Revolution: A Reappraisal.* New York: Macmillan, 1940.
Koch, Adrienne. *The Philosophy of Thomas Jefferson.* Gloucester, Mass.: Smith, 1957.
Maier, Pauline. *From Resistance to Revolution.* New York: Knopf, 1972.
Malone, Dumas. *Jefferson and His Times.* 5 vols. Boston: Little, Brown, 1952.
———. *Thomas Jefferson as a Political Leader.* Berkeley and Los Angeles: University of California Press, 1963.
Meade, Robert. *Patrick Henry: Patriot in the Making.* Philadelphia: Lippincott, 1957.
Miller, John C. *Sam Adams: Pioneer in Propaganda.* Stanford, Calif.: Stanford University Press, 1936.
Morris, Richard B. *Seven Who Shaped Our Destiny: The Founding Fathers as Revolutionaries.* New York: Harper & Row, 1973.
Nettles, Curtis P. *George Washington and American Independence.* Boston: Little, Brown, 1951.
Peterson, Merrill D. *Thomas Jefferson and the New Nation.* New York: Oxford University Press, 1970.
Schachner, Nathan. *Thomas Jefferson: A Biography.* 2 vols. New York: Appleton-Century-Crofts, 1951.
Shaw, Peter. *The Character of John Adams.* Chapel Hill: University of North Carolina Press, 1975.
Smith, C. Page. *John Adams.* 2 vols. New York: Doubleday, 1962.
Sydnor, Charles. *American Revolutionaries in the Making.* New York: Free Press, 1965.
Tudor, William. *The Life of James Otis of Massachusetts.* Boston: Wells & Lilly, 1823.
Tyler, Moses C. *Patrick Henry.* New York: Ungar, 1898.
Umbreit, Kenneth. *The Founding Fathers: Men Who Shaped Our Tradition.* Port Washington, N.Y.: Kennikat, 1941.
Wells, William V. *The Life and Public Service of Samuel Adams.* 3 vols. Boston: Little, Brown, 1888.
Wirt, William. *Sketches of the Life and Character of Patrick Henry.* Philadelphia: Thomas, Cowperthwait, 1841.
———, ed. *Patrick Henry: Life, Correspondence and Speeches.* 3 vols. New York: Scribner's, 1891.
Woodburn, James A., and Thomas Moran. *The Makers of America.* New York: Longmans, Green, 1922.

Angola

American University, Foreign Area Studies Division. *U.S. Army Area Handbook for Angola:* Washington, D.C.: Government Printing Office, 1967.
Barnett, Don, and Roy Harvey. *The Revolution in Angola: MPLA Life Histories and Documents.* Indianapolis: Bobbs-Merrill, 1972.
Bender, Gerald. *Angola under the Portuguese.* Berkeley and Los Angeles: University of California Press, 1978.
Benson, Peter. *Persecution 1961.* Baltimore: Penguin, 1961.

BIBLIOGRAPHY

Bosgra, S., and A. Dijk. *Angola, Mozambique, Guinee: De strijd tegen het Portugese kolonialisme.* Amsterdam: Paris, 1969.

Chilcote, Ronald H. *Protest and Resistance in Angola and Brazil.* Berkeley and Los Angeles: University of California Press, 1972.

Davezies, Robert. *Les Angolais.* Paris: Minuit, 1965.

————. *La guerre d'Angola.* Bordeaux: Ducros, 1968.

Davidson, Basil. *Angola.* London: Union of Democratic Control, 1961.

————. *In the Eye of the Storm: Angola's People.* Harmondsworth: Penguin, 1975.

————. "The Liberation Struggle in Angola and Portuguese Guinea." *Africa Quarterly* 10 (April–June 1970): 25–31.

Ehnmark, Andres, and Per Wasterg. *Angola and Mozambique: The Case against Portugal.* New York: Roy, 1964.

Harsch, Ernest, and Tony Thomas. *Angola: The Hidden History of Washington's War.* New York: Pathfinder, 1976.

Institute of Race Relations (London). *Angola: A Symposium: View of a Revolt.* New York: Oxford University Press, 1962.

Jack, Homer. *Angola: Repression and Revolt in Protuguese Africa.* New York: American Committee on Africa, 1960.

Kaufman, Michael T. "Suddenly, Angola." *New York Times Magazine,* January 4, 1976, 7, 40–55.

Marcum, John. "The Angolan Rebellion: Status Report." *Africa Report* 9 (February 1964): 3–7.

————. *The Angolan Revolution.* Vol. 1, *The Anatomy of an Explosion.* Cambridge: MIT Press, 1969.

————. *The Angolan Revolution.* Vol. 2, *Exile Politics and Guerrilla Warfare.* Cambridge: MIT Press, 1978.

Minter, William. "Imperial Network and External Dependency: Implications for the Angolan Liberation Struggle." *Africa Today* 21 (Winter 1974): 25–40.

Moser, Pierre A. *La révolution angolaise.* Tunis: Société d'édition et de presse, 1966.

Okuma, Thomas. *Angola in Ferment.* Boston: Beacon, 1962.

Panikkar, M. Madhu. *Angola in Flames.* New York: Asia Publishing House, 1962.

Revolution in Angola. London: Merlin, 1972.

Rossi, Pierre-Pascal. *Pour une guerre oubliée.* Paris: Juillard, 1969.

Teixeira, Bernardo. *The Fabric of Terror: Three Days in Angola.* New York: Devin-Adair, 1965.

Venter, A. J. *The Terror Fighters.* Cape Town: Purnell, 1969.

Westwood, Andrew. "The Politics of Revolt in Angola." *Africa Report* 7 (November 1962): 7–10, 31.

Wheeler, Douglas L, and René Pélissier. *Angola.* New York: Praeger, 1971.

Bolivia

Alexander, Robert J. *The Bolivian National Revolution.* New Brunswick, N.J.: Rutgers University Press, 1958.

————. *Prophets of Revolution: Profiles of Latin American Leaders.* New York: Macmillan, 1962.

Carrasco, Benigno. *Hernando Siles.* La Paz: Estado, 1961.

Céspedes, Augusto. *El Presidente Colgado.* Buenos Aires: Alvarez, 1966.

Cornejo, Alberto. *Programas politicos de Bolivia.* Cochabamba: Imprenta Universitaria, 1949.

Encinas, Mercado. *Esto es Bolivia.* La Paz: Empresa Ed. "Universo," 1956.

"El Ex-Vicepresidente Lechín, cabeza de la subversión en Bolivia." *Este & Oeste* (Caracas) 3:73 (July 15–30, 1965): 1–4.

Fellman Velarde, José. *Víctor Paz Estenssoro: El hombre y la revolución.* La Paz: Tejerina, 1954.

Hinton, Ronald, ed. *Who's Who in Latin America.* 3rd ed. Pt. 4. Stanford, Calif.: Stanford University Press, 1947.

Klein, Herbert S. *Parties and Political Change in Bolivia, 1880–1952.* Cambridge: Cambridge University Press, 1969.

Lecca, Alcantara L. *Diccionario biográfico de figuras de actualidad,* La Paz: Litografias e imprentas unidas, 1929.

Lechín Oquendo, Juan. *Lechín y la revolutión nacional.* La Paz: "Pueblo Lee," n.d.

Malloy, James M. *Bolivia: The Uncompleted Revolution.* Pittsburgh: University of Pittsburgh Press, 1970.

Osborne, Harold. *Bolivia: A Land Divided.* 2nd ed. London: Royal Institute of International Affairs, 1955.

Patch, Richard W. "The Last of Bolivia's MNR." In *AUFS Reports: West Coast South America Series.* Vol. 11. New York: American Universities Field Staff, 1964.

———. "Personalities and Politics in Bolivia." In *AUFS Reports: West Coast South America Series.* Vol. 9. New York: American Universities Field Staff, 1962.

Quién es quién en Bolivia. La Paz: Quién es quién en Bolivia, 1959.

Brazil

Carlos Marighella [biography and selected writings]. Havana: Tricontinental, 1970.

Chilcote, Ronald H. *The Brazilian Communist Party: Conflict and Integration, 1922–1972.* New York: Oxford University Press, 1974.

Davis, Shelton H. *Victims of the Miracle.* New York: Cambridge University Press, 1971.

Dos rebeldes: Camilo Torres / Carlos Marighella. Lima: N.p., 1970.

Erikson, Kenneth P. *The Brazilian Corporate State and Working Class Politics.* Berkeley and Los Angeles: University of California Press, 1977.

Fiechter, Gewges-André. *Brazil since 1964: Modernization under a Military Regime.* London: Macmillan,1975.

Jullis, F. Lamond. *Modernization in Brazil.* Provo, Utah: Brigham Young University Press, 1973.

Keith, Henry H., and R. A. Hayes. *Perspectives on Armed Politics in Brazil.* Tempe: Arizona State University, Center for Latin American Studies, 1976.

Marighella, Carlos. *Acción libertadora.* Paris: Maspero, 1970.

———. *For the Liberation of Brazil.* Harmondsworth: Penguin, 1971.

———. *La guerra revolucionaria.* 2nd ed. Mexico City: Diógenes, 1971.

———. "Minimanual of the Urban Guerrilla." In *Terror and Urban Guerrillas,* edited by Jay Mallin. Coral Gables, Fla.: University of Miami Press, 1971.

BIBLIOGRAPHY

Quartim, João. *Dictatorship and Armed Struggle in Brazil*. New York: Monthly Review Press, 1971.
Robock, Stefan H. *Brazil: A Study in Development Progress*. Lexington, Mass.: Lexington Books, 1975.
Roett, Riordan, ed. *Brazil in the Seventies*. Washington, D.C.: American Enterprise Institute, 1976.
Schmitter, Phillipe C. *Interest Conflict and Political Change in Brazil*. Stanford, Calif.: Stanford University Press, 1971.
Schneider, Ronald. *The Political System of Brazil: Emergence of a "Modernizing" Authoritarian Regime, 1964–1970*. New York: Columbia University Press, 1971.
Stepan, Alfred. *The Military in Politics: Changing Patterns in Brazil*. Princeton, N.J.: Princeton University Press, 1971.
――――, ed. *Authoritarian Brazil: Origins, Policies, and Future*. New Haven, Conn.: Yale University Press, 1973.

China

Biographical Service. Nos. 1–158. Hong Kong: Union Research Service, 1956–1957.
Boorman, Howard L. "Mao Tse-tung: The Lacquered Image." *China Quarterly* 16 (November-December 1963): 1–55.
――――, ed. *Biographical Dictionary of Republican China*. 4 vols. New York: Columbia University Press, 1967–1971.
Ch'en, Jerome. *Mao and the Chinese Revolution*. New York: Oxford University Press, 1967.
――――, ed. *Mao*. Englewood Cliffs, N.J.: Prentice-Hall, 1969.
Dittmer, Lowell. *Liu Shao-ch'i and the Chinese Cultural Revolution*. Berkeley and Los Angeles: University of California Press, 1974.
Ebon, Martin. *Lin Piao: The Life and Writings of China's New Ruler*. New York: Stein & Day, 1970.
Elegant, Robert S. *China's Red Masters: Political Biographies of the Chinese Communist Leaders*. New York: Twayne, 1951.
Emi Siao. *Mao Tse-tung: His Childhood and Youth*. Bombay: People's, 1953.
Han Suyin. *The Morning Deluge: Mao Tse-tung and the Chinese Revolution, 1893–1954*. Boston: Little, Brown, 1972.
――――. *Wind in the Tower: Mao Tse-tung and the Chinese Revolution, 1949–1975*. Boston: Little, Brown, 1976.
Hinton, Harold C. *Leaders of Communist China*. RM-1845. Santa Monica, Calif.: RAND Corporation, 1956.
Hsu, Kai-yu. *Chou En-lai: China's Gray Eminence*. New York: Doubleday, Anchor, 1969.
Hsüeh, Chün-tu, ed. *Revolutionary Leaders of Modern China*. New York: Oxford University Press, 1971.
Institute of International Relations. *Chinese Communist Who's Who*. 2 vols. Taipei: Institute of International Relations, 1971–1972.
Klein, Donald W., and Ann B. Clark. *Biographic Dictionary of Chinese Communism, 1921–1965*. 2 vols. Cambridge: Harvard University Press, 1971.
Kuo, Warren, et al. *Who's Who in Communist China*. Taiwan: Institute of International Relations, 1968.

Lee, Ming T. "The Founders of the Chinese Communist Party: A Study in Revolutionaries." *Civilisations* 13 (1968): 113–27.

Lifton, Robert J. *Revolutionary Immortality: Mao Tse-tung and the Chinese Cultural Revolution.* New York: Random House, 1968.

Liu, Shao-ch'i. *How to Be a Good Communist.* New York: New Century, 1952.

Mao Tse-tung. *Selected Works.* 4 vols. Peking: Foreign Languages, 1961–1965.

North, Robert C. "The Chinese Communist Elite." *Annals* 277 (September 1951): 67–75.

North, Robert C., with Ithiel de Sola Pool. "Kuomintang and Chinese Communist Elites." In *World Revolutionary Elites,* edited by Harold D. Lasswell and Daniel Lerner. Cambridge: MIT Press, 1965.

Payne, Robert. *Mao Tse-tung.* New York: Weybright & Talley, 1969.

Perleberg, Max. *Who's Who in Modern China.* Hong Kong: Ye Old Printerie, 1954.

Pye, Lucian W. *China: An Introduction.* Boston: Little, Brown, 1972.

———. *Mao Tse-tung: The Man in the Leader.* New York: Basic Books, 1976.

———. *The Spirit of Chinese Politics.* Cambridge: MIT Press, 1968.

Robinson, Thomas W. *Lin Piao as an Elite Type.* P-4639. Santa Monica, Calif.: RAND Corporation, 1971.

———. *A Politico-military Biography of Lin Piao. Pt. 1, 1907–1949.* R-526-PR. Santa Monica, Calif.: RAND Corporation, 1971.

Schram, Stuart. *Mao-Tse-tung.* Baltimore: Penguin, 1967.

———. *The Political Thought of Mao Tse-tung.* Rev. ed. New York: Praeger, 1969.

Schwartz, Benjamin I. *Chinese Communism and the Rise of Mao.* New York: Harper & Row, 1967.

Smedley, Agnes. *The Great Road: The Life and Times of Chu Teh.* New York: Monthly Review Press, 1956.

Snow, Edgar. "Interview with Mao Tse-tung." *New Republic.* February 27, 1965, 17–23.

———. *Random Notes on Red China (1936–1945).* Cambridge: Harvard University Press, 1957.

———. *Red China Today: The Other Side of the River.* New York: Random House, Vintage, 1971.

———. *Red Star Over China.* 1938. Reprint. New York: Grove, 1961.

Solomon, Richard H. *Mao's Revolution and the Chinese Political Culture.* Berkeley and Los Angeles: University of California Press, 1971.

Union Research Institute. *Who's Who in Communist China.* Hong Kong: Union Research Institute, 1966.

———. *Who's Who in Communist China.* 2 vols. Hong Kong: Union Research Institute, 1969–1970.

U.S. Department of State, Division of Biographic Information. *Leaders of Communist China.* Washington: U.S. Department of State, Division of Biographic Information, n.d.

Wales, Nym. *Red Dust: Autobiographies of Chinese Communists as told to Nym Wales.* Stanford, Calif.: Stanford University Press, 1952.

Wu, Eugene. *Leaders of Twentieth-century China: An Annotated Bibliography of Selected Chinese Biographical Works in the Hoover Library.* Stanford, Calif.: Stanford University Press, 1956.

BIBLIOGRAPHY

Colombia

Alvarez García, John, ed. *Camilo Torres: Biographia, platforma, mensajes, medellin.* Bogotá: Carpel-Antorcha, n.d. [1966?].
Alvarez García, John, and Christian Restrepo Calle, eds. *Camilo Torres: Priest and Revolutionary.* London: Sheed & Ward, 1968.
Broderick, Walter J. *Camilo Torres: A Biography of the Priest-Guerrillero.* New York: Doubleday, 1975.
Colombia: An Embattled Land. Prague: Peace and Socialism, 1966.
Del Corro, Alejandro, ed. *Camilo Torres: Un símbolo controvertido 1962–1967.* Cuernavaca: Centro intercultural de documentacion, 1967.
Diario de un guerrillero colombiano. Buenos Aires: Freeland, 1968.
Dos rebeldes: Camilo Torres / Carlos Marighella. Lima: N.p., 1970.
Gally, Hector, ed. *Camilo Torres: Con las armas en la mano.* Mexico City: Diógenes, 1971.
Gerassi, John, ed. *Revolutionary Priest: The Complete Writings and Messages of Camilo Torres.* Harmondsworth: Penguin, 1973.
Guzmán, Germán. *Camilo Torres.* New York: Sheed & Ward, 1969.
———. *El Padre Camilo Torres.* Mexico City: Siglo XXI, 1968.
Habegger, Norberto. *Camilo Torres: El cura guerrillero.* Buenos Aires: Peña, 1967.
Maldonado, Óscar, et al. *Camilo Torres: Christianismo y revolucíon.* Mexico City: Era, 1970.
Maullin, Richard. *Soldiers, Guerrillas, and Politics in Columbia.* Lexington, Mass.: Lexington Books, 1973.
Pareja, Carlos H. *El Padre Camilo: El cura guerrillero.* Mexico City: Nuestra América, 1968.
Perry y Cía, Oliverio, ed. *Quién es quién en Colombia.* 2nd ed. Bogotá: N.p., 1948.
Ramsey, Russel W. "Critical Bibliography on *La Violencia* in Colombia." *Latin American Research Review* 8 (Spring 1973): 3–44.
Rojas, Robinson. *Colombia: Surge el primer Vietnam en América Latina.* Santiago: Prensa latinoamericana, 1970.
Torres, Camilo. *Revolutionary Writings.* London: Herder & Herder, 1969.

Cuba

Alexandre, Marianne, ed. *Viva Che! Contributions in Tribute to Ernesto "Che" Guevara.* New York: Dutton, 1968.
Bonachea, Rolando E., and Nelson Q. Valdés, eds. *Che: The Selected Works of Ernesto Guevara.* Cambridge: MIT Press, 1969.
———, eds. *Revolutionary Struggle, 1947–1958: The Selected Works of Fidel Castro.* Vol. 1. Cambridge: MIT Press, 1972.
Camilo Cienfuegos: People's Hero. Havana: Minrex, 1962.
Castro, Fidel. *History Will Absolve Me.* New York: Fair Play for Cuba Committee, 1961.
———. *The Road to Revolution in Latin America.* New York: Pioneer, 1963.
Casuso, Teresa. *Cuba and Castro.* Translated from the Spanish by Elmer Grossberg. New York: Random House, 1961.

Draper, Theodore, *Castroism: Theory and Practice*. New York: Praeger, 1965.
———. *Castro's Revolution: Myths and Realities*. New York: Praeger, 1962.
Dubois, Jules, *Fidel Castro: Rebel-Liberator or Dictator?* Indianapolis: Bobbs-Merrill, 1959.
Ebon, Martin. *Che: The Making of a Legend*. New York: Universe, 1969.
Gadea, Hilda. *Ernesto: A Memoir of Che Guevara*. New York: Doubleday, 1972.
Galeano, Eduardo. "Magic Death for a Magic Life." *Monthly Review* 19 (January 1968): 13–21.
Gerassi, John, ed. *Venceremos! The Speeches and Writings of Ernesto Che Guevara*. New York: Macmillan, 1968.
Gonzáles, Luis J., and Gustavo A. Sánchez Salazar. *The Great Rebel: Che Guevara in Bolivia*. New York: Grove, 1969.
Guevara, Ernesto. *Guerrilla Warfare*. New York: Random House, Vintage, 1961.
———. *Reminiscences of the Cuban Revolutionary War*. New York: Grove, 1968.
Harris, Richard. *Death of a Revolutionary: Che Guevara's Last Mission*. New York: Norton, 1970.
James, Daniel, ed. *The Complete Bolivian Diaries of Che Guevara and Other Captured Documents*. New York: Stein & Day, 1968.
Karol, K. S. *Guerrillas in Power: The Course of the Cuban Revolution*. Translated from the French by Arnold Pomerans. New York: Hill & Wang, 1970.
Kenner, Martin, and James Petras, eds. *Castro Speaks*. New York; Grove, 1969.
Lockwood, Lee. *Castro's Cuba, Cuba's Fidel*. New York: Macmillan, 1967.
Mallin, Jay, ed. *Che Guevara on Revolution*. New York: Dell, 1969.
Martin, Dolores Moyano. "A Memoir of the Young Guevara." *New York Times Magazine*, August 18, 1968, 48 plus.
Matthews, Herbert L. *The Cuban Story*. New York: Braziller, 1961.
———. *Fidel Castro*. New York: Simon & Schuster, 1969.
Morton, Ward M. *Castro as a Charismatic Leader*. Lawrence: University of Kansas, Center of Latin American Studies, 1965.
Peraza Sarausa, Fermin. *Personalidades cubanas*. Havana: Anuario bibliografico cubano, 1959.
Revolución (Havana Daily), October 28, 1961.
Rojo, Ricardo. *My Friend Che*. New York: Dial, 1968.
Sauvage, Leo. *Che Guevara: The Failure of a Revolutionary*. Englewood Cliffs, N.J.: Prentice-Hall, 1973.
Scheer, Robert, ed. *The Diary of Che Guevara*. New York: Bantam, 1969.
Sinclair, Andrew. *Che Guevara*. New York: Viking, 1970.
Verde Olivo (Organo de las Fuerzas Armadas Revolucionarias) (Havana) 1 (October 29, 1960). Issue devoted to the first anniversary of the death of Camilo Cienguegos.
Weyl, Nathaniel. *Red Star over Cuba*. New York: Devin-Adair, 1961.
Wilkerson, Loree A. R. *Fidel Castro's Political Programs from Reformism to "Marxism-Leninism."* Gainesville: University of Florida Press, 1965.
Youngblood, Jack, and Robin Moore. *The Devil to Pay*. New York: Coward-McCann, 1961.
Zorina, A. M. *Kamilo Sienfuegos: Geroi kubinskoí revolyutsii* (Camilo Cienfuegos: Hero of the Cuban Revolution). Moscow: State Scientific Publishing House, 1966.

England

Abbott, Wilbur C., ed. *Writings and Speeches of Oliver Cromwell.* 3 vols. Cambridge: Harvard University Press, 1937.
Adamson, J. H., and J. F. Folland. *Sir Henry Vane: His Life and Times, 1613–1662.* Boston: Bambit, 1973.
Ashley, Maurice P. *Cromwell.* Englewood Cliffs, N.J.: Prentice-Hall, 1969.
———. *The Greatness of Oliver Cromwell.* London: Hodder & Stoughton, 1957.
———. *Oliver Cromwell: The Conservative Dictator.* London: Cape, 1937.
Brett, Sidney R. *John Pym, 1583–1643. The Statesman of the Puritan Revolution.* London: Murray, 1940.
Cooks, H. F. L. *The Religious Life of Oliver Cromwell.* London: Independent, 1960.
Drinkwater, John. *John Hampden's England.* London: Thorton, Butterworth, 1933.
———. *Oliver Cromwell: A Character Study.* New York: Doubleday, 1927.
Firth, Charles H. *Oliver Cromwell and the Rule of the Puritans in England.* New York: Putnam's, 1900.
Fraser, Antonia. *Cromwell: The Lord Protector.* New York: Knopf, 1973.
Gardiner, Samuel R. *Cromwell's Place in History.* London: Longmans, Green, 1910.
———. *History of the Great Civil War, 1642–1649.* 4 vols. London: Longmans, Green, 1893.
———. *Oliver Cromwell.* London: Goupil, 1899.
Hexter, J. H. *The Reign of King Pym.* London: Oxford University Press, 1941.
Hill, Christopher. *God's Englishman: Oliver Cromwell and the English Revolution.* New York: Dial, 1970.
———. *Puritanism and Revolution.* London: Secker & Warburg, 1958.
———. *The World Turned Upside Down: Radical Ideas during the English Revolution.* New York: Viking, 1972.
Hosmer, James K. *Young Sir Henry Vane.* Boston: Houghton Mifflin, 1899.
Judson, Margaret A. *The Political Thought of Sir Henry Vane the Younger.* Philadelphia: University of Pennsylvania Press, 1969.
Lacey, Robert. *Robert, Earl of Essex.* New York: Atheneum, 1971.
Rowe, Violet A. *Sir Henry Vane the Younger.* London: Athlone, 1970.
Smith, Goldwin. *Three English Statesmen.* London: Macmillan, 1868.
Snow, Vernon F. *Essex the Rebel.* Lincoln: University of Nebraska Press, 1970.
Walzer, Michael. *The Revolution of the Saints: A Study in the Origin of Radical Politics.* Cambridge: Harvard University Press, 1965.
Wedgwood, Cicely V. *Oliver Cromwell.* New York: Macmillan, 1956.
Williamson, Hugh R. *John Hampden.* London: Hodder & Stoughton, 1933.

France 1789

Aulard, A. *The French Revolution.* 4 vols. New York: Scribner's, 1910.
Barthou, L. *Mirabeau.* London: Heinemann, 1913.
Bax, Ernest B. *Jean Paul Marat: The People's Friend.* Boston: Small, 1901.
Beesley, A. H. *The Life of Danton.* London: Longmans, Green, 1899.
Belloc, Hilaire. *Danton: A Study.* New York: Scribner's, 1899.

Beraud, Henry. *Twelve Portraits of the French Revolution.* Boston: Little, Brown, 1928.

Brinton, Crane. *A Decade of Revolution, 1789–1799.* New York: Harper, 1934.

Carlyle, Thomas. *The French Revolution.* New York: Putnam's, 1902.

Christopher, Robert. *Danton: A Biography.* New York: Doubleday, 1967.

Cobban, Alfred. *The Social Interpretation of the French Revolution.* Cambridge: Cambridge University Press, 1965.

De Jouvenel, Henry. *The Stormy Life of Mirabeau.* New York: Book League of America, 1929.

Gosselin, L. T. *Robespierre's Rise and Fall.* London: Hutchinson, 1927.

Gottschalk, Louis R. *Jean Paul Marat: A Study in Radicalism.* New York: Blom, 1966.

Hall, E. B. *The Life of Mirabeau.* New York: Putnam's, 1912.

Higgins, F. L. *The French Revolution as Told by Contemporaries.* Boston: Houghton Mifflin, 1939.

Korngold, Ralph. *Robespierre and the Fourth Estate.* New York: Modern Age, 1941.

Lefebvre, Georges. *The Coming of the French Revolution.* Princeton, N.J.: Princeton University Press, 1949.

Lewis, George Henry. *The Life of Maximilien Robespierre.* London: Chapman & Hall, 1899.

Madelin, Louis. *Danton.* New York: Knopf, 1921.

———. *Figures of the Revolution.* Freeport, N.Y.: Books for Libraries, 1968.

Mathiez, Albert. *The Fall of Robespierre and Other Essays.* New York: Knopf, 1927.

Rudé, Georges, ed. *Robespierre.* Englewood Cliffs, N.J.: Prentice-Hall, 1967.

Siéyès, Emmanuel Joseph. *What Is the Third Estate?* [1789]. New York: Praeger, 1964.

Thompson, James M. *Leaders of the French Revolution.* New York: Harper, Colophon, 1967.

———. *Robespierre.* New York: Appleton, 1936.

Vallentin, Antonia. *Mirabeau.* New York: Viking, 1948.

Warwick, Charles F. *Danton and the French Revolution.* Philadelphia: Jacobs, 1908.

———. *Mirabeau and the French Revolution.* Philadelphia: Lippincott, 1905.

Wendel, Hermann. *Danton.* New Haven, Conn.: Yale University Press, 1935.

Whitman, J. Mills. *Men and Women of the French Revolution.* Freeport, N.Y.: Books for Libraries, 1968.

France 1968

Aron, Raymond. *The Elusive Revolution: Anatomy of a Student Revolt.* New York: Praeger, 1969.

Bensaïd, Daniel, and Henri Weber. *Mai 1968: Une répétition générale.* Paris: Maspero, 1968.

Bourge, Hervé, ed. *The French Student Revolt: The Leaders Speak.* New York: Hill & Wang, 1969.

Brown, Bernard E. *Protest in Paris: Anatomy of a Revolt.* Morristown, N.J.: Silver Burdett, General Learning, 1974.

Buhler, Alain. *Petit dictionnaire de la révolution étudiante.* Paris: Didier, 1968.

Charrière, Christian. *Le printemps des enragés.* Paris: Fayard, 1968.

Cohn-Bendit, Daniel, and Gabriel Cohn-Bendit. *Obsolete Communism: The Left-wing Alternative.* New York: McGraw-Hill, 1968.

Dansette, Adrien. *Mai 1968.* Paris: Plon, 1971.

BIBLIOGRAPHY

Duprat, François. *Les journées de mai 1968: Les dessous d'une révolution.* Paris: Nouvelles éditions latines, 1968.

Geismar, Alain, Serge July, and Erlyn Morane. *Vers la guerre civile.* Paris: Éditions et publication premières, 1969.

Geneve, Pierre. *Histoire secrète de l'insurrection de mai 1968.* Paris: Presses noires, 1968.

Gretton, John. *Students and Workers: An Analytical Account of Dissent in France, May–June 1968.* London: MacDonald, 1969.

Johnson, Richard. *The French Communist Party versus the Students.* New Haven, Conn.: Yale University Press, 1968.

Kravetz, Marc, ed. *L'insurrection étudiante, 2–13 mai 1968.* Paris: Union générale, 1968.

Krivine, Alain. *La farce électorale.* Paris: Seuil, 1969.

Labro, Phillippe. *This Is Only the Beginning.* New York: Funk & Wagnalls, 1969.

Minutes du procès d'Alain Geismar. Preface by J.-P. Sartre. Paris: Hallier, 1970.

Le Monde (Weekly edition), May–July 1968.

Mouvement du 22 mars. *Ce n'est qu'un début: Continuons le combat.* Paris: Maspero, 1968.

Le nouvel observateur. No. 181, April 30–May 7, 1968; no. 182, May 8–14, 1968.

Penet, Jacques-Arnaud. *Un printemps rouge et noir.* Paris: Laffont, 1968.

Posner, Charles, ed. *Reflections on the Revolution in France: 1968.* Baltimore: Penguin, 1970.

Priaulx, Allan, and Sanford J. Unger. *The Almost Revolution: France 1968.* New York: Dell, 1969.

Quattrocchi, Angelo, and Tom Nairn. *The Beginning of the End: France, May 1968.* London: Panther, 1968.

Rioux, Lucien, and René Blackmann. *L'explosion de mai: Histoire complète des "événements."* Paris: Laffont, 1968.

Sale, Patrick, and Maureen McConville. *Red Flag/Black Flag: French Revolution, 1968.* New York: Ballantine, 1968.

Schnapp, Alain, and Pierre Vidal-Naquet. *Journal de la commune étudiante: Textes et documents, novembre 1967–juin 1968.* Paris: Seuil, 1969.

Singer, Daniel. *Prelude to Revolution: France in May 1968.* New York: Hill & Wang, 1970.

Spender, Stephen. *The Year of the Young Rebels.* New York: Random House, 1968.

Touraine, Alain. *The May Movement: Revolt and Reform.* New York: Random House, 1971.

Villeneuve, Paquerette. *Une Canadienne dans les rues de Paris pendant la révolte étudiante.* Montréal: Éditions du jour, 1968.

Guatemala

Galeano, Eduardo. *Guatemala: Clave de Latinoamerica.* Montevideo: Banda, 1967.

———. *Guatemala: Occupied Country.* New York: Monthly Review Press, 1969.

———. "With the Guerrillas in Guatemala." *Ramparts,* September 1967, 56–59.

Gilley, Adolfo. "The Guerrilla Movement in Guatemala." *Monthly Review* 17 (May–June 1965): 9–40.

Howard, R. "With the Guerrillas in Guatemala." *New York Times Magazine*, June 26, 1966, 8–9 plus.
Johnson, Kenneth F. *Guatemala: From Terrorism to Terror.* Conflict Studies no. 23. London: Institute for the Study of Conflict, 1972.
Ramirez, Ricardo. *Lettres du Front guatémaltéque.* Paris: Maspero, 1970.

Guinea-Bissau

Andelman, David A. "Profile: Amilcar Cabral." *Africa Report* 15 (May 1970): 18–19.
Blackey, Robert. "Fanon and Cabral: A Contrast in Theories of Revolution for Africa." *Journal of Modern African Studies* 12 (1974): 191–209.
Cabral, Amilcar. *Guinée "Portugaise": Le pouvoir des armes.* Paris: Maspero, 1970.
———. *National Liberation and Culture.* Eduardo Mondlane Memorial Lecture. Syracuse University Program of East African Studies, 1970. 15 pages, Mimeo.
———. *Our People Are Our Mountains.* London: Committee for Freedom in Mozambique, Angola and Guinea, n.d. [1971?].
———. *Return to the Sources: Selected Speeches.* Edited by African Information Service. New York: Monthly Review Press, 1976.
———. *Revolution in Guinea.* New York: Monthly Review Press, 1969.
Chaliand, Gérard. *Armed Struggle in Africa: With the Guerrillas in "Portuguese" Guinea.* New York: Monthly Review Press, 1969.
Chilcote, Ronald H. "The Political Thought of Amilcar Cabral." *Journal of Modern African Studies* 6 (1968): 373–88.
Davidson, Basil. *The Liberation of Guiné: Aspects of an African Revolution.* Baltimore: Penguin, 1969.
———. "The Liberation Struggle in Angola and Portuguese Guinea." *Africa Quarterly* 10 (April–June 1970): 25–31.
Liberation Support Movement Center. *Guinea-Bissau: Toward Final Victory.* Richmond, B.C.: Liberation Support Movement Information Center, n.d.
Magubane, Bernard. "Amilcar Cabral: Evolution of Revolutionary Thought." UFAHAMU 2 (Fall 1971): 17–87.
McCollester, Charles. "The Political Thought of Amilcar Cabral." *Monthly Review* 24 (March 1973): 10–21.
"Portrait: Portuguese Guinea.Rebel [Amilcar Cabral]." *West Africa* (London), April 18, 1964, 427.
Rudebeck, Lars. *Guinea-Bissau: A Study of Political Mobilization.* New York: Africa, 1974.

Hungary

Aczél, Tamás, ed. *Ten Years After: A Commemoration of the Tenth Anniversary of the Hungarian Revolution.* New York: Holt, Rinehart & Winston, 1966.
Aczél, Tamás, and Meray Tibor. *The Revolt of the Mind: A Case History of Intellectual Resistance behind the Iron Curtain.* New York: Praeger, 1959.
Fejtö, François. *Behind the Rape of Hungary.* New York: McKay, 1957.
Kecskemeti, Paul. *The Unexpected Revolution: Social Forces in the Hungarian Uprising.* Stanford, Calif.: Stanford University Press, 1961.

BIBLIOGRAPHY

Kovrig, Bennett. *The Hungarian People's Republic.* Baltimore: Johns Hopkins University Press, 1970.
Lasky, Melvin J. *The Hungarian Revolution: A White Book.* New York: Praeger, 1957.
Marton, Endre. *The Forbidden Sky: Inside the Hungarian Revolution.* Boston: Little, Brown, 1971.
Mikes, George. *The Hungarian Revolution.* London: Deutsch, 1957.
Molnár, Miklós. *Budapest 1956: A History of the Hungarian Revolution.* London: Allen & Unwin, 1971.
Nagy, Imre. *On Communism: In Defense of a New Course.* New York; Praeger, 1957.
Paloczi-Horvath, George. "The Life and Times of János Kadar." *New Leader,* April 8, 1957, 16–20.
Pryce-Jones, David. *The Hungarian Revolution.* New York: Horizon, 1970.
Sowcross, William. *Crime and Compromise: János Kadar and the Politics of Hungary since Revolution.* New York: Dutton, 1974.
Tibor, Meray. *That Day in Budapest: October 23, 1956.* New York: Funk & Wagnalls, 1969.
————. *Thirteen Days That Shook the Kremlin.* New York: Praeger, 1959.
The Truth about the Nagy Affair: Facts, Documents, Comments. New York: Praeger, 1959.
United Nations, General Assembly. *Report of the Special Committee on the Problem of Hungary.* New York: United Nations, General Assembly, 1957.
U.S. Senate, Committee on the Judiciary. *United Nations Reports and Documents Dealing with the Hungarian Revolt.* Pt. 90. Washington, D.C.: Government Printing Office, 1959.
Zinner, Paul. "Hungary's Imre Nagy: Revolutionist at the End." *Columbia University Forum* 2 (Fall 1958): 6–10.
————. *Revolution in Hungary.* New York: Columbia University Press, 1962.
————, ed. *National Communism and Popular Revolt in Eastern Europe.* New York: Columbia University Press, 1956.

Kampuchea (Cambodia)

Burchett, Wilfred G. *The Second Indochina War: Cambodia and Laos.* New York: International Publishers, 1970.
Caldwell, Malcolm, and Lek Tan. *Cambodia in the Southeast Asian War.* New York: Monthly Review Press, 1973.
Gettleman, Marvin, et al., eds. *Conflict in Indochina: A Reader on the Widening War in Laos and Cambodia.* New York: Random House, 1970.
Gordon, Bernard, and Kathryn Young. "Cambodia: Following the Leader." *Asian Survey* 10 (February 1970): 169–76.
Grant, Jonathan S., et al, eds. *Cambodia: The Widening War in Indochina.* New York: Pocket Books, Washington Square, 1971.
Hildebrand, George C., and Gareth Porter. *Cambodia: Starvation and Revolution.* New York: Monthly Review Press, 1976.
Kamm, Henry. "The Agony of Cambodia." *New York Times Magazine,* November 19, 1978, 41 plus.
Ponchaud, François. *Cambodia: Year Zero.* New York: Holt, Rinehart & Winston, 1978.
Poole, Peter A. *Cambodia's Quest for Survival.* New York: American-Asian Educational Exchange, 1969.

Laos

Adams, Nina S., and Alfred W. McCoy. *Laos: War and Revolution.* New York: Harper & Row, 1970.

Adams, Nina S., et al., eds. *Laos Reader.* New York: Harper & Row, 1970.

American University, Foreign Area Studies. *U.S. Army Area Handbook for Laos.* Washington: Government Printing Office, 1967.

Andelman, David A. "Laos after the Takeover." *New York Times Magazine,* October 24, 1976, 14+.

Burchett, Wilfred G. *The Furtive War: The United States in Laos and Vietnam.* New York: International Publishers, 1963.

————. *Mekong Upstream.* Hanoi: Red River, 1957.

————. *The Second Indochina War: Cambodia and Laos.* New York: International Publishers, 1970.

Champassak, Sisouk Na. *Storm over Laos: A Contemporary History.* New York: Praeger, 1961.

Dommen, Arthur J. *Conflict in Laos: The Politics of Neutralization.* Rev. ed. New York: Praeger, 1971.

Fall, Bernard B. *Anatomy of a Crisis: The Laotian Crisis of 1960–61.* New York: Doubleday, 1969.

Gettleman, Marvin, et al., eds. *Conflict in Indochina: A Reader in the Widening War in Laos and Cambodia.* New York: Random House, 1970.

Halpern, Joel M. *Government, Politics, and Social Structure in Laos.* New Haven, Conn.: Yale University Southeast Asia Studies, 1964.

————. *The Lao Elite: A Study of Tradition and Innovation.* RM-2636-RC. Santa Monica, Calif.: RAND Corporation, 1960.

————. "Observations on the Social Structure of the Lao Elite." *Asian Survey* 1 (May 1960): 25–32.

Langer, Paul F., and Joseph J. Zasloff. *North Vietnam and the Pathet Lao: Partners in Struggle for Laos.* Cambridge: Harvard University Press, 1970.

Phoumi Vongvichit. *Laos and the Victorious Struggle of the Lao People against U.S. Neocolonialism.* N.p.: New Lao Haksat, 1969.

Strong, Anna Louise. *Cash and Violence in Laos.* 2nd ed. Peking: New World, 1962.

Toye, Hugh. *Laos: Buffer State or Battleground.* London: Oxford University Press, 1968.

Zasloff, Joseph J. *The Pathet Lao: Leadership and Organization.* Lexington, Mass.: Lexington Books, 1973. (Published simultaneously by RAND Corporation, R-949-ARPA, 1973.)

Mexico

Alvarez, Alfredo. *Madero y su obra.* Mexico City: Talleres graficos de la nacion, 1935.

Atkins, Roland. *Revolution! Mexico 1910–1920.* New York: John Day, 1970.

Bassols Battalla, Narcisso. *El pensamiento politico de Alvaro Obregón.* Mexico City: Nuestro tiempo, 1967.

Borquez, Juan de Dios. *Apuntes biograficos.* Mexico City: Patria nueva, 1929.

Braddy, Haldeen. *Cock of the Walk: The Legend of Pancho Villa.* Albuquerque: University of New Mexico Press, 1955.

BIBLIOGRAPHY

Clendenen, Clarence. *The United States and Pancho Villa*. Ithaca, N.Y.: Cornell University Press, 1961.

Cumberland, Charles C. *Mexican Revolution: Genesis under Madero*. Austin: University of Texas Press, 1952.

Días Soto y Gama, Antonia. *La revolución agraria del sur y Emiliano Zapata, su Caudillo*. Mexico City: N.p. 1960.

Dillon, E. J. *President Obregon: A World Reformer*. Boston: Small, Maynard, 1923.

Dromundo, Baltasar. *Vida de Emiliano Zapata: Biografía*. Mexico City: N.p. 1934.

Gates, William. "The Four Governments of Mexico: Zapata, Protector of Morelos." *World Works* 37 (April 1919): 654–65.

Guzmán, Martín Luis. *The Eagle and the Serpent*. New York: Doubleday, Dolphin, 1965.

———. *The Memoirs of Pancho Villa*. Austin: University of Texas Press, 1965.

Harris, Harry A. *Pancho Villa and the Columbus Raid*. El Paso, Tex.: McMath, 1949.

Johnson, William W. *Heroic Mexico*. New York: Doubleday, 1968.

Lópes de Escalera, Juan. *Diccionario biográfico y de historia de Mexico*. Mexico City: Magisterio, 1964.

Madero, Francisco I. "Mis Memorias." *Anales del Museo nacional de arquelogia Historia y Etnografía*. Mexico City: N.p., 1922.

———. *Las succession presidencial en 1910*. Mexico City: Mexico editoria nacional, 1972.

Magaña, Gildardo. *Emiliano Zapata y el agrarismo en Mexico*. 3 vols. Mexico City: N.p., 1938.

Manifest Destiny (Excerpts of speeches delivered by Gen. Venustiano Carranza). New York: Latin American Heros Association, n.d.

Maytorena, José. *Algunas verdades sobre el General Alvaro Obregón*. Los Angeles: El heraldo de Mexico, 1919.

McNeely, John H. "Origins of the Zapata Revolt in Morelos." *Hispanic American Historical Review* 46 (May 1966): 153–69.

Millon, Robert P. *Zapata: The Ideology of a Peasant Revolutionary*. New York: International Publishers, 1969.

Obregón, Alvaro. *Ocho mil kilometros en campaña*. Mexico City: Bouret, 1917.

Palavicini, Felix F., ed. *El primer jefe*. N.p., 1916.

Pinchón, Edgecumb. *Zapata the unconquerable*. New York: Doubleday, 1941.

Quirk, Robert E. *The Mexican Revolution, 1914–1915*. Bloomington: Indiana University Press, 1960.

Reed, John. *Insurgent Mexico*. New York: International Publishers, 1914.

Reyes, H. Alfonso. *Emiliano Zapata: Su vide y su obra*. Mexico City: N.p., 1963.

Rittenhouse, Floyd. "Emiliano Zapata and the Suriano Rebellion." Ph.D. diss., Ohio State University, 1947.

Robles, Serefín M. "El General Zapata: Agricultor y arriero." *El Campesino*, October 1951.

Ross, Stanley R. *Francisco I. Madero: Apostle of Mexican Democracy*. New York: Columbia University Press, 1955.

Urquizo, Francisco L. *Carranza*. Mexico City: N.p., 1959.

Wilkie, James W., and Albert A. Michaels. *Revolution in Mexico: Years of Upheaval, 1910–1940*. New York: Knopf, 1969.

Womack, John. *Zapata and the Mexican Revolution*. New York: Knopf, 1969.

Mozambique

Degnan, M. "The 'Three Wars' of Mozambique." *Africa Report* 18 (September-October 1973): 6–13.

"Eduardo Chitlangu Chivambu Mondlane, 1920–1969" (obituary). *Genève Afrique* 8 (1969): 46–49.

Ehnmark, Andres, and Per Wasterg. *Angola and Mozambique: The Case against Portugal*. New York: Roy, 1964.

Henriksen, T. H. "The Revolutionary Thought of Eduardo Mondlane." *Genève Afrique* 12 (1973): 37–52.

Houser, George, and Herb Shore. *Mozambique: Dream the Size of Freedom*. New York: Africa Fund, 1975.

Kitchen, Helen. "Conversation with Eduardo Mondlane." *Africa Report* 12 (November 1967): 31–32, 49–51.

Lefort, Rene. "Liberated Mozambique." *Monthly Review* 28 (December 1976): 25–39.

Machel, Samora. *Establishing People's Power to Serve the Masses*. Toronto: Toronto Committee for the Liberation of Southern Africa, 1976.

———. *Mozambique: Revolution or Reaction*. Richmond, B.C.: Liberation Support Movement Press, 1975.

———. *Mozambique: Sowing the Seeds of Revolution*. London: Committee for the Liberation of Mozambique, Angola, and Guinea, 1974.

———. *The Tasks Ahead*. New York: Afro-American Information Service, 1975.

Mondlane, Eduardo. *The Struggle for Mozambique*. Baltimore: Penguin, 1969.

Munger, Edwin S. *Mozambique: Uneasy Today, Uncertain Tomorrow*. New York: American Universities Field Service, 1961.

Paul, John S. "FRELIMO and the Mozambique Revolution." *Monthly Review* 24 (March 1973): 22–52.

Shore, Herb. "Mondlane, Machel and Mozambique: From Rebellion to Revolution." *Africa Today* 24 (Winter 1974): 3–12.

Swift, Kerry. *Mozambique and the Future*. Cape Town: Nelson, 1974.

Van Rensburg, A. P. J. *The Tangled Web*. Cape Town: Hollandsch Afrikaansche Uitgevers Maatschappij, 1977.

Namibia

Duignan, Peter, and L. H. Gann. *South West Africa: Namibia*. New York: American African Affairs Association, 1978.

First, Ruth. *South West Africa*. Harmondsworth: Penguin, 1963.

First, Ruth, and Ronald Segal, eds. *South West Africa: A Travesty of Trust*. London: Deutsch, 1967.

Jenny, Hans. *South West Africa (Namibia)*. Windhoek: N.p., 1976.

Liberation Support Movement. *Namibia: SWAPO Fights for Freedom*. Oakland, Calif.: Liberation Support Movement, 1978.

Serfontein, J. H. P. *Namibia*. Pretoria: Fokus Suid, 1976.

United Nations Information Service. *Namibia: A Trust Betrayed*. New York: United Nations Information Service, 1975.

Northern Ireland

Bell, J. Bowyer. *The Secret Army: The IRA 1916–1970*. New York: John Day, 1971.

Coogan, Tim Pat. *The I.R.A.* London: Praeger, 1970.

Elliot, R. S. P., and John Hickie. *Ulster: A Case Study in Conflict Theory*. London: Longmans, Green, 1971

Fitzgibbon, Constantine. *Red Hand: The Ulster Colony*. New York: Doubleday, 1971.

Foley, Gerry. *Ireland in Rebellion*. New York: Pathfinder, 1971.

Hamilton, Ian. *The Irish Triangle*. Conflict Studies no. 6. London: Institute for the Study of Conflict, 1970.

Hastings, Max. *Barricades in Belfast*. New York: Taplinger, 1970.

Hull, Roger H. *The Irish Triangle*. Princeton, N.J.: Princeton University Press, 1976.

Irish Republican Army, Provisional IRA. *Freedom Struggle*. London: Irish Republican Publicity Bureau, 1973.

McGuire, Maria. *To Take Arms: A Year with the Provisional IRA*. London: Macmillan, 1973.

O'Sullivan, P. Michael. *Patriot Graves: Resistance in Ireland*. Chicago: Follett, 1972.

Sunday Times (London) Insight Team. *Northern Ireland: A Report on the Conflict*. New York: Random House, 1972.

Sunday Times (London) Insight Team, *Ulster*. London: Deutsch, 1972.

"Palestine"

Abu-Lughod, Ibrahim, ed. *The Transformation of Palestine*. Evanston, Ill.: Northwestern University Press, 1971.

Alencastre, Amilcar. *El Fatah: Os comandos áraves da Palestina*. Rio de Janeiro: Gráfica e Editôra Tacaratu, 1969.

Anabtawa, S. "The Palestinians as a Political Entity." *Muslim World* 60 (January 1970): 47–58.

British Information Service, Foreign and Commonwealth Office. *Palestine Liberation Organization*. London: British Information Service, Foreign and Commonwealth Office, 1981. 21 pages, mimeo.

Chaliand, Gérard. *The Palestinian Resistance*. Baltimore: Penguin, 1972.

Churba, Joseph. *Fedayeen and the Middle East Crisis*. Maxwell Air Force Base, Ala.: Air University, 1969.

Coaley, John. *Green March—Black September*. London: Cass, 1973.

Curtis, Michael, et al., eds. *The Palestinians*. New Brunswick, N.J.: Transaction, 1975.

Denoyan, Gilbert. *El Fath parle: Les Palestiniens contre Israel*. Paris: Albin, 1970.

Dobson, Christopher. *Black September: Its Short, Violent History*. New York: Macmillan, 1974.

Fisher, Eugene M., and M. Cherif Bassiouni. *Storm over the Arab World: A People in Revolution*. Chicago: Follett, 1972.

Friendly, A. "The Middle East—The Fedayeen." *Atlantic Monthly*, September 1969, 12–20.

Hamid, Rashid. "What is the PLO?" *Journal of Palestine Studies* 4 (Summer 1975): 90–122.

Harkabi, Yehoshefat, *Fedayeen Action and Arab Strategy.* Adelphi Paper no. 53. London: Institute for Strategic Studies, 1968.

Heradstveit, Daniel. "A Profile of the Palestine Guerrillas." *Cooperation and Conflict 7* (1972): 13–36.

Holden, David. "Which Arafat?" *New York Times Magazine,* March 20, 1975, 11 plus.

Hudson, Michael. "The Palestinian Arab Resistance Movement: Its Significance in the Middle East Crisis." *Middle East Journal* 23 (Summer 1969): 291–307.

―――. "The Palestinian Resistance: Developments and Setbacks." *Journal of Palestine Studies* 1 (1972): 64–84.

Hussain, Mehmood. *The Palestine Liberation Organization.* Delhi: University Publishers, 1975.

Juradini, Paul, and William Hazen. *The Palestinian Movement in Politics.* Lexington, Mass.: Lexington Books, 1976.

Kadi, Leila S., ed. *Basic Political Documents of the Armed Palestinian Resistance Movement.* Beirut: Palestine Liberation Organization Research Center, 1969.

Kazziha, Walid W. *Revolutionary Transformation in the Arab World: Habash and His Comrades from Nationalism to Marxism.* New York: St. Martin's, 1975.

Kelidar, Abbas. "The Palestine Guerrilla Movement." *World Today* 29 (October 1973): 412–20.

Kiernan, Thomas. *Arafat: The Man and the Myth.* New York: Norton, 1976.

Laffin, John. *Fedayeen: The Arab-Israeli Dilemma.* London: Cassell, 1973.

Mertz, Anton. "Why George Habash Turned Marxist." *Mid East: A Middle East-North African Review* 11 (August 1970): 31–37.

O'Ballance, Edgar. *Arab Guerrilla Power, 1967–1972.* London: Faber & Faber, 1974.

Palestine National Liberation Movement. *Political and Armed Struggle.* N.p. [Beirut?]: Palestine National Liberation Movement, n.d. [1969?].

Pryce-Jones, David. *The Face of Defeat: Palestinian Refugees and Guerrillas.* London: Weidenfeld & Nicolson, 1972.

Quandt, William B., et al. *The Politics of Palestinian Nationalism.* Berkeley and Los Angeles: University of California Press, 1973.

el-Rayyis, Riad, and Dunia Nahas. *Guerrillas for Palestine.* London: Croom Helm, 1976.

Sayigh, Yusif. *Palestine in Focus.* Beirut: Palestine Liberation Organization Research Center, n.d.

―――. *Toward a Democratic State in Palestine.* Beirut: Palestine Liberation Organization Research Center, n.d.

Schiff, Zeev, and Raphael Rothstein. *Fedayeen: Guerillas against Israel.* New York: McKay, 1972.

Sharabi, Hisham. *Palestine Guerrillas: Their Credibility and Effectiveness.* Washington, D.C.: Georgetown University, Center for Strategic and International Studies, 1970.

Shukairy, Ahmad. *Liberation—Not Negotiation.* Beirut: Palestine Liberation Organization Research Center, 1966.

Yaari, Ehud. "Al-Fatah's Political Thinking." *New Outlook* 11 (November-December 1968): 20–33.

―――. *Strike Terror: The Story of Fatah.* New York: Sabra, 1970.

Peru

Alba, Victor. *Peru.* Boulder, Colo.: Westview, 1977.

Añi Castillo, Gonzalo. *Historia secreta de las guerrillas.* Lima: "Mas Alla," 1967.

Béjar, Héctor. *Perú 1965: Apuntes sabre una experiencia guerrillera.* Lima: Campódonico ediciones S.A., 1969.

——. *Peru 1965: Notes on a Guerrilla Experience.* New York: Monthly Review Press, 1970.

Blanco, Hugo. *El camino de nuestra revolución.* Lima: Revolución peruana, 1964.

——. *Land or Death: The Peasant Struggle in Peru.* New York: Pathfinder, 1972.

——. *Workers and Peasants to Power! A Revolutionary Program for Peru.* New York: Pathfinder, 1978.

Bollinger, William. "The Bourgeois Revolution in Peru: A Conception of Peruvian History." *Latin American Perspectives* 4 (Summer 1977): 18–56.

Campbell, Leon. "Historiography of the Peruvian Guerrilla Movement." *Latin American Research Review* 8 (Spring 1973): 45–70.

Chapin, David, ed. *Peruvian Nationalism: A Corporatist Revolution.* New Brunswick, N.J.: Transaction, 1976.

Delfín Cataldi, Milton. "Las Guerrillas." *Revista militar del Perú* (Lima), no. 226 (1962): 67–71.

Dore, Elizabeth, and John Weeks. "Class Alliances and Class Struggle in Peru." *Latin American Perspectives* 4 (Summer 1977): 4–17.

Gadea Acosta, Ricardo. "Luis de al Puente: To the Measure of Peru." *Tricontinental* (Havana) 4–5 (1968): 47–55.

Gall, Norman. "Peru's Misfired Guerrilla Campaign." *Reporter,* January 12, 1967, 36–38.

"Guerrillas in Peru: The Real Battle." *Atlas* 10 (September 1965): 169–71.

Hillikert, Grant. *The Politics of Reform in Peru.* Baltimore: Johns Hopkins Press, 1971.

Homenaje a Luis de la Puente. Havana: Universidad de la Habana, 1966.

"Hugo Blanco: Peru's Most Successful Reformer." *Atlas* 19 (April 1970): 56–57.

Levano, Cesar. "Lessons of the Guerrilla Struggle in Peru." *World Marxist Review* 9 (September 1966): 44–51.

Maitan, Livio. "Revolt of the Peruvian Campesino." *International Socialist Review* 26 (Spring 1965): 38–41.

Malpica, Mario Antonio. *Biografía de la revolución: Historia y antología del pensamiento socialista.* Lima: Ensayos sociales, 1967.

Mercado, Rogger. *Las guerrillas del Perú.* Lima: Fondo de cultura popular, 1967.

Peru, Ministerio de Guerra. *Las guerrillas en el Perú y su repression.* Lima: Ministerio de guerra, 1966.

Pike, Frederick. *The Modern History of Peru.* New York: Praeger, 1967.

de la Puente Uceda, Luis. "The Peruvian Revolution: Concepts and Perspectives." *Monthly Review* 17 (November, 1965): 12–28.

Villanueva, Victor. *Hugo Blanco y la rebelión campesina.* Lima: Mejía, 1967.

Philippines

Abaya, Hernando. *The Untold Philippine Story.* Quezon City: Malaya, 1967.
American University, Foreign Area Studies. *Area Handbook for the Philippines.* Washington, D.C.: Government Printing Office, 1969.
Blackburn, Robin. "Rebirth of the Revolution." *Nation,* December 7, 1970, 582–87.
Buckley, Tom. "Corks in the Pacific." *Harpers,* February 1972, 28–37.
Butwell, Richard. "The Philippines after Democracy." *Current History* 65 (November 1973): 217–20.
———. "The Philippines under Marcos." *Current History* 58 (April 1970): 196–207.
Day, Beth. *The Philippines: Shattered Showcase for Democracy in Asia.* New York: M. Evans, 1974.
Durdin, Tillman. "Philippine Communism." *Problems of Communism* 25 (May–June 1976): 40–48.
Kann, Peter R. "The Philippines without Democracy." *Foreign Affairs* 52 (April 1974): 612–32.
Lachica, Eduardo. *The Huks: Philippine Agrarian Society in Revolt.* New York: Praeger, 1971.
Lansang, José A. "The Political Answer to Land Reform." *Solidarity* (Manila) 1 (April–June 1966): 66–71.
Lightfoot, Keith. *The Philippines.* London: Benn, 1974.
Muijzenbery, Otto. "Political Mobilization and Violence in Central Luzon." *Modern Asian Studies* 7 (October 1973): 691–705.
Noble, Lela Garner. "The Moro National Liberation Front in the Philippines." *Pacific Affairs* 49 (Fall 1976): 405–525.
Philippines, Armed Forces, General Headquarters. *So the People May Know.* 5 vols. Quezon City: Armed Forces of the Philippines, General Headquarters, 1970.
Pomeroy, William J. *An American Made Tragedy.* New York: International Publishers, 1974.
———. "The Struggle in the Philippines and Its Lessons." *Marxism Today* (London) 13 (September 1969): 272–77.
Shaplen, Robert. "Letter from Manila." *New Yorker,* April 14, 1973, 97–119.
Starner, Francis L. "Whose Bullet, Whose Blood?" *Far Eastern Economic Review* (Hong Kong), October 17, 1970, 23–30.
Swomley, John M., Jr. "Polarization of the Philippines." *Nation,* January 26, 1974, 101–104.
Van der Kroef, Justus M. "Communism and Reform in the Philippines." *Pacific Affairs* 46 (Spring 1973): 29–58.
———. "Communist Fronts in the Philippines." *Problems of Communism* 25 (March–April 1967): 65–75.
———. "Philippine Communist Theory and Strategy: A New Departure?" *Pacific Affairs* 48 (Summer 1975): 181–98.
———. "The Philippine Maoist." *Orbis* 16 (Winter 1973): 892–926.

BIBLIOGRAPHY

Puerto Rico

Anderson, Robert. *Party Politics in Puerto Rico*. Stanford, Calif.: Stanford University Press, 1965.

Bhana, Surrendra. *The United States and the Development of the Puerto Rican Status Question, 1936–1968*, Lawrence: University Press of Kansas, 1975.

Bras, Juan Mari. "The Struggle for Puerto Rican Independence." *Black Scholar* 8 (December 1976): 18–26.

Cabranes, José A. "Puerto Rico: Out of the Colonial Closet." *Foreign Policy* 33 (Winter 1978–1979): 66–91.

Cripps, Louise L. *Puerto Rico: The Case for Independence*. Cambridge, Mass.: Schenkman, 1974.

"Eldest Son of General Secretary of PSP Juan Mari Bras Murdered by Terrorists." *Granma* (Havana), April 4, 1976, 10–11.

Howard, Alan. "A Colony Comes Home to Roost." *Nation*, April 10, 1976, 430–33.

"International Conference of Solidarity for Puerto Rican Independence." *Granma* (Havana), September 21, 1975, 2–3.

"Interview with Juan Mari Bras." *Granma* (Havana), September 14, 1975, 6.

Lewis, Gordon K. *Notes on the Puerto Rican Revolution: An Essay on American Dominance and Caribbean Resistance*. New York: Monthly Review Press, 1974.

———. *Puerto Rico: Freedom and Power in the Caribbean*. New York: Monthly Review Press, 1963.

Lopez, Alfredo. *The Puerto Rican Papers: Notes on the Re-emergence of a Nation*. Indianapolis: Bobbs-Merrill, 1973.

McDougall, George. "Puerto Rico: On Letting the People Decide." *Worldview*, November 1978, 11–12.

Maldonado-Denis, Manuel. "Puerto Ricans: Protest or Submission?" *Annals*, no. 382 (March 1969): 26–31.

Sariola, Sakari. *The Puerto Rican Dilemma*. Port Washington, N.Y.: Kennikat, 1979.

Silén, Juan Angel. *We the Puerto Rican People: A History of Oppression and Resistance*. New York: Monthly Review Press, 1971.

Wells, Henry. *The Modernization of Puerto Rico*. Cambridge: Harvard University Press, 1969.

Wesson, Robert G. "A Different Case for Puerto Rican Independence." *Worldview*, November 1978, 8–10.

Quebec

Bernard, André, ed. *Reflexions sur la politique au Québéc*. 2nd ed. Montreal: Cahiers de l'Université du Québéc, 1971.

Burns, R. M., ed. *One Country or Two?* Montreal: McGill-Queen's University Press, 1971.

Canada 70 Research Team. *Quebec: The Threat of Separation*. Toronto: Telegram, 1969.

Cook, R., ed. *French Canadian Nationalism*. Toronto: Macmillan, 1969.

Corbett, Edward M. *Quebec Confronts Canada*. Baltimore: Johns Hopkins Press, 1967.

Daniels, Daniel, ed. *Quebec, Canada, and the October Crisis*. Montreal: Black Rose, 1973.

Dion, Léon. "Reflections on the FLQ." *Canadian Forum*, August 1963, 104–107.

Dooley, D. J. "Quebec and the Future of Canada." *Review of Politics* 27 (January 1965): 17–31.

Dumont, Fernand. *The Vigil of Quebec*. Toronto: University of Toronto Press, 1974.

Kwavnick, D. "The Roots of French-Canadian Discontent." *Canadian Journal of Economics and Political Science* 31 (November 1965): 509–523.

Meyers, H. B. *The Quebec Question*. Montreal: Harvest House, 1964.

Morf, Gustave. *Terror in Quebec: Case Studies of the FLQ*. Toronto: Clarke, Irwin, 1970.

Pelletier, Gérard. *The October Crisis*. Toronto: McClelland & Stewart, 1971.

Regush, Nicholas M. *Pierre Vallières: The Revolutionary Process in Quebec*. New York: Dial, 1973.

Reid, Malcolm. *The Shouting Signpainters: A Literary and Political Account of Quebec Revolutionary Nationalism*. New York: Monthly Review Press, 1972.

Saywell, John. *Quebec 70: A Documentary Narrative*. Toronto: University of Toronto Press, 1971.

Stewart, James. *The FLQ: Seven Years of Terrorism*. Montreal: Montreal Star Books, 1970.

Trait, Jean-Claude. *FLQ 70: Offensive d'automne*. Montreal: Les éditions de l'homme, 1970.

Vallières, Pierre. *White Niggers of America*. New York: Monthly Review Press, 1971.

Russia

Balabanoff, Angelica. *Impressions of Lenin*. Ann Arbor: University of Michigan Press, 1964.

Bol'shaya Sovietskaya Entsiklopediya (Great Soviet Encyclopedia). Vol. 38. Moscow: State Scientific Publishing House, 1955.

Bol'shaya Sovietskaya Entsiklopediya (Great Soviet Encyclopedia). Vol. 51. Moscow: State Scientific Publishing House, 1958.

Bordiaev, Nikolai A. *The Russian Revolution*. Ann Arbor: University of Michigan Press, 1961.

Bunyon, James, and H. H. Fisher. *The Bolshevik Revolution, 1917–1918*. Stanford, Calif.: Stanford University Press, 1934.

Carr, Edward Hallett. *The Bolshevik Revolution, 1917–1923*. Vol. 1. New York: Macmillan, 1951.

Chamberlin, William Henry. *The Russian Revolution, 1917–1921*. 2 vols. New York: Macmillan, 1935.

Conquest, Robert. *V. I. Lenin*. New York: Viking, 1972.

Daniels, Robert V. *Red October: The Bolshevik Revolution of 1917*. New York: Scribner's, 1967.

Deutscher, Isaac. *Lenin's Childhood*. London: Oxford University Press, 1970.

———. *The Prophet Armed: Trotsky, 1879–1921*. New York: Oxford University Press, 1954.

———. *Stalin: A Political Biography*. New York: Oxford University Press, 1949.

Fischer, Louis. *The Life of Lenin*. New York: Harper & Row, 1964.

BIBLIOGRAPHY

Hill, Christopher. *Lenin and the Russian Revolution.* New York: Macmillan, 1950.
Hingley, Ronald. *Joseph Stalin: Man and Legend.* London: Hutchinston, 1974.
Howe, Irving, ed. *The Basic Writings of Trotsky.* New York: Random House, 1963.
Krupskaya. N. K. *Reminiscences of Lenin.* New York: International Publishers, 1970.
Lenin, V. I. *Selected Works.* 12 vols. New York: International Publishers, 1943.
Payne, Robert. *The Life and Death of Lenin.* New York: Simon & Schuster, 1964.
Schueller, George K. "The Politburo." In *World Revolutionary Elites,* edited by Harold
  D. Lasswell and Daniel Lerner. Cambridge: MIT Press, 1965.
Shub, David. *Lenin.* New York: Doubleday, 1948.
Smith, Edward E. *The Young Stalin: The Early Years of an Elusive Revolutionary.* New
  York: Farrar, Straus & Giroux, 1967.
Souvarine, Boris. *Stalin: A Critical Survey of Bolshevism.* London: Longmans, Green,
  1939.
Sukhanov, N. N. *The Russian Revolution 1917: A Personal Record.* Edited, abridged,
  and translated by Josel Carmichael. London: Oxford University Press, 1955.
Theen, Rolf H. W. *Lenin: Genesis and Development of a Revolutionary.* Philadelphia:
  Lippincott, 1973.
Trotsky, Leon. *Diary in Exile.* Cambridge: Harvard University Press, 1958.
————. *The History of the Russian Revolution.* 3 vols. in one. New York: Simon &
  Schuster, 1936.
————. *Lenin: Notes for a Biographer.* New York: Putnam's, 1971.
————. *My Life: An Attempt at an Autobiography.* New York: Scribner's, 1930.
————. *Stalin: An Appraisal of the Man and His Influence.* New York: Harper, 1941.
————. *The Young Lenin.* Translated by Max Eastman, edited by Maurice Friedberg.
  New York: Doubleday, 1972.
Tucker, Robert C. *Stalin as Revolutionary, 1879–1929: A Study in History and Personali-
  ty.* New York: Norton, 1973.
Ulam, Adam B. *The Bolsheviks: The Intellectual and Political History of the Triumph of
  Communism in Russia.* New York: Macmillan, 1965.
————. *Stalin: The Man and His Era.* New York: Viking, 1973.
Voline, Boris. *12 Militants Russes.* Paris: Librairie de l'humanité, 1925.
Wolfe, Bertram D. *Three Who Made a Revolution.* Rev. ed., New York: Dial, 1964.
Wolfenstein, E. Victor. *The Revolutionary Personality: Lenin, Trotsky, Gandhi.* Prince-
  ton, N.J.: Princeton University Press, 1967.

South Africa

Arnold, Millard, ed. *Steve Biko: Black Consciousness in South Africa.* New York: Ran-
  dom House, 1978.
Benson, Mary. *South Africa: The Struggle for a Birthright.* London: Penguin, 1966.
Carter, Gwendolen N. "African Nationalist Movements in South Africa." *Massachu-
  setts Review* 5 (Autumn 1963): 147–64.
Feit, Edward. *African Opposition in South Africa.* Stanford, Calif.: Hoover Institution
  Press, 1967.
————. *Urban Revolt in South Africa.* Evanston, Ill.: Northwestern University Press,
  1971.
Hoagland, Jim. *South Africa: Civilizations in Conflict.* Boston: Houghton Mifflin,
  1972.

Johns, Sheridan. "Obstacles to Guerilla Warfare: A South African Case Study." *Journal of Modern African Studies* 11 (June 1973): 267–303.

Kahn, Ely J., Jr. *The Separated People: A Look at Contemporary South Africa.* New York: Norton, 1968.

Legum, Colin, and Tony Hodges. *After Angola: War over Southern Africa.* New York: Africana, 1976.

Legum, Colin, and Margaret Legum. *South Africa: Crisis for the West.* London: Pall Mall, 1964.

Nkosi, Lewis. "Robert Sobukwe: An Assessment." *Africa Report* 7 (April 1962): 7–9.

"Profile [of Robert Sobukwe]." *Black Star* (London) 1 (May 1963): 1–4.

Roux, Edward. *Time Longer Than Rope: A History of the Black Man's Struggle for Freedom in South Africa.* Madison: University of Wisconsin Press, 1964.

Shamuyarira, N. N. "Revolutionary Situation in South Africa." *African Review* 4 (1974): 159–80.

Stubbs, Aelred, ed. *Steve Biko: I Write What I Like.* London: Bowerdean, 1978.

Woods, Donald, *Biko.* New York: Paddington, 1978.

Uruguay

Costa, Omard. *Los Tupamaros.* Mexico City: Era, 1971.

Foland, Frances. "Uruguay's Urban Guerrillas." *New Leader* (London), October 4, 1971, 8–12.

Generals and Tupamaros: The Struggle for Power in Uruguay, 1969–1973. London: Latin America Review of Books, 1974.

Gerassi, John. *Toward Revolution.* Vol. 2. London: Weidenfeld & Nicolson, 1971.

Gerassi, Marysa. "Uruguay's Urban Guerrillas." *New Left Review* (London), no. 62 (July/August 1970): 22–29.

Gilio, María Esther. *The Tupamaro Guerrillas.* New York: Ballantine, 1973.

———. *The Tupamaros.* London: Secker & Warburg, 1972.

Labrousse, Alain. *Les Tupamaros: Guérilla urbaine un Uruguay.* Paris: Seuil, 1971.

———. *The Tupamaros: Urban Guerrillas in Uruguay.* Harmondsworth: Penguin, 1973.

Max, Alphonse. *Tupamaros: A Pattern of Urban Guerrilla Warfare in Latin America.* The Hague: International Documentation and Information Centre, 1970.

Mercader, Antonio. *Tupamaros: Estrategia y acción.* Montevideo: Alfa, 1969.

Moss, Robert. "Urban Guerrillas in Uruguay." *Problems of Communism* 29 (September–October 1971): 14–24.

Nuñez, Carlos. *Los Tupamaros: Vanguardia armada en Uruguay.* Montevideo: Provincias unidas, 1969.

d'Oliveira, Sergio L. "Uruguay and the Tupamaro Myth." *Military Review* 53 (April 1973): 25–36.

Porzecanski, Arturo C. *Uruguay's Tupamaros.* New York: Praeger, 1973.

Weinstein, Martin. *Uruguay: The Politics of Failure.* Westport, Conn.: Greenwood, 1975.

Vietnam, North

Aptheker, Herbert. *Mission to Hanoi.* New York: International Publishers, 1966.

Fall, Bernard B., ed. *Ho Chi Minh on Revolution.* New York: Praeger, 1967.

227

BIBLIOGRAPHY

—————"A Talk With Ho Chi Minh." *New Republic,* October 12, 1963, 19–22.

—————*The Two Viet-Nams.* New York: Praeger, 1963.

—————*The Viet-Minh Regime.* New York: Institute of Pacific Relations, 1956.

—————"Vo Nguyên Giap—Man and Myth." In Vo Nguyên Giap, *People's War, People's Army.* New York: Praeger, 1962.

Fenn, Charles. *Ho Chi Minh: A Biographical Introduction.* New York: Scribner's, 1973.

Fischer, Ruth. "Ho Chi Minh: Disciplined Communist." *Foreign Affairs* 33 (October 1954): 86–97.

Halberstam, David. *Ho.* New York: Random House, 1971.

Hammer, Ellen J. *The Struggle for Indochina.* Stanford, Calif.: Stanford University Press, 1954.

Hoang Van Chi. *From Colonialism to Communism: A Case History of North Vietnam.* New York: Praeger, 1964.

Ho Chi Minh. *Prison Diary.* Hanoi: Foreign Languages, 1972.

Honey, P. J. *Communism in North Vietnam.* Cambridge: MIT Press, 1963.

—————. *North Vietnam Today.* New York: Praeger, 1962.

Huyen, N. Khac. *Vision Accomplished? The Enigma of Ho Chi Minh.* New York: Collier, 1971.

Lacouture, Jean. *Ho Chi Minh: A Political Biography.* New York: Random House, 1968.

Lancaster, Donald. *The Emancipation of French Indochina.* London: Oxford University Press, 1961.

Lê Duân. *Forward under the Glorious Banner of the October Revolution.* Hanoi: Foreign Languages, 1967.

—————. *The Vietnamese Revolution: Fundamental Problems, Essential Tasks.* Hanoi: Foreign Languages, 1970.

Neumann-Hoditz, Reinhold. *Portrait of Ho Chi Minh.* Hamburg: Herder & Herder, 1972.

O'Neill, Robert J. *General Giap: Politician and Strategist.* New York: Praeger, 1969.

Our President Ho Chi Minh. Hanoi: Foreign Languages, 1970.

An Outline History of the Vietnam Workers' Party. Hanoi: Foreign Languages, 1970.

Pham Van Dong. *Achievements of the Vietnamese People's War of Resistance.* Hanoi: Foreign Languages, 1955.

"Profiles [of Vietnamese Leaders]." Portion of a typescript (pp. 25–50) supplied by Vietnam Working Group, U.S. Department of State, Washington, D.C., 1973.

Sainteny, Jean. *Ho Chi Minh and His Vietnam: A Personal Memoir,* Chicago: Cowles, 1972.

Shaplen, Robert. "The Enigma of Ho Chi Minh." *Reporter,* January 27, 1955, 11–19.

Truong Chinh. *Forward along the Path Chartered by K. Marx.* Hanoi: Foreign Languages, 1969.

—————. *President Ho Chi Minh, Beloved Leader of the Vietnamese People.* Hanoi: Foreign Languages, 1966.

—————. *Primer for Revolt: The Communist Takeover in Vietnam.* New York: Praeger, 1963.

—————. *The Resistance Will Win.* Hanoi: Foreign Languages, 1960.

Vo Nguyên Giap, *Banner of People's War, the Party's Military Line.* New York: Praeger, 1970.

—————. *Big Victory, Great Task.* New York: Praeger, 1968.

———. *The Military Art of People's War.* New York: Monthly Review Press, 1970.
———. *People's War, People's Army.* New York: Praeger, 1962.
Warner, Denis. *The Last Confucian.* New York: Macmillan, 1963.

Vietnam, South

Aptheker, Herbert. *Mission to Hanoi.* New York: International Publishers, 1966.
Biographie des membres du Gouvernement révolutionnaire provisoire de la République du sud Vietnam et son conseil des sages. Saigon: Giai Phong, 1969.
Burchett, Wilfred G. *The Furtive War: The United States in Laos and Vietnam.* New York: International Publishers, 1963.
———. *Vietnam: Inside Story of the Guerrilla War.* 2nd ed. New York: International Publishers, 1965.
Carver, George A. "The Faceless Viet Cong." *Foreign Affairs* 44 (1966): 347–72.
Commission for the Foreign Relations of the South Vietnam National Front for Liberation. *Personalities of the South Vietnam Liberation Movement.* N.p.: Commission for Foreign Relations of the South Vietnam National Front for Liberation, n.d.
Coney, Michael Charles. *The Communist Insurgent Infrastructure in South Vietnam: A Study of Organization and Strategy.* Washington, D.C.: American University, Center for Research in Social Systems, 1966.
Fall, Bernard. *The Two Vietnams: A Political and Military Analysis.* 2nd ed. New York: Praeger, 1967.
Fitzgerald, Frances. *Fire in the Lake: The Vietnamese and the Americans in Vietnam.* Boston: Little, Brown, 1972.
Lacouture, Jean. *Vietnam: Between Two Truces.* New York: Random House, 1966.
Langguth, A. J. "The Lengthening Shadow of the N.L.F." *New York Times Magazine,* April 7, 1978, 28–29 plus.
Pike, Douglas. *Viet Cong: The Organization and Techniques of the National Liberation Front of South Vietnam.* Cambridge: MIT Press, 1966.
"Profiles [of Vietnamese Leaders]." Portion of a typescript (pp. 25–50) supplied by Vietnam Working Group, U.S. Department of State, Washington, D.C., 1973.
Race, Jeffrey. *War Comes to Long An.* Berkeley and Los Angeles: University of California Press, 1972.
Raskin, Marcus G., and Bernard B. Fall, eds. *The Vietnam Reader.* New York: Random House, 1965.
Tanham, George K. *Communist Revolutionary Warfare: From the Vietminh to the Viet Cong.* Rev. ed. New York: Praeger, 1967.
Van Tien Dung. *Our Great Victory: An Account of the Liberation of South Vietnam.* New York: Monthly Review Press, 1978.
La vérité sur le Front national de libération du sud-Vietnam. Supplement to *Est & Ouest* (Paris), no. 377 (February 1–15, 1967).
Who's Who of the Republic of South Vietnam. Saigon: Giai Phong, 1969.

Zimbabwe (Rhodesia)

Africa Research Group. *Race to Power: The Struggle for Southern Africa.* New York: Doubleday, Anchor, 1974.

BIBLIOGRAPHY

Barber, James. *Rhodesia: The Road to Rebellion.* London: Oxford University Press, 1967.

Byers, C. J., ed. *Dictionary of South African Biography.* Vol. 3. Cape Town: Tafelberg-Uitgewers, 1977.

Carter, Gwendolen M., and Patrick O'Meara. *Southern Africa in Crisis.* Bloomington: Indiana University Press, 1977.

Clements, Frank. *Rhodesia: A Study of the Deterioration of a White Society.* New York: Praeger, 1969.

Day, John. *International Nationalism: The Extra-territorial Relations of Southern Rhodesian African Nationalists.* London: Routledge & Kegan Paul, 1967.

Jacobs, Walter D., et al. *Terrorism in Southern Africa: Portents and Prospects.* New York: American African Affairs Association, 1973.

Legum, Colin, ed. *Africa Contemporary Record.* New York: Africana, 1976.

Mlambo, Eshmael. *Rhodesia: The Struggle for a Birthright.* London: Hurst, 1972.

Mtshali, B. Vulindlela. *Rhodesia: Background to Conflict.* New York: Hawthorn, 1967.

Nash, Rebecca. "Interview with Dr. Masipula Sithole [brother of Ndabaningi Sithole]." Dayton, Ohio, University of Dayton, African Studies Department, November 4, 1977.

Rotberg, Robert. "From Moderate to Militant: The Rise of Joshua Nkomo and Southern Rhodesian Nationalism." *Africa Report* 7 (March 1962): 3–4, 8, 22.

Shamuyarira, N. N. *Crisis in Rhodesia.* London: Deutsch, 1965.

Sithole, Ndabaningi. *African Nationalism.* 2nd ed. New York: Oxford University Press, 1968.

———. *Threshold of Revolution.* London: Oxford University Press, 1977.

Todd, Judith. *Rhodesia.* London: MacGibbon & Kee, 1966.

Wilkinson, Anthony R. *Insurgency in Rhodesia.* London: International Institute for Strategic Studies, 1973.

Young, Kenneth. *Rhodesia and Independence: A Study in British Colonial Policy.* London: Eyre & Spottiswoode, 1967.

INDEX

Index

233

About the Authors

Mostafa Rejai received his Ph.D. from the University of California, Los Angeles, and is now Distinguished Professor at Miami University (Ohio), where he has also been the recipient of an Outstanding Teaching Award. He is coauthor (with Kay Phillips) of *Leaders of Revolution* (1979) and author of *Comparative Political Ideologies* (forthcoming), *The Comparative Study of Revolutionary Strategy* (1977), and *The Strategy of Political Revolution* (1973). He is editor of and contributor to *Decline of Ideology* (1971) and *Democracy: The Contemporary Theories* (1967). He has coauthored *Ideologies and Modern Politics* (1971, 1975, 1981) and edited *Mao Tse-tung on Revolution and War* (1969, 1970). He has contributed to *Perspectives on World Politics* (1981), *Handbook of Political Conflict: Theory and Research* (1980), *The Theory and Practice of International Relations* (1974, 1979), *Dictionary of the History of Ideas* (1973), and *The New Communisms* (1969). He has been an associate editor of the *Journal of Political and Military Sociology* since its founding in 1973. His articles have appeared in social sciences and humanities journals in the United States and Europe.

Kay Phillips received her Ph.D. from the University of Cincinnati and is now associate professor and assistant chair in the department of sociology and anthropology at Miami University (Ohio). In addition to articles in professional journals, she is coauthor (with Mostafa Rejai) of *Leaders of Revolution* (1979) and is currently working on two projects: *Organizational Change and Cultural Evolution* and *Demographic Change and the Rise of Capitalism.*